IT'S
NEW WORLD!

Jeff Jeffries

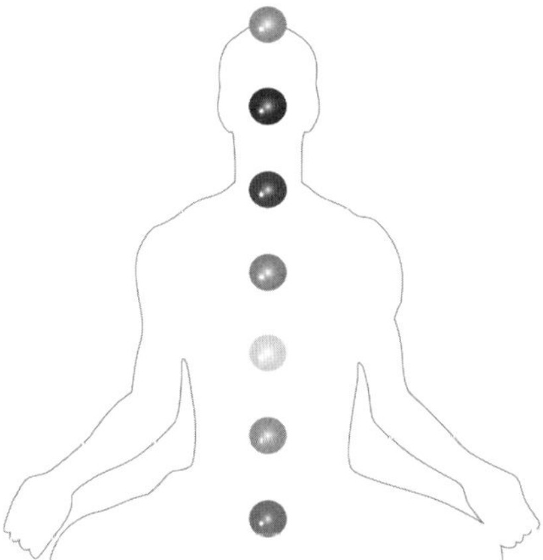

Published by Intelligent Energies Ltd
www.intelligentenergies.com

IT'S A WHOLE NEW WORLD!

Published by Intelligent Energies Ltd

www.intelligentenergies.com

First published in Great Britain 2012

CONTENTS

ACKNOWLEDGEMENTS

My book and my growing understanding of the implications for Intelligent Energies are the result of twenty years of my life plus twenty years of the support of others – particularly my family.

My wife Brenda went with me through every step of our early years of discovering about healing for Jenny and then the years of my own development as a healer – not to mention many more years of tolerating my commitment to my theories and to my book; very little would have come of all this without her!

My sons Mike and Dave have also given me every encouragement and help along the way when many might have despaired of a parent determined to establish a whole new world!

Jenny for being Jenny and for having a soul willing to face her difficulties and allowing me to learn!

I am also grateful to my wider family, friends and friends of friends who trusted me and allowed me to practise and learn – especially Nicola. Particular thanks also to Ann our friend who as a former Head of Science in a major Comprehensive school trusted her own experiences of my healings and assessed my manuscript with kindness and insight; also Anthony who trusted me with his own growth towards psychic understanding – and also advised on my manuscript.

I have also been guided, without either of them being aware of it, by Professor Sir Richard Dawkins whose books 'The God Delusion' and 'Climbing Mount Improbable' clearly spell out the scientific view of the sort of issues I address and Bill Bryson who describes 'science' with spectacular clarity in his ' A Short History of Nearly Everything'. Thanks to both authors I was better able to establish my own truths in pursuit of a 'fourth perspective' about which I write. I must stress that I am not implying that either writer endorses anything I have to say but their skills have indirectly helped my own thinking and I genuinely appreciate their work.

I have also quoted from the wisdom of Albert Einstein because so much of what he understood and had to say encourages us all to explore wider horizons than the familiar ones.

Finally thanks to Julie from Jem Design Studio with whom I have worked on several projects and who skilfully assembles exactly what I want – even when I am not at all clear about what I do want!

Jeff Jeffries

— INTRODUCTION —

'We shall require a substantially new manner of thinking if mankind is to survive'

Albert Einstein

It all started with a quest to find help for my daughter, Jenny, who was born with learning difficulties; by the time she was nine years old I already knew that 'the system', if left to itself, would fail her. I had decided the time had come to do something more though I cannot say I was looking for anything in particular, just for that little bit extra from somewhere outside of the UK's education/health structure that might make a difference for her. I certainly didn't know how or where to start – there was no effective internet twenty years ago – but soon after I made the conscious decision to find some way forward options seemed to come to meet me. Even when those opportunities did appear I had no idea of just how far they would take me but in the end I had worked my way into the heart of present-day debates about the planet and our place in an amazing healing universe. I did find help for Jenny, very quickly as things turned out; it was help that came in a remarkable way that redefines the way we see the universe and our lives within it. I did indeed find a whole new world.

Essentially my story is about what I found to help Jenny but much more than that it is also the story of how, in doing so, I came across the truth about our universe – how we can all connect to its interactive forces to benefit ourselves and others, and how it all works. Whether or not you currently know about or believe in techniques such as Reiki healing, water divining, religion, positive thinking, yoga, crystal healing, telepathy, the healing abilities of animals, or any of the other fields that lie outside of science, you owe it to yourself to understand the common thread that makes all of them practical realities. Despite the astonishing progress made by science, if you only accept scientific thinking as the basis for life then you will never see the whole picture; to fulfil your own potential you need to examine that common thread for yourself.

So much happened on my own journey to answer so many of today's doubts and puzzles that I knew I had to bring it all out in book form. It is a book that harmonises and explains topics that we have come to see as incompatible but which, in fact, complement each other easily and naturally. It is, however, a book that could only be written by a layman who would not be bound by loyalties to science, religion or the cause of mysticism – the three perspectives that have led human understanding but which have long been controversial in their different ways and needlessly at odds with each other. The truth is that differences of opinion about the nature of existence still rage as fiercely now as they ever did and are never going to be determined by any single one of those three belief systems to which humankind has always turned. The answers to our questions rest within a force which joins them together, something which connects mainstream science and aspects of religion to that third set of beliefs loosely described as the metaphysical – the field with which, despite my own initial scepticism, I became very familiar.

The simple truth is that our culture now predominantly concentrates on 'nuts and bolts' detail. Scientists mostly reduce everything to basic constituent parts; they will weigh and measure and try to fathom what they have. Anything can be limited to its base essentials – the *Mona Lisa* as oil on canvas or a football match with all its skill, passion and endeavour to 22 men kicking a ball about. Science likes to capture everything in such easy terms, yet everyone knows it is not enough. Surprisingly for many people, one of the most significant people to have recognised the limitations of such a perspective was Albert Einstein – one of the finest scientists who ever lived and all the greater because he acknowledged the wider view that includes spirituality, intuition and a universal power. There are many quotes attributed to him which amply illustrate his wider understanding and values as well as his practical genius; I have used a few of those quotes to prove how right he was and to encourage others to look more closely at the scientific interpretation.

The problems humankind has had in understanding the true nature of the universe and life within it is that our three traditional perspectives have each come to be held as all-or-nothing certainties – generally speaking, people commit themselves to religion or to science or to claims about psychic gifts. There are exceptions, of course, but as a convenient, crude generalisation we individuals have mainly built our outlook around one or other of those three forces. Science has been gaining the ascendancy over the past three hundred years or so and now sets the main structure for western civilisation in particular. Surprisingly, the first lesson I learned when I took those early steps towards finding help for Jenny was that the scientific model is not so much wrong as incomplete and even partly misleading. The second lesson I learned was that I had to tell people why we needed a wiser, more complete understanding – something that I felt needed its own identity on which I could focus Einstein's observation that we need 'a new manner of thinking'. I have termed that identity the 'Fourth Perspective', a way of life that makes room for all three previous perspectives – and then adds something more besides. It is no exaggeration to say that what I have discovered amounts to another 'Renaissance' – an overworked claim, I know, but in this case one that really is no less important for the world than the rebirth of civilisation from medieval times.

Religion does see a much bigger picture; to believe in God is to recognise the universal force at work that, typically, science does not. Religious believers enjoy an overview that starts with an affinity with the active power that guides the universe but focuses mainly on specifics that have been handed down over the centuries. While religion captures the fact of that universal power, believers interpret it quite precisely according to stories, doctrines, beliefs and worship that go back thousands of years; for many it is something that no longer engages with a modern world.

For their part, healers and others in various practices that can best be regarded as non-scientific are a bit weak on overviews and tend to concentrate on the gift that they use as an end in itself. They often recognise a general spiritual foundation for their various healing, dowsing or clairvoyant abilities, but their gifts are treated mostly as outputs. Remarkable as these genuine techniques are, they are seen as individual demonstrations of something that happens to be possible. The experiences of healers and others in the many fields that are considered 'paranormal' are not brought into the grand overview that both science and religion address in their different ways.

We therefore have a modern society which separates out our understanding of one universe into three often conflicting cultures; none of them can claim to be complete until science, religion and the psychics join forces and share in the truth that has been there for 14 billion years. Over human time on earth we have come close to grasping it, only to see it slip away again. Despite our technical advances and the cautionary advice of Einstein we have been unable to see beyond three different ways to view life on and around one planet – until one father set out to find extra help for one child with a learning disability.

I not only found that help, I also found secrets of the universe and incredible new healing techniques that inspire a new reality.

Jeff Jeffries
www.intelligentenergies.com

1
FIRST STEPS THAT CHANGED EVERYTHING

'Common sense is the collection of prejudices acquired by age eighteen"

Albert Einstein

Unintentionally at first, I began to pull together a new perspective on life and the universe in an unlikely way from clues, evidence and proof through a chain of events that began one summer's day in 1989. With my family I was on holiday at a campsite somewhere in the south of England. In an unlikely setting I found an opportunity that proved to be the first stepping stone towards a dramatic understanding that was to mean so much to me as well as all those around me. I no longer believe the choice of our holiday location that year was a coincidence; nor do I believe that subsequent encounters that were to lead me to new discoveries happened by chance. In those days, however, such beliefs were not part of my reckoning; I relied only on what I regarded as common sense, an attitude that is valuable but which can be very limited.

There is in fact a prelude to my whole story, and this concerns our daughter, Jenny. Although we were not to recognise it for a number of years, Jenny was born with significant learning difficulties; those difficulties became the trigger that started my wife and me on a fascinating journey of discovery for both of us. Like most parents we have always tried to do the best for our children – always trying to get the best schooling and, in Jenny's case, the best additional support for her special needs, giving her practical and other help wherever we could. Sometimes our efforts to support her went well and sometimes it all seemed an impossible struggle against the system and almost against life itself. On those occasions all parents of children with special needs will inevitably feel more than a little down and weary of our lot in life. All we can see at those times are the difficulties, one after another stretching into the future. The rewards just disappear for a while.

On one of those gloomier occasions one wet day, while walking from my office to my car, I began to dwell on some of this. Although I was – and remain – of no religious faith, I found myself doing what many others throughout the ages have done when they felt their backs were against the wall. Regardless of my belief system I mentally asked God for help for Jenny. I believe this was a significant moment for me because I remember so well doing it and remembering anything in detail is not my strong point. To be able to recall so clearly how it happened, exactly where I was, the weather at the time and the way I was feeling, picturing it now with such clarity, shows that it was indeed a highly significant moment.

Alas, having asked for help from any 'Almighty' source there may be I found no obvious response as I continued my walk in the rain. There was no vision, no crash of thunder or celestial voice by way of reply and Jenny was in no way better or at all different when I arrived home. However, what did happen a few weeks later when we were holidaying on that campsite was that for no obvious reason I broke the habit of a lifetime (well, fifteen years or so!) and bought a midweek morning paper. This is something I almost never do and the fact that I did it on holiday at that small caravan campsite, where they happened to have a copy of the *Guardian*, made it even more unlikely.

The significance of that spontaneous change of habit was that the newspaper I picked up carried a report of the work of an impressive-sounding new healer based in London named Seka Nikolic. Although I knew virtually nothing about the subject of healing, as I read the article I immediately connected what the journalist had to say with Jenny's disabilities. We have all seen newspaper accounts about claims made by those who say they have special healing gifts and in that sense it was a topic that had always struck some sort of chord with me whenever I read the stories. Nowadays we hear a lot more about healing and natural remedies than we did in 1989 and so, at that time, the *Guardian* article gave me more detail about the healing process than I had ever known. I was instantly intrigued by what Seka had to say about healing and her technique as it was described in the article; the piece also carried a case study about the success Seka had enjoyed in treating one of her patients, a lady who was suffering from the debilitating condition known as ME.

In her article the journalist recounted how she herself had been impressed when Seka briefly demonstrated how she worked with clients. During the demonstration Seka was able to create physical sensations by putting her hands close to the journalist's body. I now know that feelings of warmth are almost always reported by clients when healers work on them, though a number of other sensations are also experienced that I will talk about later. Even more impressive to me at that time, however, was that the article also talked about the healer's ability to diagnose intuitively, and accurately, the reporter's health problems. Seka's technique to diagnose was also simply to move her hands around her 'client's' body but without making any actual physical contact. In her own conclusion, the journalist left her readers to make up our own minds about the validity of healing on the basis of Seka's demonstration, her explanations and the testimony of the ME patient.

It seemed to me that the unmistakable sensations the reporter experienced while Seka was working on her amounted to pretty strong evidence that something real must have been going on. Likewise, the case study about ME quoted by the journalist was very positive about the help given by the healer; the patient's comments were very encouraging and I found myself convinced that it was unlikely that all of this was something about which intelligent people could possibly be mistaken.

I decided that the coincidence, of having found the newspaper report in this unlikeliest of ways, was too much of an 'invitation' to ignore; almost overwhelmingly I felt I had to book Jenny an appointment with Seka to see if anything could be done for her. I was also captivated by this whole new topic and its possibilities, and was keen to judge for myself what healing really was all about. When I came back to earth I did see a problem in that the healer was a distance away in London and charged something like £35 per session for children. This was not an insignificant sum of money to me twenty years ago and would be in addition to travel and hotel costs. It was not to be taken lightly for what, as keen and optimistic as I was, I had to anticipate were very uncertain gains.

I actually carried the cutting from the newspaper in my wallet for some months before I rang Seka's office to make an appointment. I am not sure why I took so long, though it was probably a combination of facts. The whole business was entirely outside anything I had ever been involved with before and there were those financial costs, along with the need to travel to London and the lingering doubts over whether this could ever be anything but a confidence trick of some sort. I had no experience of healing or anything like it and, despite my genuine fascination, that belief system of mine was still nagging away at me. I could not avoid the question that is still often asked of me: if there is such a thing as healing, why do we not know more about it already and why are the hospitals still full?

It took me quite a while, but eventually I came to realise that if I had encountered Seka as someone who happened to live down the lane and who charged no money, then I would have taken Jenny to see her without a second thought. In those circumstances I would have tested out the newspaper report for myself and been in a position to judge these claims about healing. It was plain, therefore, that the only thing standing in my way was the effort of getting to London and the need to pay some money. I decided that Jenny deserved the chance to meet Seka, whatever the cost or inconvenience to me or my family, and I eventually did ring Seka's practice to make the arrangements.

Without going into too much detail about Jenny and her condition in those days, the fact was she could barely speak more than two or three words at a time, even though she was ten years old; she also had poor balance and 'motor skills'. She was and is a delightful girl and it was saddening to know that she really had no life of her own; mostly she would play a little by herself but otherwise she simply sat with us, apparently taking in what she could until it was time to 'move somewhere else'. In simple terms, she was coping as well as she could with her learning disability while we did the best we could to help but with no signs of long-term improvement.

Going to see Seka, when the time came, was a nervous occasion for us; it was make or break in respect of any real hope of gains for Jenny and if Seka couldn't help, we knew the future would be a difficult one for all of us. Certainly medicine couldn't offer any solution, natural progress was painfully slow and successive schools had achieved no obvious breakthrough for Jenny. When we went to see Seka, therefore, I was hopeful that she could unlock Jenny's problems in some way but I could not bring myself to be confident that she really would be able to do so. I was also very much on my guard and not about to succumb to flattery, false promises or self-delusion.

At the time, Seka was operating from a smart practice in Golders Green in North London which was where the three of us, Jenny, my wife and I, eventually headed on that first trip. Once inside the building we immediately climbed stairs (very difficult for Jenny) into a bright, modern and comfortably welcoming environment. We were met by Seka's sponsor and 'practice manager', Clive, who was friendly and helpful; over a cup of tea, as we waited, he told us something about Seka and her healing gift. It is a story that has since been well documented in many newspapers and magazines – stories that nowadays mention that from time to time she is asked to treat royalty and other famous clients. She has also worked on TV with the hypnotist and hypnotherapist Paul McKenna, but in those days such things were still way into the future. Although such matters are now much more familiar to people, at that time it felt like we were entering another world.

That first visit was in fact for a diagnosis by Seka who showed natural empathy with Jenny as soon as they met. Her manner was gentle and kindly, she talked and asked questions unhurriedly and built links with us and with Jenny without being at all effusive or in any way insincere. As it turned out, that initial visit strengthened my commitment but still left questions in my mind. In our discussions with Seka, I had already described Jenny's problems as we saw them, giving all the information I could on the basis that, regardless of Seka's own reputed ability to diagnose, there was no point in keeping her guessing about why we were there. It was from this basis that Seka went on to tell us what she thought were Jenny's medical condition and her needs.

As I recall it, the diagnosis was simply that Jenny had a balance problem, also that the part of her brain that controlled her development was not working properly and finally that the two halves of her brain were not properly connected. My uneasy reaction at the time was that if that were the diagnosis, and if it were accurate, then that would indeed be all Seka could be expected to say. But the fact remained that although that exact diagnosis had never been given to us before, it provided no conclusive proof of Seka's abilities. To establish Seka's real ability had become hugely important to me; if she had a real gift and the phenomenon of healing genuinely existed, then I was on the edge of something truly exciting – something to change my world completely! In addition to seeking help for Jenny, it was becoming essential to me that I uncovered the truth.

As an aside I was later to have very real evidence of Seka's natural diagnostic skills. One day while I was in her waiting room, I talked about Seka's abilities with another patient. This lady had been most impressed with Seka who, simply by holding her healing hands a few centimetres from the lady's body and passing them over and around her, was able to tell her client that she had no gall bladder! There was no way Seka could have known this; it was not on any records that Seka had access to and the patient did not undress to reveal any scar. The lady told me she was totally mystified but did indeed confirm to Seka that the gall bladder had been removed some years previously. By any standards, the ability to diagnose intuitively in this way is totally remarkable and in its own way it immediately challenges science. In fact the ability is not confined to Seka alone though it is not exactly a common gift in my experience.

After giving us her diagnosis of Jenny's condition, Seka said she thought she could improve Jenny's prospects if we wanted to take her for treatment. My wife and I returned home to reflect on everything we had seen and been told; there was no point in discussing it with Jenny because, so far as we knew, she did not have the ability to understand what the issues were and would not be able to give either an informed consent or a refusal. In any case, we would not have wanted to raise her hopes even if she had been able to enter into the conversation and tell us her wishes; it was a decision we would have to make on Jenny's behalf, and hope that for her sake we would get it right.

In the event neither of us had much hesitation in agreeing to book a session of treatments in what we felt sure were Jenny's best interests and so we arranged to visit Seka again some weeks later. As we knew from the newspaper article, the treatment would consist of Seka passing her hands over and around Jenny about 12 centimetres from her body, the same method she used when intuitively diagnosing. The difference between the two is that when Seka is using the technique to heal, she consciously withdraws what she calls negative energy with one hand while introducing good healing energy with the other. Seka believes this combination of removing and replacing energy, almost like a blood transfusion, is the best way to help the body to repair itself. Interestingly, as part of this technique, Seka briefly draws the negative energy into her own body and then immediately expels it. Because of the nature of such a way of working, one condition she would not treat is cancer because she regarded that energy as too dangerous and uncontrollable to take into herself. Naturally enough I saw these as yet more astonishing concepts; they were way outside anything I had previously considered, but I was willing to let them run their course.

From having read about how Seka carried out her healing I did have some idea of her claims that energy was at the root of healing. I knew she talked about working in, and with, the energy fields of her patients and that in the early days she described her process as 'bio-energy' healing. I now know that accepting the existence of active energy is the biggest hurdle for anyone to have to clear in order to be able to take on board the facts about healing. It was something that I quickly had to acknowledge, something which would later lay the ground for the much wider implications at the heart of what I have to say. I will go into the concept of healing energies in more detail later, but in essence all healers use methods similar to Seka's; everyone works through:

- An energy mass, which is sometimes known as the aura. In a sense it is the energy equivalent of the whole human body. It is bigger than the body and possibly exists throughout the inside of the human frame as well as extending beyond it. Some psychics can 'see' this energy field outside the body and, from its colours and condition, say they can use their gift to analyse health issues. It is also thought that this energy mass comprises seven distinct levels.

- Energy flows running along channels and meridians throughout the body and which can be likened to the 'lines' of our nerves and blood circulation systems. It is the energy flows that are manipulated with needles in the Chinese art of acupuncture; in the spring of 2009 the UK authorities formally accepted acupuncture as a bona fide treatment – with no idea of how it could possibly work! I believe reflexologists tap into the same channels and that a physical massage also probably affects the energy flows in a similar way, bringing results that go way beyond what you would expect just from the manipulation of tissue.
- Energy centres, or chakras as they are usually known. To complete the analogy with our physical bodies they can be regarded as reflecting our major organs and endocrine system. There are usually said to be seven major chakras running from a point just above the top of the head, down the body via the area of the forehead, the throat, the centre of the chest, the solar plexus and the lower abdomen to the base of the spine. There are also thought to be minor chakras in the area of each of our joints.

A simplified illustration of the chakra points is shown on the front cover and the title page of the book.

Although my wife and I understood something of the general principles involved, we were not really familiar with that level of detail when the day of our appointment with Seka eventually arrived and we set off to get actual healing treatment for the first time. Jenny was due to have five daily sessions in that first week and we were looking forward to what was in store; in the event we were soon in for high drama of a type that we could never have imagined. Once the preliminaries were over, Seka asked us to leave Jenny alone with her in her treatment room because, quite understandably, she did not want the distraction that comes from having anxious and curious parents hovering over her when she needed tranquillity for her healing. As we settled in the waiting room, however, we were suddenly shocked to hear Seka next door scream out loud, causing her interpreter to rush through to see what on earth was happening. After a few anxious moments for us as we wondered whatever was happening it transpired that, as she was putting her hand into Jenny's body energy field, Seka had felt a tingling sensation so severe she felt it was as though she had been given an electric shock!

It apparently caused Seka pain for some considerable time afterwards and, despite all her experience, it was for her a unique happening, something she spoke of and was able to laugh with us about on many an occasion afterwards. At the time the sceptic in me did wonder if it had been a trick to win our faith, but I soon learned that Seka had no need for such theatre; reality was to be even more impressive! For us, however, it was a dramatic introduction to the sheer power of human energy fields and an event that none of us is ever likely to forget.

After the excitement, order was resumed and the first session started again while we remained in the adjoining waiting room. After about half an hour Seka returned with Jenny and, in answer to our questions, told us that she had felt a lot going on while she was carrying out the healing and that she was hopeful of making at least some improvement for her over the sessions to come. This, of course, was music to our ears but we would only be able to believe her prognosis totally when we saw something tangible for ourselves.

We were in fact just a little disappointed that there was no improvement that we could see as a result of that first day's treatment, though Seka did tell us that it was too soon to expect any obvious changes in Jenny, especially given the nature of her problems. However, from the second healing session the following day, Jenny amazingly began to show unmistakable changes and gains. The changes we noticed in her, though apparently small, were as dramatic as they were captivating. It is important to stress that Jenny had no real idea what was happening to her; there is no way she could have understood the concept of healing or willed herself into experiencing any sensations or improvements. Nonetheless, early in that first week we had the vital evidence that we had hardly dared to hope for. Holding Jenny's hand we realised she felt so much 'lighter'. Jenny had always been a child whose arm seemed to weigh heavily when you were holding her hand to walk with her; she would always be at least a pace behind so that you were practically dragging her along. I suddenly realised as we left Seka's rooms at the end of the second session and walked towards our hotel that Jenny definitely felt distinctly 'lighter' and was keeping up with me without the usual pulling. It was only a slight improvement in the grand scheme of things but you know your own child, and we were now experiencing a totally unexpected improvement in her; moreover it was a change that could actually be measured, even if only subjectively. There was no possibility that we could have been fooling ourselves into seeing an improvement that had not really happened – beyond question, and against the odds, Jenny was not the same as when we arrived!

Soon there were other gains to be seen over those first three or four days. First, Jenny was able to reach behind her and fasten her skirt, a movement that hitherto she would not have thought to try and did not have enough dexterity to manage. She also walked down the stairs from Seka's rooms on her own, holding the bannister with one hand while carrying a bag in the other. For the first time in her life she also took stairs alternately rather than putting both feet on the one step. This achievement, such progress in so short a time, was way beyond anything she had shown before. Later in the hotel room she jumped across a narrow gap between two beds – another new skill; she soon began, not exactly to talk, but to gabble rather than using just two or three words. Provided we knew what it was she was talking about we were able to understand her much better than ever before. These were such big steps forward for all of us that my wife and I could not stop ourselves from enjoying the moment; we sat by Jenny's hotel bed with big, silly grins all over our faces, watching her embark upon new skills and new hope!

The improvements we saw were consolidated over about four further visits to London; as I recall, the weeks all involved three or five treatments of one session per day. Jenny's improvement continued throughout this time though not as dramatically as during that first week. Seka then advised us to discontinue treatment for a while to try to let Jenny benefit and develop naturally from the gains that had been made. By now the improvement in Jenny's communication meant she was able to make us understand something of what she experienced during the time she was being treated. Although it was necessary to push her, and interpret, she told us that while Seka had been working on her it felt as though cotton wool was being pulled out of her head! This was one of the earliest indications we had that Jenny was in fact a lot more aware, and was taking a lot more in, than we had realised and certainly a lot more than she was capable of giving out. I would never have thought she knew that cotton wool existed or that she could connect such imagery to what was happening to her at Seka's hands.

In case there are doubts, this awareness on Jenny's part would still have been at a far lower level than that of knowing what a healer might do for her in ways that could trigger wishful thinking, or willing herself to show the gains we had seen. We were discovering a new daughter and could not have been more delighted!

We accepted Seka's advice to take a break in treatment but later took Jenny back for another week of healing to see if we could build on what had been done. There were no major gains from that additional week and we decided to see how she continued to develop. This is one of the facts about healing that we simply have to accept even if it is something that does not fit into any recognisable pattern. Sometimes progress does reach a sort of plateau which, though amounting to a significant improvement, is less than a full cure at that point in time.

To us, however, Jenny was now living proof that, whatever the mechanics might be, healing was real. She had made unmistakable progress that could not be put down to coincidence or any sort of self-will and had also experienced sensations during the healing process that left us in no doubt that genuine activity was under way. The realisation fascinated me. I could not understand how anyone would not go to visit a healer who had so clearly demonstrated an ability to help. I became evangelical, telling anyone and everyone I met and who had any sort of problem where they might go for help; I was even tempted to tell strangers in the street who were obviously suffering some disability or another that they really ought to give Seka and her healing a try! Although I managed to avoid going over the top in quite that way nothing could stop me from remaining committed to the cause of understanding and spreading the word about what I was seeing.

Even so, for a time, I still made the mistake of believing healing to be a constant and ready means of miraculously curing anything and anyone regardless of the circumstances. I would learn later that this is not what happens but it was all part of my excitement at what was happening around me. Clearly I had much to learn but learning about all of this was exactly what I wanted to do; I talked to Seka as much as she had time for and read as many books as I could find on healing and related topics. Having realised that healing was for real, I knew that this new metaphysical world had much more to offer and was there to be examined with a fresh, if still critical, eye.

Having found complementary medicine, my quest to understand more about it soon took me to see an acupuncturist in order to find out if he could tackle the problem of my high blood pressure that had been diagnosed a few years earlier. As I briefly mentioned, acupuncturists treat their patients by inserting, and sometimes vibrating, needles at specific points in the human frame. They use the energy flows of the body as the focus for their healing, releasing 'blocked' energies and balancing them to restore health. In my case the practitioner was able to give me some immediate help with my hypertension but only for a short time; the problem always returned within a couple of days after each session of treatment with him and eventually I decided to call a halt to it.

Nonetheless, acupuncture is a beneficial form of healing that has existed in China for thousands of years and is now readily available all over the UK. There are countless reports of its success, not only as a treatment, but occasionally as the only anaesthetic for some people undergoing surgery, which many happily accept. I have to say that it is not an anaesthetic process for surgery that I would undergo myself, though it is a powerful testament to what acupuncture can achieve.

In addition to my own brush with acupuncture for my hypertension, I can relate to experiencing something similar to the anaesthetic effect in quite an offbeat way. I cannot recall how experienced in healing I was at the time, if at all, but I do know it was when I was a 'nervous patient' when it came to dentistry. I never went for any check-up and dreaded the times when I needed any treatment – which therefore was usually for toothache! Something of the kind must have struck when I was working away from home and needed to find a dentist in a city thirty miles from my local practice. When I asked my secretary Sue for a recommendation, and admitted I was nervous, she suggested I visit a dentist used by a number of her friends, saying that he used a technique which they had all found painless and comfortably stress-free. It was not actually a worry about pain that bothered me – it was more a psychological hang-up about dentistry, but I liked the promise of comfortable and stress-free so decided to try him out.

I think Sue called his technique aqua-pressure, which led me to assume that instead of needles there would be water pressure jets of some kind – I was so keen to avoid the usual experiences that I even wondered if they were used instead of the drill! Nervous, but full of hope, I made an appointment and went to see the miracle man. On my arrival I was introduced to the dentist, who happened to be quite elderly, and told him why he had been recommended. We went into his treatment room where, very professionally, he asked me a lot about my general health, took notes, examined me and told me about his method of, yes, *acupressure*. Nothing to do with safe water jets, but connected to acupuncture theories including, he told me, that the ear is seen as representing a foetus because of its shape and that the lobe of the ear is seen as a baby's head. All very fascinating, and quite technical as an introduction to his dentistry – to which we then came as I sat in the dreaded chair.

At this point he suddenly said, 'Just wait a moment while I get what I need'; this also had a ring of hi-tech reassurance about it – until he rummaged in his desk drawer and brought out two spring-loaded clothes pegs! One of them he put on one of my earlobes, and the other on the flap of skin between thumb and index finger, as he assured me that these were seen as points that inhibited pain and calmed anxiety. As you might imagine, I was not at all convinced; one of the world's most nervous dental patients was about to have his tooth drilled by an unknown man, without any anaesthetic and aided only by two clothes pegs! What was that about comfortable and stress-free? My thoughts as he came at me were: Sue, if I get out of this ordeal with my memory intact, you are dead!

That dentistry turned out to be absolutely painless, and totally comfortable. Because my mouth was not numbed I could feel what was going on, but without any pain. I had a better sense of the treatment rather than suffering any fear of the unknown, and when it was over I had none of that unpleasant numbness that lasted half the day and caused you to dribble from the moment you rinsed your mouth. Without doubt it was the most comfortable dentistry I ever received.

My first contacts with principles of acupuncture and acupressure may have been somewhat mixed, but much more important than that treatment I had received for my hypertension was the fact that the acupuncturist was about the only person, then or since, in a position to tell me about a book on an Indian, human, 'god' named Sai Baba. It was a book which proved to be another significant stepping stone on my route to understanding and acquiring direct healing knowledge.

Sai Baba's story is breathtaking in its account of 'miracle' events surrounding him and his whole life, and is immeasurably challenging to western ideals. I have of course no way of being able to vouch for any of it but if just a small percentage of what he claims and what is said about him is valid then we have so much still to learn. I regret that it is not a debate on which I can throw any light though the book had a life-changing impact for me when I read that if anyone wants something and they want it sincerely and for the right reasons they should call for it in Sai Baba's name and it will be granted. By this time I knew that, other than to see Jenny's continued progress, I wanted to be a healer like Seka more than anything else in the world. Sai Baba's fascinating book seemed to offer me a 'heaven-sent' way into developing the gift.

Over a number of nights I held the book and repeatedly asked for healing skills in the name of Sai Baba. Alas, again, there was no discernible response to my new attempt at 'prayer' and no evidence that I had been given any new abilities but still I continued.

Then, one Sunday morning, after about three weeks of this I found myself nursing a gentle headache and instinctively put my hands over my eyes. Within about half a minute, and much to my surprise, blue colours began to shimmer past my closed eyes; instinctively I kept my hands in place, fascinated by the experience. To my even greater surprise and joy, within a very short time my headache had disappeared and I suddenly felt fine. Just then my eldest son appeared and said (oddly) that he could 'smell petrol' and that it was giving him a headache. Half joking I said 'I can cure headaches, my son', and before he could stop me, put my hands on his head. He allowed me to do this for a few minutes and then said that his headache had gone.

Of course he might well have been saying that in order to get away from a suddenly deranged parent who was clearly best avoided at that moment! Whether he was or not, and I have asked him since but he cannot remember, I now had something very encouraging on which to build as a potential healer. My first patient, understandably enough, was then me again. Working more than thirty miles away from where I lived meant I had to drive every day for an hour or more from home to my office in rush-hour traffic. For parts of that journey I was able to put my hand on my shoulder where I was suffering the effects of fibrositis. This is by no means a recommended way to give healing – or even to drive – but regardless of such drawbacks I found I was definitely beginning to notice an effect from my attempts. The sensations of warmth that I experienced were not very strong, but something was undoubtedly happening. The joint loosened and the pain lessened as the condition I was trying to treat eased and then disappeared after a few days of this self-help. I still have a 'weakness' with my shoulders but it has never returned as fibrositis and, for all practical purposes, I had been able to cure myself of a painful condition that had previously bothered me on and off for quite a number of years. That success, as you might expect, thrilled me and gave me even more resolve to continue with my quest.

I next began to extend my healing skills by practising on my family and friends; it was not safe for anyone to mention any disorder from a stiff muscle to the beginnings of a cold without being leapt on by me, determined to establish or strengthen this new gift. More than once I have stood in a motorway service station car park giving hands-on healing to try to cure hiccups in a reluctant and severely embarrassed child. Again, not what healing is about, but I was, literally, feeling my way and anxious to avail myself of every opportunity to progress.

I quickly found any number of useful books on healing techniques; nowadays there is also much information on the internet but the books soon helped me familiarise myself with the process and mechanics of healing and develop my new ability. As my skills and confidence grew, some of my nature asserted itself to the extent that I found myself reluctant to follow other people's ideas and techniques unless I felt comfortable with them, though I spent some time as a probationary healer with the National Federation of Spiritual Healers (NFSH) which offers training and support to their members. I was glad I joined them because it helped me come to terms with a very different set of values, though it was not long before I decided that I wanted to go solo. From that moment, and ever since, I found that I much prefer to operate according to my own instincts and standards. I am never comfortable following the guidance and ways of others, or signing up to any preset procedures. Even so, it was useful to have gained insights into the way in which people tend to work with the healing power – if only as a means to develop my own approach. It is not the purpose of this book to provide operating instructions for new healers but there are still many books as well as the websites out there that will help you if you are interested and the NFSH is probably still a good starting point.

As I found more opportunities to develop healing skills, one of the first signs that things were happening for me was that I was able to 'feel' the energy in people that Seka had talked to me about in the very early days. What I soon discovered was that as I reach into someone's energy field, my hands start to tingle as if with very fine 'pins and needles'; this is something you can easily establish for yourself and I will show you how in a later chapter. Thankfully I have never suffered the pain reported by Seka when she first dipped into Jenny's energy mass, but I do always feel distinct tingling. The feeling is nothing to do with anything like pins and needles actually happening for real in my own body; I am definitely feeling my patient's energy but it does come across as that sort of sensation. In addition, as I move my hands around their field I can tell if there is a 'bump' in it that feels different from the rest of the energy. This unevenness in the energy field always represents the point at which my healing should first be directed.

With the help of my family and a few close friends who were willing to let me try my hand, my gift continued to develop to the point where it was unmistakable. There was no possibility of delusion on anyone's part; too many successes, and clear physical sensations during the process, left me and others in no doubt that something worthwhile was happening. In some ways I was now ready to look further afield for patients, but in other ways I still lacked the assurance to present myself to the world as a genuine practitioner. Fortunately my wife had no such inhibitions and regularly told anyone she discovered to be in need of help that her husband was ready and able to oblige.

Thanks to her input and much 'word of mouth' a steady stream of patients turned up over the months and then years. At first, as with all new beginnings I was learning more and more almost with every passing day and every new client. Regular experiences with the different people who came to me for help were all enabling me to strengthen my abilities and my understanding of this entirely new dimension to my life. I recorded many of the cases just to help me gather the evidence of my own abilities and then added others later once I had decided to write this book. The next chapter is about just some of my case studies.

2

WHO SAYS THERE IS NO EVIDENCE!

Case Studies

'The only source of knowledge is experience'

Albert Einstein

Our time with Seka – the discussions we had enjoyed, the work she had done on Jenny and its obvious impact on her – had made a huge impression on me. It made me realise beyond any doubt that this little-known, controversial and somewhat vague area of human activity was indeed genuine.

Not only that, it was also provable and measurable, but most important of all it was not just academic and had ceased to be something for me just to admire from a distance; instead I was thrilled to have found that I too had a practical healing gift.

I became committed to a 'new' capacity that the world has for benefiting humankind – and that was only the beginning. I had not only found a vital step forward for my daughter, I had also taken us all way beyond present familiar boundaries and explanations. Almost overnight, my experiences had changed my perspectives and stretched my belief systems. Common sense physics, that status quo within which most of us understand and conduct our lives, was no longer the most reliable arbiter of what is possible in this world. I had long discarded my scepticism and accepted that successful healing proves there is no reason to let anything hold us back from exploring other truths for ourselves. The remarkable facts about the mechanics of healing are the basic foundation to support even greater revelations about the universe that science has not yet grasped.

I knew the truth about healing conclusively from my growing first-hand experience as a practitioner myself. Case histories are a crucial part of the proof of the healing process and I am keen to present some of mine as vital evidence. I recognise from my own early doubts, and the reactions I have so often seen and heard since, how the rest of the world can be hard to convince; those of us who know healing intimately have a duty to make that knowledge accepted as the fact that it is. Over many years I have been successful in helping very many patients, all of whom have come to me by recommendation. Almost all have seen their health improve as a result, sometimes dramatically so. The examples I have chosen from my caseload show something of the range of people and the different conditions I have met; they are typical cases but special in that they illustrate particular features of healing that help demonstrate its variety, strength and impact.

—— Cathy ——

I have given Cathy a number of treatments for various problems and I will mention a couple more instances later. I am particularly pleased with the time I worked on her eye infection, which the doctor had said was a dust allergy and was something that cropped up annually in summer. Her GP advised Cathy to keep the house well vacuumed and to stay away from obvious sources of dust but he was unable to bring any relief to her discomfort; his conclusion was that she would just have to live with it. Healing treatment involved working in Cathy's energy field close to her eye rather than actually touching the infected area; treating her this way removed the discomfort by the end of just one session. Cathy recently told me she has never been troubled since by a problem that used to upset her every single year. (This covers the last 18 years to 2010.)

—— Julie-Anne ——

Julie-Anne is a close family friend. When she first heard my healing stories she did not really know what to make of them but was not about to accept any claims at face value alone; she was properly sceptical, though with an open mind. This is exactly the right attitude, as was the way in which she made up her mind – she simply asked to try some healing for herself.

The problem we tackled was a nodule of some kind on her finger. It had been there 'for as long as I can remember', she told me; she was in her late twenties at the time. I gave her one session of gentle healing, touching the skin near the tip of her finger and working in the energy field around it. Julie-Anne told me she felt warmth in the finger and then a couple of days later was able to report that the nodule which had been there for most, if not the whole, of her life had gone. Julie-Anne was surprised, not to say amazed, by what had happened, but was readily convinced by what she experienced. Very few of my clients have come to see me with advance expectations of success, even if I have been able to help them before; but all of them leave knowing that the healing force is a reality.

—— Barbara ——

Barbara was one of my early clients, introduced to me by my wife when I was too self-conscious to be able to encourage patients for myself. She was suffering from headaches and discomfort around her eye and ear and came to me for a small number of sessions.

During the healing process Barbara felt the healing force at work through sensations of warmth and 'pulling' that focused at a point behind her eye, rather than in the eye or in her ear. We conducted two or three sessions before the time came for her to attend a hospital appointment that had already been arranged. Those hospital tests later showed that Barbara had a tumour which, unexpectedly, lay behind her eye; the test results became the first medical suggestion that there was anything amiss in that specific location although this was exactly where Barbara had picked up the healing effects.

Unfortunately for me she didn't come back for more treatment once the medical diagnosis had been made and I have no idea what help I might have been able to give her had my treatment continued.

I must stress that Barbara was obviously right to seek orthodox treatment; no responsible healer would ever come between a patient and their GP or hospital specialist. It is important whenever a healer sees a client to find out whether there has been a proper medical diagnosis and always to encourage their client to visit their doctor and to tell them that healing is proposed or being undertaken.

That is why I regard healing as complementary rather than alternative; we are there to support but there are grave dangers in a healer winning trust and reliance at the expense of orthodox treatment.

—— Marion ——

We shall meet Marion later in my story but I got to know her through the business she ran with her husband. At the time I treated her she was suffering from a painful elbow joint that meant she could not lift even small weights; just trying to pick up a kilo of sugar brought on too much pain for her.

In all, I gave her three sessions of healing by holding her elbow and arm during which she told me she felt considerable warmth. Each session eased the pain more, allowing heavier weights to be lifted. The problem disappeared after the third treatment.

—— Curtis ——

Curtis was related to Marion and I met him while healing her; she had responsibility for him and with his agreement gave me permission to heal.

Curtis had two large warts 'all his life' on the back of his hand; he was aged about 14 at the time and was waiting for surgery when he reached 16. To avoid actually touching the warts I loosely covered them with a piece of kitchen towel and worked mainly in his energy field.

The first healing session led one of the warts to start to bleed. I stopped at that point but healing continued over three more sessions in the following days. After the end of the third session the first wart fell off, as did the second not long afterwards without further treatment.

—— Maurice ——

Maurice was tricked into seeing me through a conspiracy involving his wife and a mutual friend. I did not know that he had been brought to me under false pretences and, until he arrived at my home, he had no idea that the purpose of the visit was to receive healing. Of course, when this dawned on us we each had the option of putting a stop to it or letting it go ahead. As the two conspirators had expected, Maurice, having got that far, reluctantly agreed to let me carry on even though he did not believe in the possibility of healing in any way; his views, of course, were the reason he had been misled in the first place.

Maurice's problem was bad circulation that made it too painful to walk 'more than twenty yards' before movement became too painful. Healing, over a few sessions, gradually eased the pain considerably and allowed him to enjoy more relaxed and easier movement over much greater distances.

Converted to a 'believer' by his direct experience, he tiled my bathroom as a thank you but then didn't come back for more sessions that, for all I know, might have cured the condition completely; whether it did in fact clear his problem completely remains unknown to me. As I mentioned earlier, it does seem to be a feature of healing that a plateau can sometimes be reached, as it did when Seka treated Jenny. I regret that I can give no clear explanation for why this happens but it does seem that the greatest gains take place early on and clients do sometimes stop treatment before achieving complete cure. It is worth adding that this pattern is also found within orthodox medicine when early gains too are made before the impact slows down later in the treatment!

—— Hilda ——

Spondylitis was making it impossible for Hilda to turn her head more than a few degrees either side. She had suffered this for many years and was actually resigned to it; in fact the reason she asked for help was not about her neck, rather it was to see if I could deal with severe pain she was now having at the bottom of her back. Hilda became very significant to me in that it was while treating her that I first experienced a sensation that I call 'sympathy pain' which I sometimes feel in my own body as an indicator of where to concentrate treatment.

Because the pain was at the bottom of her back, that is where I first began to work on her; I could feel she had lumps and bumps of tight energy there and at first I took them as the usual signal for me to begin working at those points. It was while doing so and about ten minutes into the treatment that I felt a stab of pain in my shoulder just at the base of my neck. At first I ignored it, thinking I had simply had a brief pain of my own, but when it hit me again a few seconds later – this time with two sharper twinges – I tried moving my attention to that same spot on Hilda's shoulder. Immediately she told me she was feeling the strong warmth of healing flowing into her and, from that moment on, the session gave me no more painful stabs. Thinking about it afterwards it became very clear to me that something in the healing process had known that I was not working in the right area and had communicated in order to pass that information on to me. For this to happen was perhaps a reduced version of the ability to diagnose that Seka had demonstrated from the very beginning. In the same way that information can be passed on as a diagnosis, it seemed that some useful information about where to treat the patient was coming into the process to help me. For me to be able to access the 'prompt' in this way was to prove a hugely important revelation, far more than I realised at the time.

I continued healing Hilda for about six sessions which gave her virtually free movement of her head. As she put it, this made her neck feel 'better than for twenty years'. For some reason during those sessions I was unable to help the lower backache for more than a day at a time; perhaps more treatments would have helped, but Hilda decided to call a halt once the rate of her progress started to slow down. It is conjecture, but it is also possible that the problem in her neck was affecting the lower back and that the neck had to be dealt with first. I did not see her for long enough to be certain whether or not I could also have eventually relieved her back pain permanently.

—— Julie ——

Julie was a work colleague who eventually came to me to say that she was enduring a repetitive strain injury. Typing had become very painful for her; it had been building up during the day and meant that she spent her evenings in great pain with her arm resting on cushions.

This debilitating condition was leaving her unable to do anything at home other than very light housework. At first she could cope during the day at work because the pain would ease overnight, but eventually it caught up to give her problems during the day as well. It was this deterioration that had prompted her to ask me for help.

I gave her healing three times on successive days which eased the pain more and more each time until the problem disappeared on the third visit. During the first healing session Julie told me she felt 'explosions of warmth down my arm' as the healing kicked in, bringing quick help for her problem. I found this a very graphic confirmation of one of the familiar healing sensations.

—— Dave ——

Dave was an amateur footballer who came to see me one Sunday afternoon with a hamstring injury he had picked up the previous day. He told me that it was something that happened about once a season and always took at least three or four weeks to clear. He limped up the steps of my house with obvious difficulty for us to begin the healing session, but after receiving only fifteen minutes' treatment he was able to walk out with absolutely no sign of any limp. By any standards this was a very significant improvement, virtually amounting to a cure in a spectacularly short time.

As he was leaving Dave told me that 'the leg feels lighter', which is a common reaction after healing and perhaps mirrors that change we noticed in Jenny when she first saw Seka. He rang me next day to say there was only slight discomfort remaining and that this was only apparent when he ran upstairs. He did not need to see me for any further treatment.

For a while I became healer to Dave's football team and actually carried out some work on players during a visit by the then manager and other officials of a football club who were then only recently relegated from the Premiership. The officials took an interest in what we were doing and talked about healing to me and to the player I was working on. He happily confirmed the benefits of what I did but the club never followed up my offer to demonstrate healing to their professionals.

I actually came to know socially a professional football coach who has also worked in the Premiership – in fact he was an occasional member of my pub quiz team. One evening, just as the quiz was finishing, he walked into the room with a very obvious limp which turned out to be from an Achilles tendon problem. It was quite early in my 'career' as a healer but, plucking up my courage, I told him about healing and offered to see if there was anything I could do to help. He was immediately interested and, in the middle of a busy pub, put his leg up on a stool and invited me to begin. True to form he soon felt the warmth of healing and after about twenty minutes found the pain had disappeared. He immediately tested his ankle out and was quite shocked to find he could walk perfectly well.

Before that evening the problem had persisted for some weeks, despite being attended by the club's medical team who had all the modern treatment facilities at their disposal. He was amazed by the experience and has mentioned his fascination to me since on more than one occasion.

—— Leighton ——

Leighton was a near neighbour, a teenager who was very tall for his age at the time and who suffered frequently from painful knees. He also comes into the category of patients who would have preferred not to bother with healing but was pressured into it, this time by his mother. Their GP had said the pain was a common problem among young people who were growing tall quickly and nothing could be done.

Leighton turned up to see me with his mother and showed all the signs of preferring to be somewhere else, interested only in getting the embarrassment over with as quickly as possible. Fortunately for him the one healing session removed the immediate pain, which never recurred.

—— Louise ——

Louise is a friend who had met with a skiing injury some time previously; it had left her regularly in pain which gave severely limited movement and sometimes caused her back to 'lock' altogether. When that happened she found it too painful even to leave her bed. I gave her one or two sessions of healing per week for about six weeks. She felt the usual sensations of warmth and gentle 'pulling' which gradually took the pain away to leave her with free movement, and no longer needing to take pain-killing tablets.

An interesting aside to this occurred when her hospital consultant called Louise in for an unscheduled appointment. It transpired that a scan of her back taken, coincidentally, after the healing sessions was so different from a previous X-ray that he needed an explanation. Louise told him what we had done but he showed no interest in following up anything with me, even though he had the evidence in front of him. Apparently his only response had been that 'it does happen'. I must admit I was slightly surprised when he did not wish to discuss his patient's rapid and unusual improvement with me. Then again, in a way how could he? His professional structure and working hierarchy are in tune only with a different outlook and there is no easy way for him, or any professional, to see beyond it.

The next three case studies are meant to eliminate a convenient argument that is common among people who have doubts about healing. Sceptics who have not tried it themselves like to suggest that somehow the outcome is solely dependent on what the patient believes or expects. For some, this is the faith part of what is sometimes called 'faith healing'. In reality this phrase is rarely used these days because it is misleading. It implies either religious faith – which is certainly not a requirement – or it suggests that results are due to patients simply convincing themselves that the healer will make them well again. In fact virtually all the patients I see make it plain to me that they are not expecting any success and that they are there pretty much as a matter of last resort. There is no way that the vast percentage of clients could ever be convincing themselves into generating their own recovery on the basis of their having such total confidence and belief in what we offer. If confidence in the practitioner were all it took to cure someone, then you would expect this to be where orthodox medicine would have an overwhelming advantage. There should be enough belief in the NHS for patients to have been cured long before they feel any need to seek out complementary help. In addition, as I have said, very few clients come to me professing any confidence in what may happen. Faith, of any kind, is not an issue.

Another explanation sometimes provided by orthodox medicine for the success of complementary medicine is that complementary therapists achieve results because they have more time to spend with every client. We are assured that the increased attention we can lavish on the sick is the secret ingredient that brings forth a cure. In other words the claim is that people with no healing gift can effect cures through nothing but spending time with the patients; if that is so, orthodox medicine should solve unemployment and halve the NHS bill by drafting in those who are out of work to sit and talk to sick people!

A positive outlook undoubtedly helps any treatment but the case studies that follow all rule out belief or expectation as the answer. In different ways they show that healing is a very real aspect of life, one that must be accommodated into our understanding and our culture.

— Cathy —

Cathy had one of those slender pink moles sticking out about 3 or 4 millimetres from her neck. I had already successfully healed her on more than one occasion before she asked me if I could do anything about the mole; she told me it only troubled her when it got caught by clothing or jewellery and she was only seeking treatment because I had already proved able to help her with more intrusive problems. I said that I thought it unlikely that I would be able to help her this time because a mole seemed to me to be more of a natural feature than something I would call a disorder. We both agreed that success was unlikely but that there was no harm in trying.

I gave Cathy healing in the usual way but at the end, although she had felt a little of the usual warmth, nothing had happened to the mole and we agreed that it would have to go down as something that I could not do anything with.

Next day, however, she came back excitedly to show me that, overnight, the mole had started to flatten and I could see that it was now clearly drooping downwards. Encouraged, we did another session and, to the surprise and delight of both of us, the mole fell off a couple of days later.

—— Baby ——

My wife and I were at a wedding reception and found ourselves seated next to the parents of a new baby who had been fed and was clearly suffering from tummy ache. The baby was restless, to say the least, crying and obviously in discomfort. This was apparently par for the course after feeding and the parents had never found an answer. With their permission I gave healing; the baby soon stopped crying and fell asleep within minutes. The parents said this was simply unheard of. The baby, of course, knew nothing about any of it but she was presumably pleased in her own way!

—— Minka ——

Minka was our very large cat – fat and contented, the vet used to say. One day she limped into the house with a damaged back leg. We took her to our vet who said that there was severe tendon damage due to her probably having got it caught or trapped somewhere.

He also said a complete cure was going to be unlikely as she was too heavy; although she was not exactly actively energetic she would nonetheless move about too much to give it the rest it needed. The vet's prognosis was that he expected the injury to go into continued decline leading to arthritis. We took Minka home without her having received any treatment.

We were disappointed that she was going to have to continue suffering and so, that evening, I gave her some healing. She could clearly feel something going on, even though I was operating in her energy field and wasn't actually touching her. While I did so, her looks and body language showed she could feel sensations of some kind and probably much the same as I know are experienced by humans.

After a while I did begin to touch her to give 'contact' healing which included much holding of her back leg and, surprisingly, she allowed me to do this for the rest of that session. She permitted the same course of treatment the following day, but when I tried a repeat session on a third day she refused. She wouldn't permit me to hold the leg at all for any more healing and, by way of making her feelings known, tried to nip me. She then casually jumped down from the settee, which is where I had been treating her each time, and left the room without a backward glance. The day after that she was walking very much better and very soon after that there was no sign of any problem at all.

The same injury did return some years later, possibly after another incident on one of her many nocturnal trips. The same few sessions of healing produced the same 'cure'; again she would only tolerate my holding her limb a few times while she perhaps felt she was getting benefit from healing. Somehow she seemed to know it was for her own good, but once the problem was under control she would not allow any more treatment. Typically of cats she showed no sign of gratitude, but I am pleased to say lived happily and free of pain before she sadly reached the end of her life.

All of the above case studies are based on the familiar concept of hands-on or 'contact' healing. The cases predominantly involve touch, though sometimes working just in the patient's energy field in the way that Seka had first demonstrated. This direct approach is not the only means of giving healing, however; healers can also 'send' the energy over vast distances to their clients with the same effects and effectiveness as when they give it through contact. This form of healing from a distance really does begin to push open the unknown.

The procedure is known as absent, or distant, healing and I first came across this amazing feature when Seka conducted an experiment in which she sent absent healing to a large number of patients at the same time. She had asked my wife if she would be willing to get involved in this intriguing trial. My wife readily agreed and, at the appointed time, went into a bedroom at home to see what would happen. Soon after Seka was due to start the healing from her base in London, my wife began to feel very relaxed and later felt as though there was a gentle swaying movement happening to her as though she were rocking softly in a small boat. My wife found it a relaxing and totally unexpected experience.

I do not recall that Seka was trying to deal with any medical situation when she sent healing to my wife – it was more a matter of seeing how many of the patients involved at the same time could detect any sensations. In the event I seem to remember the figure was around fifty or so.

The fact that my wife did pick up on healing being transmitted from some two hundred miles away really did put everything we were experiencing into a new dimension that is still largely unknown to most people. It made a terrific impression on both of us that first time, though as I grew in experience I was later to come to realise that most, and possibly all, healers can use this technique. When you stop to think about it, the fact that we can send healing to be received by our patients anywhere in the world is truly remarkable.

No matter how often I do it, I am always in awe that such a thing is possible. I want to say more about the mechanics of it and the amazing implications later.

While I prefer the hands-on approach, and to be in the company of anyone I am trying to help, I'm always happy to send healing to my clients if that is preferred for any reason.

The following case studies give an impression of this wonderful phenomenon.

—— Pat ——

Pat was a work colleague of my wife and was the first patient with whom I tried distant healing. She had suffered whiplash injuries in a car accident and had been living on painkillers for over a year with much sick leave from her job. I never actually met Pat but sent her three healing sessions over the period of a week or so. So far as I recall Pat's home was just over ten miles from where we lived. During the sessions of distant healing she felt heat in her neck just as if I had been healing her from within the same room. The effects were equally successful; by the third treatment all her pain had gone. From then on she had no need for painkillers and experienced none of the previous sick absences from work. She was as delighted as I was with the outcome of my first attempt at distant healing, telling me over the phone that it was 'now a pleasure to be able to do my ironing, gardening and carry my own shopping'. The relief she felt at being released from her pain was very evident in her voice as well as in the words she used.

What I have already referred to as sympathy pain as a healing signal in the earlier case study involving Hilda also cropped up while I was working on Pat. During one of the sessions I felt tingling in my jaw even though I was not concentrating on that area and didn't know whether or not Pat might have had a problem there. I was directing the healing to deal with the whiplash as usual when I felt the tingling and could do no more than simply continue with it. It later turned out that, in Pat's words, her jaw had given her trouble from time to time, by seeming to dislocate itself. She went on to say that she too had unexpectedly felt the warmth in her jaw during her treatment and that it felt much better afterwards. I was subsequently told it no longer gave her a problem.

—— Cathy ——

Cathy, the one with the mole and the dust allergy, was living about two miles away from us when she asked if I would send healing to deal with a cyst that the doctor had advised would have to be removed through surgery. I was happy to try to oblige though privately I did think it seemed to be quite a tall order.

The next morning she couldn't wait to tell my wife at work that she had received the healing and, as usual, had enjoyed the warm relaxation that accompanies it. Even so she had been amazed by the results; overnight, the treatment had 'miraculously' flattened the cyst so that it had virtually disappeared completely. By way of proof she even insisted that my wife should see for herself what had been achieved. There was no need for surgery or any other treatment, which is an outstanding result for one 30-minute session of healing from two miles away.

In fact Cathy falls into the category of a patient for whom I seem to be completely on the same healing wavelength and we have had a number of good successes. On one occasion I was sending her distant healing when, as she later told me, she was lying in bed and saw an image of my head in her room with gold light shimmering out of and around it.

When I heard of this my immediate reaction was that she must have been drifting off to sleep and that this was some form of a dream state.However, a couple of years later I read in a healing book that it has sometimes been reported by patients that they have seen the face of the healer during distant healing. I've no idea how common it might be but it is the only time that this has ever been reported to me from one of my healings. Neither Cathy nor I knew that such a thing was possible – it happened because it happened and it was only much later that I found it verified as a known occurrence within the field of healing.

What would be really interesting about that phenomenon would be if the healer's face appeared to someone who did not know the healer's features but who could then pick their photograph out, based purely on the image that had appeared in the vision. If only it had happened to one of my clients whom I have never met we would be able to hold a sort of psychic identity parade – but I digress.

—— Ian ——

Although there had been no formal diagnosis, Ian believed he was suffering from chronic fatigue syndrome, or ME. I agreed to send absent healing to him over a distance of probably 25 miles. Ian later reported that, during the healing, he had experienced warmth in his back but also a very dramatic example of a feeling of 'heaviness' that is one of the more occasional sensations that patients report happening to them during a healing session. In fact he told me he felt that he was pinned to the bed but, as he put it, 'sucked down from underneath rather than pressed from on top'.

This powerful sensation lasted for about forty minutes and eventually began to bother him so much that he described it as an 'oppression' and forced himself off the bed to prove that he could break free. This is one of the very rare times anyone has reported a sensation that did not suit them during healing. One or two have mentioned a degree of nausea or dizziness but almost everyone enjoys every healing experience. The feeling Ian called oppression may well be a stronger version of what others refer to as a feeling of 'heaviness'; in any event it was something that Ian easily dealt with by putting a stop to it of his own accord.

On another occasion when I sent distant healing to Ian he told me that he had felt the opposite effect; he seemed so light that he had to touch the bed to make sure he wasn't floating above it. It is interesting to note, yet again, that the concept of someone feeling 'lighter' as a feature of healing is mentioned.

Ian found that the healing and some advice I was able to give him helped him break free of the problem within a few short weeks. I will explain more about that advice later.

—— Daniel ——

Daniel brings together an example of someone who was being healed from a distance and also did not know that healing was taking place. He could not, therefore, help the process in any way, or 'fool' himself into any improvement. He was about 18 months old at the time, suffering development problems and having to be fed through a tube into his tummy; he was also struggling with chest infections for most of the time.

He is the grandson of a friend who passed on my offer of help to Daniel's mother who seemed a bit reluctant to go ahead with it until, as we did with Jenny, she eventually decided that her son deserved the opportunity to try healing no matter how unlikely she thought were the chances of success.

The first time I treated Daniel I went to see him at his home. I initially spent some time talking to his mother about the healing process in order to help her understand what it was all about and to reassure her that it was perfectly safe for me to use healing in order to try to help him. As I was doing so Daniel immediately crawled across to see me, which was very unusual for him; apparently, he was very wary of strangers and for him to come over so readily was a big surprise. His interest in me did not last long, however, and he soon took himself off. With an 18-month-old baby who had no knowledge of what I was trying to do for him – and a whole world around him to explore – I soon realised that even though he would come over to me the circumstances for healing were less than ideal. Whenever I put my hand to his chest or his back (depending on which way he twisted and turned) he would never give me more than a few seconds to work on him before he was moving off to look at something more interesting.

To try to distract him we persuaded him to watch one of his videos sitting on the carpet in front of me. Gradually this tactic meant I was at least able to give several bouts of close healing that lasted no more than a couple of minutes each time and without actually touching him. It was clear, however, from the way that he kept turning round to look at me that this limited process was giving him some sort of sensation. This became even more obvious when he started wriggling his shoulders while I kept my hand two or three centimetres behind him and with his attention back on the video.

Although Daniel was definitely receiving the healing energy, the circumstances were proving difficult and so to try to make it easier I agreed with his mother that I would start to send him distant healing a few days later. This was itself a novelty for me because on every other occasion I had used absent healing it was with the knowledge of a patient who was expecting me to do it at an agreed time. I had no idea whether it would work if the client were unaware that it was due to happen. Intrigued as to what the result might be, I sent the healing at the appointed time and, so far as I could tell from my own reactions, it felt as though the healing was working as normal. Success was soon confirmed when, later that day, his mother rang me to report that the healing had clearly got through to him because he again kept wriggling his shoulders throughout the session just as he had when I was there.

On another occasion I worked on him Daniel drifted off to sleep at the time I was sending the healing. This was unheard of for him at that time of day and he then slept solidly for two hours. A relaxed feeling, even a brief sleep, is also something that often happens during a healing session – including to adults.

I sent healing to Daniel a number of times and I am satisfied that it provided help, because it was reported back to me that he was showing gains. His mother told me that on one of the days I had sent healing he went on to have 'the best day of his life' and that he had been without symptoms of 'chestiness' for longer than she had ever known.

An interesting sideline to Daniel's case is that while I was explaining to his mother about healing on the first day, I asked her if she had any health problem that I might use to let her experience for herself the healing sensations that Daniel might feel. She told me that she had no adverse health conditions but she had been noticing an unexplained discomfort in her tummy; it was not severe and she had done nothing about it. I put my hand close to her tummy, moving it around as I searched for the bumps in her energy field that would tell me where the weak spot was. I soon found the area I needed to work on and as she duly felt the warmth of healing, she confirmed that I had hit the right spot. I did not give her healing for long because my intention was only to give her an insight into what should be happening to Daniel.

It was a week or two later that I realised that the point of mum's unexplained pain was around the area where her baby's feeding tube went into his tummy. When I telephoned her to ask her if it was indeed near that spot she said that she had never noticed before, but that was exactly where it was.

The case of Daniel nicely illustrates that distant healing is every bit as real as contact healing and that there can be no question of mind over matter or some version of the placebo effect if a baby is so evidently experiencing healing sensations at the time healing is being sent. It provided yet more fascinating evidence of the crucial fact that a definite power is at work, and also brought out another variation on the appearance of sympathy pains that can connect a healer to their client; in this case they were actually connecting a mother to her baby.

Because I do always send healing at a time agreed with the patient there is room for people to wonder whether clients are creating their own sensations of healing without receiving genuine inputs from me. Daniel's case proved that genuine interaction, whether direct contact or at a distance, does take place; it also supports the claims initially made to me by Seka, that interactive transfers between energies must be an essential part of how healing works. The next case study also covers an occasion when I was able to get more corroboration of this from an adult in an unexpected way; this is the story of Margaret.

—— Margaret ——

Margaret had been suffering for many years with backache. She had been prescribed many forms of analgesic, had tried massage, used a pain-easing machine and heat treatment, but had never obtained complete relief. She was introduced to the idea of healing by her sister who is a friend of mine and our efforts began with two sessions of contact treatment at her sister's house. Margaret had noticed a definite improvement in her condition on each occasion and this prompted her to try distant healing at an arranged time for what would be the third session.

The time agreed was 7 pm – though I wrongly believed that it had been fixed for 7.30. Just before 7 pm, unknown to me, Margaret sat down comfortably ready to receive the healing but then 7 o'clock came and went and nothing happened for her; five past, ten past – but still nothing. By now she was quite aware of the sensations she could expect during a normal healing session and was disappointed to feel nothing on this occasion. She had to conclude that this method of 'absent healing' which she was trying for the first time did not work for her.

However at 7.30 I rang her to apologise for the fact that I was actually running late – for what I had believed to be a 7.30 appointment! I told her I would in fact not be able to begin the healing process as arranged and would need to delay it.

Margaret was kind enough not to mention that it should have started half an hour earlier and we simply agreed to begin at a new time of 7.45 pm.

This time Margaret did feel the warm sensations to her troubled back area and again obtained relief from the nagging pain. As she later told her sister, she had genuinely believed that she was going to receive the healing at 7 pm and 'if it is all in the mind then that is the time I would have felt the benefit'. The sensation of healing had not begun until I began the process for real from my home some miles away at the later time!

My final example combines most of the features of healing that I have been keen to bring out in my selection of case studies, but also illustrates the need for we healers to be careful with our clients at all times.

—— Ian ——

Ian was a young lad of maybe 11 or 12 at the time. He was the son of a friend and was in pain, suffering from a broken leg. His mother brought him to see me and I proceeded with the usual sort of session which gave some help but, naturally enough, didn't solve the problem altogether; broken bones are not cured overnight.

Some days later his mother rang to ask if I would try again but, for convenience, she suggested that this time I used absent healing (over a distance of fifteen miles or so) rather than contact. Of course I agreed and sent the healing at the arranged time. Very soon, and while I was still working on him, his mother was on the telephone urgently asking me to stop because it was 'freaking him out'. I said I had no idea if I could just switch the process off like that but I would try, and would certainly do nothing further to keep it going. I also said I felt sure Ian would be able to stop it himself by simply willing himself against it. As it turned out, one way or another, the healing did then cease without further upset for my young client.

I was talking to Ian again recently, having long forgotten this incident, which probably happened about fifteen years ago; although we see each other occasionally the subject of that session had never cropped up until he happened to remind me. He told me that the direct, hands-on, healing session that I had first carried out with him had itself taken him by surprise; he had only come along that day to pacify his mother (where have I heard that before?) and had never expected anything to happen. He said that, to his amazement, he had felt the heat of healing through his plaster cast and had been happy to accept what was happening. He went on to say that he had felt willing to try it from a distance but when he had started to feel the healing sensation for real, on his own in his room and with me a long distance away, he couldn't take it. Using the same phrase so many years later, he told me he 'just freaked out'.

We agreed that if it were to happen now, for a more mature person it would not be a problem. However, it was a lesson for me not to take clients or the healing process for granted; as healers we do need to be careful at all times. As a welcome postscript, the good news was that Ian was able to tell me that the plaster on his broken leg had been taken off a few weeks earlier than normal – which is not a bad result for one session and a bit!

For me and my clients, all of these experiences and case studies amounted to absolute proof of an interactive mechanism that delivers healing, both directly and across distances. In a general sense I have shown that the mechanism is indeed some form of energy exchange; this concept is by no means new but my selection of cases contains more proof and stronger arguments than I have usually seen. The fact that healing is successful in the ways I have described is critically important in demonstrating the need to update our orthodox understanding which steadfastly denies all possibility of a healing force. In my next chapter I want to spell out in more detail exactly what healers know that everyone should learn about.

3
WORKING WITH THE MYSTERIOUS ENERGIES

'The most beautiful thing we can experience is the mysterious. It is the source of all true art and all science'

Albert Einstein

Millions of people throughout the world regularly experience and benefit from healing, a fact that seriously challenges the certainties held by those who doubt that anything is relevant to our universe outside the framework that we are generally recommended to accept. However, it was not only the outcomes of my work with individual clients that made me realise how far scientific knowledge lagged behind reality. Over the years I saw how the process itself, the subtleties and the physical presence of those energy mechanisms prove the limitations of everyday science in many other ways. By transmitting the healing 'agent' to distant clients I have broadly ruled out that healing depends on any direct physical contact and this moves us further towards a whole new world. Before we can go there, however, there is much more that I have to make clear about what is going on when the healing is doing its work – the practical facts of healing that justify what I have to say about our healing universe.

The question that is most often asked of all healers is 'can anyone do it?' The answer to this is yes, at least up to a point; I do not believe that literally everyone *can* do it to a truly useful level but most, if not all of us, could develop some ability. Those who do have ability can improve their gift and, as with all skills, the more it is practised the better it becomes. It is also the case that some of us are going to be far better at it than others, which is not unusual in any field. There are many who are competent in art and some who are so gifted as to be held up as 'maestros'. Then there are others who, like me, are totally incompetent, not able to draw anything better than slightly recognisable, let alone praiseworthy! It is the same for healers; no matter how hard we try we will only reach the highest level within our own competence, but in simple terms, yes – we can all do it. We can all join the healing force, but relatively few of us ever get round to 'trying our hands', so millions of people are not going to know how good they may be if they were to give themselves a chance.

Unlike art, sports or academic subjects, our aptitude for healing is not often tested. To some extent this is because healing seems to have an air of mysticism around it that initially deters people from having any involvement, whether as potential practitioner, client, or even as interested observer. This is deeply unfortunate and unnecessary; there is no call whatsoever for a 'mystical' approach and clouding the topic in mystique has done the world no favours. Healing is not spooky, nor is it unworldly or supernatural in any way; it is entirely practical and grounded. It is as important to me to deflect any elements of mysticism as it was to present the case studies that give proof that something real is happening. The actual mechanics of healing are vital to understanding the greater mysteries of the universe and that is why I want to spend this chapter dealing with the practicalities involved.

I have said that, for me, it was the book about Sai Baba that took me into becoming a healer. What I cannot know is whether that experience of asking for the gift in his name did actually transform me into a healing practitioner. I will never really know whether I was helped by making that plea to Sai Baba or if it simply brought out a skill that had always been there, untapped and just waiting to be tried, tested and developed. No matter, reading that book set me off on the path to becoming a very effective healer. The first lesson, therefore, is that if you want to know whether you can heal, be serious about it, but in essence just give it a go and judge what happens for yourself. For millions that will be all that is needed to prove the point.

For me, the process of learning to be a healer was not so much about seeking out direct practical training or instruction; it was more a matter of finding out exactly what was my version of the gift and then gaining confidence and familiarity in the things that I could do as an individual. During their learning process all those who become healers will spend time absorbing everything about the fact that healing is physically real. Regardless of their past beliefs, they will soon be certain that they are in the midst of a highly effective and powerful force which, for most of us, transforms our understanding. As our healing power grows we find a greater appreciation of spiritual values opening up for us; at the same time, we have to address the practical matter of how to deliver healing to those who need it. Each time I conducted a session I learned more about the practicalities; as those practicalities became more familiar I came to know more and more about the forces that were at work.

I think it is important that this account of what I now know, and how I got there, moves forward in much the same way as I did. I therefore want now to describe in some detail what I do, and what I encounter as a healer virtually every time I conduct a healing session.

I first make a patient feel welcome and as relaxed as possible. Then, having talked a little about healing theory and how I will conduct the session, the first practical step I take to get the ball rolling is to relax myself. I calm my mind and mentally ask to be connected safely to the healing energy for the benefit of my client. When I am ready, which only takes a few seconds, I put my hands a few inches from the patient and within their energy field at the general location of the problem that they have described. Usually at this point I quickly feel the tingling that I get from my client's energy field and will usually feel the differences within their field that I know can guide me to where the healing process should first be directed.

I mentally ask for the healing energy to flow, and with my hands remaining in the client's field I usually feel aware that healing energy is beginning to channel; I get my sense of this through barely perceptible sensations of warmth and even the merest vibration around my hands. Having worked briefly just around the patient's energy field I soon get my focus and put my hands actually on the spot on their body where I am moved to direct the healing. If I am not happy that the healing has got under way I will scan their whole body at the energy level to see if I can identify a better spot to start the process.

Sometimes it does take a little longer for me to be satisfied that healing sensations are coming through but when I do feel a connection my patient usually confirms that it has started. Clients mostly pick up on the feel of a healing sensation at about the same time as I do, or sometimes a minute or two later. Occasionally they will not recognise anything at all at this point, though this will not mean that the healing is not working – just that they are unable to detect it themselves. Whatever feedback they give me I will carry on with the healing for as long as I am happy that something is happening. It is rare for anyone not to feel one or more of the usual sensations that regularly accompany healing and at some point in the session, as they get used to the experience, almost all clients will sooner or later confirm they can feel its effects. Whatever the strength of any sensation that either I or my client detect, only the end of the session will reveal how much has been achieved for them, and sometimes it can even take them until the next day to be sure about their gains.

Often when I am actually touching a patient, as opposed to working simply in their body's energy field, I can feel the movement of energy in their body as the healing interacts. When this movement is present I can feel it whether from what seems to be a point deep in the body or one that is very close to the surface; interestingly, if I am working on the head I can even feel movement on the skull where there is little flesh between my hands and the bone. In about a third of cases the patient can also pick up a feeling of movement. The sensation is as though there are undulating waves gently coming up through my hands; you could imagine that muscles or flesh are rippling under your fingers, but you know they are not – it is the motion of energy that you can feel.

Throughout the session, as well as at the beginning, by moving my hands around the patient's field I am constantly drawn to where I sense that the healing process should be concentrated by those differences in the texture of the energy that I can feel. It seems to be that there is some sort of hierarchy of these locations because, having dealt with whatever shows up as the most obvious spot and treated it, I can then find I am drawn to another spot somewhere else. The indication to move on often coincides with a feeling I get that the first spot has somehow 'had enough'. This is more of an instinct on my part than anything obvious happening to the healing flow, but almost always I find another place to work on as soon as the first one has subsided and this goes on until the healing session comes to an end.

During the session I will ask my client about what seems to be happening – whether they are feeling any sensations, if there is any change or improvement in the condition they came to see me about, and so on; for me, there is no need to conduct healing in total silence, though other healers prefer to do so. It is important for both healer and patient to focus gently on the healing and so it is better not to indulge in social chit-chat, but I think that healing feedback while I am working is a good thing.

Ending a healing session is a matter of recognising that this natural process has done all that it can for the time being; again, it is partly a matter of instinct. As with much else we humans do, something inside us tells us when enough is enough. In my case I will usually start to feel that the healing power itself is petering out, that it is somehow running out of steam, which prompts me to check with the patient if they are still feeling the healing effect as strongly as they did. Often they will agree that it does seem to be subsiding, but if not they usually feel it easing off not long afterwards. It is at that point I will look at the clock – usually to be surprised at just how quickly the thirty minutes or so have passed.

Once a healing session has ended, the patient virtually always tells me how relaxed they felt during the process – not just comfortable but in a state almost approaching drowsiness. It is important now to allow the patient time to 'come round' from the session before talking in any detail about what was happening or what progress may have been made. When we do talk about it, as well as telling me how relaxed they are, most will tell me that physical gains have been made from the healing. Depending on the condition, and the rapport with the patient's energy, the improvement may even amount to complete relief, but more usually it is a matter of having made distinct, measurable progress. Very rarely am I told there has been no noticeable benefit, though sometimes patients report a feeling of muscle stiffness for about five to ten minutes after a session, which can temporarily disguise any improvement. Once this initial discomfort has gone, however, there is usually recognisable relief from some or all of the symptoms for everyone.

Often, I can sense for myself that the healing is bringing relief as the corresponding part of my own body registers a sensation of relaxation while I am working on that area of my patient's body. This is another variation of the sympathy signal though, for me, it is not something that can be called upon to happen to order. Unfortunately, when I do get these signals there are occasions when I get mixed up so that the feeling can turn up in me as the mirror image of the actual location for the patient. By this I mean that a pain or a sense of relief in my left shoulder will relate to a condition that in real life rests in the client's *right* shoulder. That may not seem very efficient; it would never be welcomed in the orthodox physical world, but with healing, that's just the way this particular aspect works for me.

The cause of such 'crossed wires' may just be that my own sensitivity to what is happening is at its limits. Whatever the reasons, for me the many variations within the healing process that are unpredictable but frequently repeated confirm the reality of healing; I am in no doubt that they help illustrate that there is indeed a physical exchange that is taking place between the healer and patient.

There is another feature that may be related to those 'crossed wires' that also sometimes crops up to affect healing. This happens when the area of a patient's body to which I am attracted by their disturbed energy is not directly the spot where the patient is feeling discomfort. This is particularly the case with the back, when I may feel tingling in the client's neck which directs me to work there even though the client's pains are in their lower back, or vice versa. We do not know enough about how the human energy system works to be able to explain exactly how or why this happens, but there is a consensus, shared with practitioners of acupuncture, that blockages in body energy flows lead to health problems which can impact at another point in the body. The energy blockage may be well away from where the problem shows up as pain, and probably happens because the interruption to the energy flow means it has not been able to do its job properly which then leads to an impact further down the line.

I know that orthodox medicine will also cite the possibility that the confusion is brought about by what they know as 'referred pain'. This could explain some instances, but not the full range of signals that we healers pick up on.

Another interesting feature of joining the healing energies to our patients is that the link between them and the healing process continues for some time after we have finished 'channelling'. Many patients tell me that they can feel the healing energy flowing for an hour or more after my direct involvement has stopped. This has led to a convention among healers that the healing process in fact goes on for 24 or even 48 hours, though without the patient usually being able to detect it for anything like that length of time. There are many cases where there are more gains subsequent to the healing session than are felt actually at the point when the healing from the healer concluded.

I had a patient with a 'bad back' who travelled to me from Halifax for help. He usually left in as much pain as when he arrived, which is probably an example of that effect of temporary muscle stiffness that can sometimes follow treatment, though for my Halifax client it lasts for much longer than in anyone else I have healed. The upside is that he always knew from his own experience that the healing would continue helping him and that he would feel very much better the following day. This pattern has been repeated a number of times, but unfortunately he has never been able to come for a significant run of treatments that might have solved his problem altogether. His gains are quick and last for a number of weeks after one of our healing sessions but then the problem recurs.

The natural span for a healing session with me seems to be 25 to 40 minutes. If all the indications are that the healing is fading but the time that has passed is significantly less than that, there is rarely any point in pressing on in the hope that it will reactivate. If we have read the indicators right and the power is petering out, there is nothing we can do to get more out of it. On the odd occasion in my early days as a healer when I tried to squeeze too much out of a healing session I found that I simply depleted my own energy levels to the point of feeling nauseous. This caused me discomfort and did nothing more to benefit my patient.

In my case studies I included examples of one of the most amazing experiences in the whole field of healing – that of absent, or distant, healing. During this treatment the process works with the same effectiveness and, most tellingly, often with the same physical sensations for both healer and patient as if they were in the same room. It is a technique that puts the practicalities of healing on to a level that goes beyond even that of contact healing. It is obvious that healing at a distance cannot rely on touch or the proximity of healer and client. To be able to heal successfully in this way offers the strongest and most direct evidence that the truly active part of the healing process is outside of we healers who are merely acting as channels. There is no sensible way in which we could directly pass energy to a client on the other side of the world, somewhere in a suburb of a town or city we don't know, if all we have to use is our own physiology. There is so much more to it, and it is an issue I will be returning to explore later.

When I am sending healing I begin to think about the absent patient and try to lock on to wherever they are by facing in what I think is roughly their direction. I concentrate for a few moments and then stretch my hands out in front of me before I sway them slightly from side to side, in a wide arc. The motions I make are a bit like the movement of a compass needle as it hovers either side of its mark before settling to show the direction of north. I always sway my hands from side to side searching for a 'channel' or corridor through which I should direct the healing energy. I have to say that I am never quite clear whether or not I do end up literally pointing in the direction of where my patient is waiting – although that would seem the most logical. Because healing does not always work as we might expect there has to be a possibility that what I have identified as I sway my hands is simply an 'opening' that is suitable for me to transmit the healing, regardless of where it may actually point geographically.

Whatever the nature of the channel that I am able to lock on to in this way, the direction in which to send the healing always becomes clear. I gain a physical sense of having found a more open 'window' guiding me to where the absent healing should be directed – down that segment of the arc through which I had swung my hands and where the magnetic pull feels weaker than at each side of it. For some reason I believe that this is where I should send the healing and since I have had many successes in working this way, I have to believe I am getting it right.

As an example of this process, about five or six years ago a friend of a friend telephoned me to ask if I could send healing to deal with some floating material in his knee; this, he told me, was a problem that would otherwise need surgery. I was not particularly hopeful that I could deal with such physical debris in this way and warned him that it may not succeed. I did not know of him before his call and was therefore only able to attempt healing by my concentrating on getting healing to be sent to 'George in Glasgow' who needed help with his painful knee – that was all the information I had. On that basis I turned towards where I thought Glasgow, and he, might be positioned in Scotland from where I was living, put my swaying technique into effect and did my best. From this vague background on my part the healing was delivered precisely as intended – as I discovered when 'George in Glasgow' later rang me back to say that he had felt heat at the time I transmitted the healing and that, against all the odds, his knee now felt fine after just one treatment. He was very grateful, and I must admit I was particularly delighted with that success.

A similar illustration of all of the features of this incredible absent healing process involved another client I also knew only by her first name and where she was living in a particular district of my town. I had no actual address for her and, as with 'George' I did not know much else about her. She was called Barbara (a different Barbara from the one in my previous case study) and had been put in touch with me to see if I could help with her back problem; my only contact with her was by telephone. Somehow, again, the healing power would have to find the right person from very sketchy information. Certainly, at the human and physical level, I could never have found her house myself, even though the district was not too far from where I lived; nor would I have ever recognised her if I saw her in the street.

I sent distant healing to her by my usual method on a couple of occasions and doing my best to concentrate treatment on her lower back. Each time, when she telephoned with feedback, she told me she had received it on cue, but as sensations that were acting on her neck rather than in her back where she was expecting them. In some ways she was disappointed that it would only set to work on her neck, though she had to admit that she was still quite pleased with the outcome in that she soon found that she was able to turn her head properly and was therefore able to drive more comfortably. It is another example of the healing power knowing far more about what is needed than either client or healer. I never met Barbara and she didn't stay in touch long enough to see if she would get help further down her spine.

One final example of what I regard as a fascinating, and revealing, aspect of healing concerns a call I received from my cousin in the armed forces in Germany, who had damaged his shoulder some weeks earlier. Orthodox medical treatment from the military had failed to make any impression on the injury which troubled him most because it prevented him from playing football, something that I personally sympathised with. He had been advised that the next stage of treatment would have to be cortisone injections and he told me that he was not keen for this to be done. I immediately offered to do what I could to help and, as usual, arranged to send healing at an agreed time.

The first session happened on a Sunday afternoon; it was important for me because at that time it meant I would be sending healing the furthest distance that I had so far tried – from England to Germany. In principle, I knew the actual distance the healing would have to travel should not make any difference, and that there was no reason to worry that the force would be affected by a few hundred miles. Nonetheless, if I were successful it would reveal a little more about the capacity of the healing power to find its mark. After I sent the healing, therefore, I was a little more anxious than usual as I awaited feedback from him – partly for the selfish reason that I did want to chalk up what would be a personal long-distance success, and partly of course because, as always, what mattered most to me was knowing that healing was bringing relief from pain or suffering whatever the distance.

My cousin later rang me to say that at the time I had sent the healing he had indeed felt very strong sensations in his shoulder, particularly of warmth but which soon turned to slight pain. There are those who say that the healing process should never bring on any pain but I find that in a small number of cases it does. On these occasions the pain is never strong enough to be described as unbearable but it is a sensation that sometimes, for reasons that are not obvious, some patients do feel. No one has ever asked me to stop on account of the pain, and having been subjected to physiotherapy I can honestly say that no one has ever even hinted that they felt anything like the agony I went through when I was trying to get help for my own shoulder during a session of absolutely brutal, physical treatment.

Over the next week or so I sent another two or three bouts of healing to my cousin and about ten days after his first telephone call to me, he was able to confirm that the problem had disappeared and that he was now back to playing football.

This method of absent healing is indeed pretty much as effective as the direct healing that we give when the healer and client are in the same room and, as I said, helps prove that there must be something 'physical' to connect healer and patient, regardless of how far apart they may be. In addition to the body energy that is a part of the physical make-up of all of us, long-distance healing can only be sent if there is some power that enables a healer's force to be directed and channelled, so as to be received almost instantaneously by the client. We know that healers, and others from different cultures throughout the world, have always insisted that there is in fact a vast external energy field within which everything in the universe sits. All 'hands-on' healers agree that natural healing takes place by their being able to channel healing energy from this outside universal source. We are all very clear that what we do does not emanate exclusively from somewhere within our own bodies.

Healers believe that during a hands-on healing process, the healing power is routed from the external force into the *healer's* personal energy system; the healer immediately channels it on and into the energy system of the patient. The patient's own energy field is boosted by this healing power and temporarily becomes super-efficient at its natural task of keeping the body in good order. As I mentioned when I was writing about Seka, the entire business of channelling healing energy is similar to giving a blood transfusion that can help the body to mend itself, the healing version being a 'transfusion' of healing-energy impulses that greatly enhance the body's capacity for self-healing. The essence of healers, therefore, is that in some way they are wired up to be able to make the essential connection between their client and the available external healing force.

I have already touched on the very telling evidence that while this transfer of energy is taking place there is a narrow range of physical sensations that virtually all patients repeatedly report happening to them. Patients may feel only one of the sensations from this small and familiar range, though frequently they can detect combinations of two or three during any one session; certainly patients can expect to experience more than one of these reactions if they have more than one treatment. Additionally, as I have said, almost all patients tell me that they feel exceptionally relaxed during and after a healing treatment; this is often so powerful that a number even fall asleep for a short time while I am working on them. The fact that clients do experience these common reactions has always seemed to me to be as important as the results of healing treatment in terms of furnishing proof that an active force is at work.

The most frequently reported sensations are:

- heat (by far the most repeated)
- a pronounced and unusual sense of relaxation
- tingling
- pulling or pulsing
- a sense of heaviness
- cooling
- internal tremors – possibly the release and flow of blocked energy.

Sensations experienced by patients are usually very strong indeed and always unmistakable. As with the overall effects of healing, they come as a complete surprise to the first-timer, very often seriously challenging their belief systems as well as their expectations. When they do come across it for the first time many of my clients will say something like 'it may be coincidence, but I did feel warmth – and the pain has reduced'. I am sure that their hesitation is mostly because they do not want to let themselves believe they really are on the edge of something that could ease or even resolve their health problem, especially if it has been of a chronic nature. People do not want to build up their hopes too quickly and it often takes gains over two or three sessions before they allow themselves any real confidence.

Whether the healing method I use is contact or absent, from my experience an overall rule of thumb is that more than 95 per cent of my patients do feel something going on very soon after I start a session and then go on to tell me they have enjoyed distinct benefits from the treatment. If people feel the process of healing having an impact as it is happening and then feel an improvement in their condition almost immediately, and if it happens time and time again regardless of the expectations of healer and patient, then a reasonable deduction is that there is something at work – something well worth understanding. It shows that there is more going on than some sort of self-delusion or an undue 'influence' on the part of the healer. If the healing sensations that clients experience vary, it is even more unlikely that the process has anything to do with meeting known expectations; hundreds of clients are not likely to self-generate the same range of familiar sensations.

At the risk of becoming too technical, let me throw in some basic observations:

- Something like 60–70 per cent of my clients gain complete relief of their symptoms provided they do not call a halt to the process too early. Some do break off their visits to me because they are happy with their progress even though it may be less than a cure; some find it too much for their belief system; and I suspect some feel they do not want to keep 'troubling' me because I rarely take any money.
- Healers seem often to have a particular affinity with some conditions but are less successful with others – as though they are not on the same wavelength as the condition.
- It is also possible for a healer to be on a particularly close wavelength to some of their clients at the human energy level, which will greatly aid the healing process. It is likely that when a healer has such a good rapport with both the condition and the particular patient they are more likely to get those amazing results that grab the headlines. Conversely if either the patient or the condition is not on the healer's wavelength, successful treatment will be more difficult.
- Occasionally there are clients who actively block the healing process whether they intend to or not. Some, psychologically, do not wish to get well regardless of the type of treatment, while others cannot really accept the implications if they allow healing to work. I've actually had one patient tell me that he'd been nagged into seeing me but was determined not to let it work and if it did work he wouldn't admit it!
- In all treatments, orthodox or complementary, much really depends on the cause of the condition. If the cause remains then, no matter how effective the treatment

(and no matter what type of treatment), the condition is likely to return to some degree or another. If someone is made ill by eating the wrong food or living beneath an electricity pylon, or if their physical symptoms arise from emotions or any other cause that is not removed, they cannot be surprised if they get ill again.

While that might seem a defensive list of background features I mention them to aid understanding and to explain at least some of the reasons why healing can vary and why, in some cases, it may not be 100 per cent effective. The success rate for good healers is nonetheless astounding, particularly when you think that almost everyone who seeks our help does so because orthodox treatment hasn't worked for them. This means we often find ourselves dealing with conditions that orthodox practitioners have not found easy to treat, but we still enjoy a success rate, and in a timescale, that would delight any physician.

There is no need for any sense of competition in this. Healing is hugely effective and in some cases more efficient than orthodox medicine; on the other hand, modern health provision is better structured, better supported and has many techniques and practices that are better suited to patients' needs than our means of healing can claim. Between the two, however, so much more could be achieved to deal with sickness in an enlightened way if the two perspectives of medics and psychics could join forces.

The success rates for healing and healers vary as they do in orthodox treatments. If you read reports of healers' achievements or see them on television you will often be struck by the dramatic way in which the healers appear to be able to help. You may feel entitled to believe from this that the healer is a miracle worker who can cure anyone of anything at the flick of a finger. Don't be tempted to believe any such thing; the fact is that you will always be told the best examples of our successes for obvious reasons – they are intriguing and encouraging events for us as healers and can be expected to be equally fascinating to others. There is great mileage all round in highlighting how a healer has cured a condition in a single dramatic event; it certainly makes for more exciting PR than if the cure comes in ten or a dozen sessions over several weeks.

Provided 'miracle' accounts are true and accurate there is probably nothing wrong with presenting them for public consumption but we make rods for our own backs and do no service to healing if we allow clients or the public to think that miracles are the norm and more or less guaranteed. I too have had my share of dramatic successes but there are also times when it's a much harder slog and, though very rarely, frustrating times when no help seems to be given at all. Because both healers and their patients are all individually different and the true cause of patients' conditions is also not constant – or may well not even be known – the healing process can be less predictable than many of us would like.

Whatever we make of the detail, there is no getting away from the fact that healing is a genuine form of therapy that works by means of an interaction between energies for the benefit of humans and animals. Healing input can be given by millions of people who have whatever it takes to perform the service and everyone in the world should be free to enjoy its effects. Small wonder that I was thrilled to find out about it in the first place – and even more thrilled to establish myself as someone capable of using healing energies to help others.

For me to have become a practising healer, however, proved to be only the beginning of my fantastic journey. It did provide the hard evidence that there is more to the universe than we commonly believe, but I was soon to find how the influence of energies is even more widespread throughout the universe, and in all our lives, than I had yet realised.

4

ADVANCING THE ARGUMENT and the evidence

'To raise new questions, new possibilities, to regard old problems from a new angle, requires creative imagination and marks real advance in science'

Albert Einstein

So, the evidence shown through successful healing strongly demonstrates the presence of interactive energies all around us as well as within us. I am very aware that even though this is a simple truth for healers, it is still seen as a trite, and even controversial, statement in other circles. Outside the healing experience the idea of body energies and the presence of a vast universal energy force has rarely been accepted by most westerners; it is considered at least unorthodox, if not impossible. There seems little general sympathy for the conviction held by millions of healers and their clients worldwide that everything, and everyone, exists within the area of a universal energy field that surrounds not only the earth but our whole solar system and indeed reaches across the entire universe. For healers and their clients, however, energies and the role they play in our cases are readily self-evident.

The mechanism that conducts healing is a mixture of the body energies of healer and client, jointly supported by the external energy. It is as if we are all beings who are fundamentally made from energy, living in a sea of related universal energy with which we are as one. What I have been saying so far proves this and immediately distances what healers know from everything that we are all generally taught to expect as we move through life. Healing is one of the most obvious ways that we can demonstrate the presence and impact of energies but there is no reason to believe that this is all that the universe has to offer; the obvious question to ask about the forces of healing is: 'what else can such mechanisms do – what else could they reveal?' So far as I know this has never been asked before – certainly I have never seen much of an answer – but as I set about dealing with the question for myself I was soon to discover that energies do have many other influences and connections across the universe, and within our lives. Once I had established the truths about healing, many other aspects of real physical forces beyond our everyday understanding just turned up. They arrived in their own ways in an order that appeared to be nothing more than randomly diverse – I just had to piece them all together as and when I could; this proved to be a task that became easier and more obvious the more I opened my mind.

Over the next few chapters a sense of the threads of immense energies will emerge and will illustrate something of the links that exist between them. They vary and escalate in power but are unmistakable once you begin to look at the evidence. They connect like the pieces of a jigsaw puzzle – the sections may have some appeal in their own right but they only show their full impact when they make up the bigger picture.

My knowledge of healing was, and remains, the cornerstone of everything I believe. Countless individual cases – my own and those of thousands of other healers – constantly emphasise how energies contribute immensely in our personal lives. For clients to feel those physical reactions as healing affects their bodies is usually enough to satisfy them that they are in the hands of a genuine healer and that, whatever they may have expected, a bona fide interactive treatment is taking place. The sensations they feel are strong in themselves and an effective way to rule out most, if not all, initial doubts and predispositions that many people have when they first visit a healer. They also deal particularly well with the favourite response from anyone who wants only to refute healing – the claim that it is all down to placebo, as if this explains everything!

In truth, the placebo effect is not fully understood at all but it is the general label given to instances in which a patient derives a benefit from being given remedies that have no known active ingredient. Placebos are given consciously during trials to volunteers who anticipate that what they are being given can, or will, be helpful. The placebo tests that I have read about all rely on this factor of the patient believing that the treatment to be given is expected to be effective. They are 'deceived' into anticipating that they will see a benefit while, unknown to them, they are being ministered with a dummy medication. In terms of 'belief' in what is happening to them they are being manipulated to have confidence in the treatment they are receiving; a proportion – sometimes quite a high proportion of them – then do go on to show signs that they have benefited from the 'medication'.

The placebo experiments are fascinating, but the process

does not match what happens during treatment by a healer. When a placebo is involved the patient does not feel sensations from the dummy medication in the way that people receiving healing usually report. Most of my clients expect nothing at all when they first come along to receive healing; they quickly admit to having real doubts that the treatment can do anything for them and none of them is deceived into believing otherwise. I am afraid that trying to draw comparisons between a session of healing and what is happening during a structured placebo trial misses the point completely – they are vastly different in nature, intent and expectation. I have had no involvement with placebo trials but as a healer my belief is that the placebo effect occurs in those medical trials because in some circumstances it becomes possible for people actually to heal themselves; they are able to connect naturally to the healing energies in a version of the ways in which healers generally make contact to help their clients. I am sure that when someone who is somehow in tune with the energies receives their dummy tablet, it acts as a focus for that person to attract the universal energies to interact with them so as to make a healing gain.

If this were what is going on it would represent a practical, cause-and-effect explanation that science is currently finding hard to match from its own perspective. I can certainly say, beyond question, that healing is not an incidence of the placebo effect – but the placebo effect might well be an incidence of the healing force at work!

What also supports healing as a practical means of treating people is clear from my earlier case studies, particularly those in which clients are not even able to know that healing is taking place. They cannot therefore be calling on any other factor – including the placebo effect – to account for the gains that were made. In addition there are also those cases in which something previously unknown or unexpected crops up during healing treatment. I am thinking here of Barbara who first felt healing at work in a tumour behind her eye that none of us had known to be present and those many instances in which healing shows that it is required somewhere in a client's body other than the perceived location of their pain. To that we can also add those signals that I receive as sensations in my own body to indicate that I need to vary what I am doing. When these interactions happen we learn even more than we do from the healing sessions themselves.

There are also other times when I have had experiences that are outside the range of typical healing reactions; these always add an extra twist to our understanding. One interesting study concerns an incident that took both my client and me totally by surprise; it also shows why it is not just desirable, but essential, for healers to work hand in hand with orthodox practitioners in an atmosphere of mutual trust and support.

The case began as I finished healing my client Marion, the lady I have already mentioned in one of my earlier case studies. After her treatment Marion's husband, Jim, unexpectedly asked me to treat his arm which he said was very painful – so much so that he could not raise it above shoulder level. He demonstrated how difficult that was for him and told me that it had been troubling him for some time but he could get no satisfactory help or even any positive diagnosis from his doctor. He then explained that the problem had started shortly after a visit to hospital where he had been given an injection and he was convinced there was a connection between that jab and his painful problem.

I agreed to see what I could do, but had no expectation of what, if anything, I might find. Nonetheless, I began to move my hands around in his energy field, 'scanning' his arm and shoulder, checking for the usual telltale signal of increased tingling or 'bumps' in his energy field that would show me the source of his problem – or at least the area where I should direct treatment. I quickly found a point in his arm where his energy field felt different but just as it was registering with me Jim immediately shot out of his seat, holding his arm and crying out that I had given him an electric shock!

His rather dramatic reaction shocked and surprised me as well. I had certainly never witnessed anything like it before, though it later put me in mind of the pain that Seka had felt when she first treated Jenny. Then, of course, it had been the healer who had felt the shock; this time it was the patient. I persuaded him to try again and, although there was nothing that I had actually done as part of the healing process that was any different from my usual technique, I decided to make my healing passes slower and gentler. At no time had I actually touched him or done anything physical that could have caused any pain, but I determined to be more relaxed in order to calm things down as best I could.

As I started the healing again, I was relieved to find there were no more shocks of any kind and I was able to continue the healing as normal. Once we had settled into it a little, he turned to me and said, 'I'll tell you what, the place where I got the shock and where you are working is exactly where they put that bloody needle into me'.

He had been wearing a long-sleeved shirt so there was no way I could have known where that spot was, and I hadn't really had time to consider what he had been saying about the possible source of his problem. There had been no need to start from any particular point because I expected my scanning to signal where to work and whether there was anything I could do. Because he had been wearing his shirt and we both knew

I had not jarred him as I healed him, it is obvious that the healing process had worked out for itself where the problem lay and transmitted the information on to me, guiding me to where I needed to give treatment. Even if I had touched him it seems unlikely to me that he would feel it as what he called an electric shock, or what I would term an unexpected 'super tingle'. This is clear evidence that a range of signals is generated during healing as specific features or responses in respect of what is going on, though I had no idea exactly what had happened in energy terms to trigger that reaction in Jim.

At the end of the session his arm was much more comfortable though there was not much improvement in his degree of movement. We carried on healing for several weeks with probably two sessions per week on average. The outcome was always the same – comfort for a day or two but no overall improvement, no lasting gains. I kept advising him to go back to his GP or the hospital consultant but he refused, saying he had no confidence in either of them; he told me he had been to them repeatedly and their examinations had brought neither help nor diagnosis.

Eventually we reached a natural break as I went away on holiday. On my return I went to see him again and was shocked to be told that a few days after I had gone, and while he was returning from another fruitless trip to his doctor, he had collapsed in the street and had been rushed to hospital. There they had discovered that the problem was a massively septic arm caused, he again insisted, by a dirty needle with which he had been injected. In the end he had to undergo massive surgery to clear the huge infection.

My purpose in recounting this, of course, is not to take a swipe at orthodox medicine. I have no idea why his condition could not have been detected earlier, but these things happen.

My point is that if the existence, role and reliability of energies could have been taken seriously by the doctor, then the medics could have had a clear idea from me where the source of the problem was, and known sooner that there was indeed a real problem to be treated. Unfortunately, that degree of rapport and understanding has not been reached; instead a client came to rely on me for any comfort I could give and the medical profession was effectively sidelined. In just a few short days, when my help had to stop temporarily, it nearly cost him his life when he collapsed immediately after a visit to his doctor, which again had unfortunately not helped.

In the event, he bought my wife and me a watch each for the fact that, as he saw it, I had been saving his life for weeks. I must say that the healing must have been doing an incredible job if it were keeping massive infection at bay like that. Sadly there is insufficient trust, respect and co-operation between orthodox and complementary medicine; we have not joined forces and between our disciplines it could be argued we nearly killed him!

In fairness, and to their credit, there are many from a medical background who are open-minded and willing to treat the topic of healing with more respect. Encouragingly a significant number of GPs have developed the healing gift for themselves and are happy to use it alongside their orthodox skills for the benefit of their patients. Others work with healers and complementary therapists as a helpful additional resource to the same end and there are some areas of the UK that have set up doctor/healer liaison committees to try to make sense of it at a practical level.

Unfortunately, this is all pretty much ad hoc with not enough overall structure – not enough is taught in our schools, universities and teaching hospitals, or across society, that would prepare anyone to give or receive healing or even to acknowledge that it exists as a practical, physical certainty. It is a weakness in the system that is illustrated by another case in which I sent absent healing to Neil – he is the son of a friend of ours who had been knocked off his motorbike and suffered a fractured wrist. He was prepared to try healing but the actual arrangements had been made through his father who did have some knowledge of what healing can do. When I sent Neil some healing at the agreed time I had never spoken to him, I knew nothing about him personally and I had no details of his injury – I just went about the healing process in my usual way and waited for feedback.

Neil called me a couple of days later in order to let me know how it had turned out for him. He did not have a lot to say but confirmed that he had felt warmth in his wrist when the healing was being channelled and that he was pleased to see that, afterwards, it definitely felt 'better', allowing him to gain more movement. I remember saying that I was not sure that investigating movement in this way was a wise thing to be doing to a broken wrist, but Neil said he was confident it would be OK. I offered another session when he felt like it and that is how we left things.

Next day his father happened to ring again to set up some healing for another friend and took the opportunity to tell me that Neil was indeed pleased with the healing I had sent. It transpired that it was something about which his son had been sceptical and even a little nervous beforehand but that, afterwards, he knew it had improved things. During my chat with his father I also learned that Neil was in fact a health professional who had really preferred to rely on orthodox treatments within his own field but had turned to me for healing because his injury had not been making the progress that, professionally, he would have expected.

A few days after that, Neil contacted me again to let me know that he had now had the plaster cast removed and seen his NHS physiotherapist. At first the physio had forecast that it would be about three weeks before Neil would be able to drive his car but when he actually tested the wrist, much to his own amazement, the physio changed the forecast to one week. This has to count as another outstanding result for one healing session, especially as the reason that Neil came to me was that his progress up to then had been too slow. To have accelerated his recovery provided a pleasant bonus for Neil and a good way for him to discover the world of healing energies.

As well as confirming my theme that prior confidence or expectation has nothing to do with the success of healing, that story also shows how Neil, as a health professional, was unfamiliar with healing; it is therefore another indication of how the health service is missing out hugely by not taking the subject seriously enough. Some hospitals, and many hospices, do have access to complementary medicine though it does not amount to a standard provision of routine therapy. To my understanding it is more in the nature of something that may be available when orthodox treatment has little or nothing to offer – somewhere as an afterthought rather than a supporting part of the front line.

The prime difficulty for our health professionals, as well as for science and academia generally, is still the question: 'what are the mechanics by which healing can be delivered?' Without an answer to that it is hard to have confidence that healing could be helpful; it becomes virtually impossible for medics to recommend patients try healing for themselves, although English law does permit GPs to do so. As a healer it is easy for me to repeat the general explanations that healing is simply delivered by energies but despite being accurate that is not really robust enough for someone trained in medicine to make any sense of. At worst it might be seen as a sinister evasion and, at best, an unproven claim which the western world should not rush to take on board.

The presence and effects of energy are certainly the only realistic explanation as to how it is possible for healers to transfer healing and health gains to clients, whether directly or from thousands of miles away. For as long as it remains only a theory, however, it will fail to convince, but fortunately I can actually demonstrate very clearly the existence of interactive body energy on which the explanation of healing depends. This is done by means of a simple experiment that any of us can easily conduct. In my experience of discussing, demonstrating and even some lecturing on the subject of energies, I have found that at least 30 to 40 per cent of people can easily feel their own energy field for themselves – first time, without any practice. This is how you can try to do the same for yourself:

Stand or sit comfortably with your elbows bent and hands pointed in front of you palms apart, as though holding a skein of wool that someone is rolling into a ball. With your hands out and relaxed, fingers loosely apart, you need to imagine electricity flying around and between your hands. Then after a few seconds, as you keep the mental image going, stay relaxed but concentrate a little on whether you become aware of anything happening in your hands or fingers. You may feel a sensation of warmth or tingling, possibly in the fingers or the palms of your hands – it may be localised or more general.

Whether or not you do feel anything, you should then bring your palms quite close together – not touching, but to maybe 5 to 10 centimetres apart – and then take them back out again to a distance of 30 to 40 centimetres. Repeat this movement so that you are gently and quite slowly drawing your hands together and taking them apart. You should be moving your hands together and away softly and loosely a number of times as if playing an imaginary concertina – though in a flowing, elegant style rather than in a stiff or robust manner. The essence is on quite relaxed movements to and fro; ten or twelve times should be enough to notice a distinct sensation.

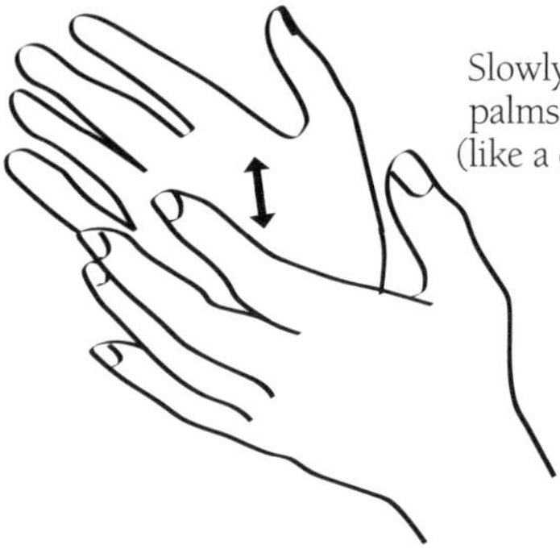

If it doesn't work for you, ask others to try instead, while you watch the results. I have found it helpful to include one or two women as they do tend to be more sensitive to the sensations than men; up to 50 to 60 per cent of women who have tested it out for me were able to feel that tingling sensation that is sometimes accompanied by warmth. Whether or not people do experience something in that way, many will also be able to recognise what seems like a ball of magnetism either pulling or showing subtle resistance between their hands as they repeat their movements. Do not look for strong or violent sensations – they are more restrained but very unmistakable. The more this is practised, the clearer the feelings become so everyone should be prepared to repeat the exercise more than once before deciding it is not going to work.

Anyone who does feel their own body energy in this way will usually find it possible also to feel the body energy of other people; this really underlines the reality of body energy because you will realise that it is not just a sensation from your own hands, you really feel it as another person's field. This is how you go about it:

Begin by facing the person who has agreed to let you feel their energy; both people need to be standing about a metre apart. Put your hands up to a comfortable height, about level with your chest and with your palms facing your partner. Hold your hands up in this way for a few seconds – they should be comfortably just about 30 centimetres or so from your shoulders as if warding someone off rather than being totally outstretched in front of you. Now move slowly towards your partner using gentle forward movements pushing and withdrawing (but without ever touching your partner) to try to detect their energy in the same way you could feel your own by the movement of your hands in the previous experiment. Just make the pushing motion backwards and forwards with your hands while slowly stepping closer and then away from the other person until you can feel the same tingling field as you felt with your own energy. This is your partner's body energy.

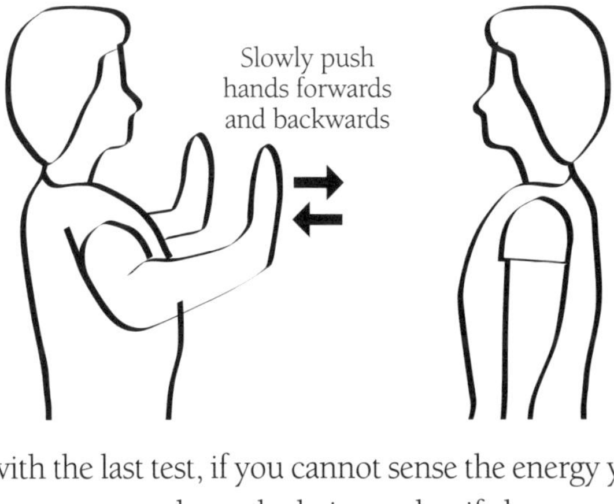

As with the last test, if you cannot sense the energy yourself, get others to try and watch their results; if they are doing it right, then out of three or four people who try it, at least one should succeed. If all those who try have actually felt their own body energy then the success rate may well be higher than that.

Another experiment can now be conducted to prove that it really is your partner's energy field you are finding; more importantly this one also shows how the energy fields we possess actually change and interact in a very subtle way. If you are able to feel another person's energy field in the way I described above, now try this additional variation:

First, ask your partner to think of something pleasant, something that they like, that appeals to them. When you are both settled feel for their energy field as described above and notice how far away from their body their energy field reaches at the point where you start to feel it.

If you do it immediately after you first detected their field it is now likely to be a bit wider than it was a minute or so earlier as their mood perhaps changes from uncertainty and inquisitiveness the first time round to being more relaxed. If it is the same 'size' do not worry; it simply means they were already happy and relaxed while you were checking them before. Just make yourself familiar with how far you are from them at the point at which you can detect their field.

Now move on to the real test by inviting them to think of something really sad or unpleasant for them – perhaps to remember a serious dislike of theirs or to think about anything that would alarm or trouble them. Step away and then repeat your previous movements to come forward to feel their energy field again. This time you will find that the whole field is much closer in to their body. The energy field has become distinctly tighter and more concentrated; instead of being open and extended as it was when they were pleased, you will find it altogether more restricted.

It is important that you do not leave anyone for long in this pool of negative, tighter energy, so you must make sure to finish the experiment by telling them to think pleasant thoughts again as they did at the beginning, thereby relaxing and widening that energy field. Test them again to be certain that their energy field has indeed returned to its relaxed positive state.

With a little practice, particularly with the same person, you can invite them to choose which two states they want to generate, without telling you, and by feeling for the distance of their energy field you will be able to work out whether their field is tight or open. From this you can tell them whether they have chosen happy and positive or negative and sad thoughts.

I have had feedback from people who have passed the exercise on to others who have confirmed that it worked just as well wherever and whenever it was attempted. In my earlier days of healing I attended a communications course as part of my day-to-day job. One of the exercises was for each of us to lecture the rest of the course for a short time on a topic of our own choice. Such blank canvasses are often difficult to fill but I soon decided to tackle the topic of these energies. I thought it would be an interesting enough subject for my audience – and familiar enough to me that it would require little advance preparation on my part! The talk did seem to go well and a lively discussion followed, both in the training room and in the bar afterwards. Many years later my work brought me back into contact with one of the other course members, a senior and very independently minded colleague, who, out of the blue, reminded me of my talk and told me he had repeated the experiment of detecting energy many times since with different friends and always proved its success. He and they had always found it a fascinating demonstration.

These experiments can indeed be entertaining diversions, but they become much more than a party trick when you begin to think about some of the implications. Consider what impact there could be on your body, including your mind and emotions, if your energy field, which is supposed to keep you well, is being tightened and hindered in this way. This could easily happen, for example if we meet up with real sadness, upset or other forms of unpleasantness – just as we create in that earlier experiment when the subjects deliberately put themselves into a negative state. Is it not obvious that our energy, as it becomes tighter and closer, would be less able to do its job of keeping the body in good order as effectively as it would when it was full and unconstrained? Consider also the reverse – how much more effectively our energies will keep us well if we can relax and enjoy life, perhaps aided by yoga, meditation, positive thinking and laughter.

Because sensing energies in this way does not work equally for everyone, scientists are forced to have a bit of a problem with the concept since getting the same result with every experiment is the cornerstone of what they are and what they do. Repeatability is what confirms scientists' perceptions and proves their theories. I can respect that approach but it is also true that it is not always the only valid way to make judgements. We have no idea what governs our individual ability to pick up these energy fields, but after all why should we all be the same? We do have different aptitudes, and widely different tastes and emotions. Some people are crippled with hay fever simply from leaving their home, while others wouldn't know that pollen existed unless they read about it.

We have no reason to expect everything to be homogenised. In the world of orthodox medicine modern drugs come with a long list of side effects which may affect different users in different ways – if at all! There are variables between individuals almost wherever you look; detecting body energy is an objective physical exercise but, nonetheless, to be successful does depend on a personal facility that, apparently, not everyone has, or if they do it is not as easily accessible to them as it is for those who pick it up quickly. However, with the odds of about one in three or four people showing the ability first time, you will not need to involve too many others in the tests before you are satisfied that energies that interact with our minds and bodies really do exist.

Having seen how healing works for us through the transfer of good energy into this interactive system, we must also be prepared to recognise the opposite inevitability – body energy which has somehow become constrained by internal or external influences will indeed be less effective in keeping us well. It is also likely that any ill effects would be greater if the body energy were to continue to be restricted on a long-term basis, through stress for example. From our present knowledge of our physiology we would not allow muscles or the blood supply to be restricted in a similar way for long because we know that the consequences would be damaging. The same applies to constricted body energies – it is not the natural way for them to be, they do their job less well, and our health suffers, whenever they are not fully operational.

The experiments I have just described show how our mental states can vary the energy to a greater or lesser extent; things change according to whether we feel confident or not, optimistic or pessimistic, relaxed or tense, comfortable or uncomfortable and so on. Such states will affect the way our energy is able to function, and our minds and bodies will carry the consequences. Few people these days, and especially those in orthodox medicine, would challenge the notion that a positive outlook aids recovery from illnesses and helps promote a balanced and healthy life. I believe that what I have just been describing about body energy illustrates exactly how that works, and I doubt that anyone has a more convincing explanation.

Earlier I talked about the universal power – the vast external energy field which healers believe covers the entire universe and through which we can channel healing to anyone, anywhere on earth. Unfortunately there are no individual direct experiments I can suggest that would allow you to demonstrate to yourself the existence of this wider energy, but when you think about it, the evidence for its role in healing is very convincing, even if we cannot put our fingers on it in the literal way we can for body energy.

As a healer I know that I do not provide the healing service solely from somewhere within my own body because I have learned that if I try to heal any one person longer than the natural process is available to me, then my own energy physically starts to drain and I begin to feel weak and nauseous. I can, however, heal a large number of different patients, one after the other, without experiencing those symptoms – providing I do not try to work longer than the outside energy is active for each individual client. In other words, I use outside energy on each patient until that external help fades out. If I then move on to another patient, I can restart the healing process and can keep that energy active; it is only if I stay too long with any one patient that I quickly start to become drained.

If we examine that healing system as a whole we can see that it is geared to ensuring that patients receive the right amount of healing energy channelled through the healer; provided we stop working on each client as soon as that channelled energy closes down, we will not deplete our own energy. I know that fifty minutes, say, can be too long in respect of a single patient and lead to my feeling weak, but as much as four or five hours is entirely comfortable when more than one person is being treated successively for about half an hour each. If I were delivering something that only had its source within me, it is logical to assume that I could give the four or five hours of it to one or two people with no detriment to me. It does not happen that way, leaving me in no doubt that during healing we are not working alone from something deep within us but are indeed channelling from outside our personal energy systems.

There is another piece of evidence to take into account that helps to establish for sure how energies are so bound up with our health. Quite often when I am out and about and not thinking at all about healing I can suddenly feel energy being drawn from me through being in close proximity to someone who is ill and needs healing energy. When we were chatting about her work in the early months of treating Jenny, I remember Seka telling me that this happened to her, although she did not tell me anything about it in detail. In my case, however, I find that it is something that happens inadvertently so far as the person who is draining my energy is concerned but it brings on the same unexpected sensation of weakness that happens to me when I try to heal a client for longer than the outside healing force is permitting. Again I clearly feel that I am quickly becoming nauseous and soon begin to feel my energy disappearing. This impact on my well-being is in contrast to what goes on during my healing sessions when I am giving energy to people properly, consciously using the externally channelled energy which keeps me freshly topped up and leaves me with no ill effects. The surprise draining by nearby strangers in need of an energy boost is an intrusion, a natural search for healing energy by someone whose own energy is failing them.

This phenomenon of losing energy to people inadvertently has happened to me many times, and is well known to all healers. It can happen fleetingly and instantly – perhaps for less than thirty seconds when passing someone closely in a crowded situation – or for longer when I spend time in the company of someone whose energy is weak. We do not really know how serious that person's problem has to be before the healing energy starts to get drawn out of us; nor do we know whether some particular level of compatibility between the healer and their impromptu client is needed for the drain on energy to kick in, apparently of its own accord. Whatever does trigger this exchange of energy, it very much underlines that healers do usually give their treatments through the external force and that they must always consciously make their connection to that power if they are to make sure they are generating a safe healing energy boost for their client without causing their own energies to diminish.

Some years ago, one of my daughter's teachers suffered meningitis and shortly after her return to work, still weak, she came to visit us in our home. This was an odd thing in itself and I do not recall what actually prompted the visit. I am, of course, tempted to suggest that she was somehow drawn to me for help in the way that I was drawn to Seka all those years ago – who knows? In any event, when she arrived she looked really ill, her face was grey and she seemed weak in herself, but during our conversation both my wife and I felt the sensation of being weakened ourselves as, unknowingly, Jenny's teacher took some of our vitality. Our energy was gradually drawn away from us but, conversely, when the teacher left an hour or so later she was actually pink and looked to be in much more robust health. We were the ones looking grey and weak; my wife is not a healer but her energy was drained as easily as mine.

Similar instances of energy being dissipated in this way also happen to many people visiting patients in hospital. Very often the patient is much improved after the visit; this is often put down to the psychological impact of having a visitor, while the visitor goes home feeling distinctly less well. What is happening is that the energy system of the patient is naturally absorbing a boost of healing from their visitor's own body energy – which of course starts to become depleted. The visitor will probably notice that they feel weakened in some way but will probably put it down to 'hospitals', or the stress of their visit.

If you are in the company of someone who is significantly unwell, there is a convention among healers that the way to protect yourself against the possibility of this unwanted use of your energy is to sit with your hands and fingers held together forming a steeple, unobtrusively pointed towards them, to ward off the intrusion. This is a stereotypical clergyman's pose said to have arisen, consciously or not, from the fact that clergymen have visited sick people over the centuries and this pose has emerged to help them to avoid their energy fields being affected by the weak energy fields of their parishioners.

Recognising that our body energy does indeed exist and that it can be affected by external influences is key to understanding matters affecting our health that are otherwise inexplicable to orthodox medicine. These energies are not vague concepts, popular with psychics to explain the inexplicable. In reality energies are aspects of physical matter; they are interactive but exist in different forms. Some of them have the practical impact in healing that I have talked about, and to which I will return, but others have different and quite damaging ways to affect us. Concerns about the potential impact on our health of mobile phones and radio masts is the most obvious and familiar example but there is also another form of energy that is so invasive and dangerous that I want to devote the whole of the next chapter to it.

5
NEUTRALISING THE MOST INVASIVE ENERGY ON EARTH
in a room near you?

'A man should look for what is, and not for what he thinks should be'

Albert Einstein

Some energies are local, others are personal; energies can also be seen as universal in the sense that all the different types of energies are found everywhere, while some are universal in the sense that they are part of what makes up the universe at large, in the way that gravity is. Although my main aim is to use my knowledge of energies as an introduction to even bigger issues to illustrate the ways in which you can enhance your life, it is arguable that the most useful practical purpose for my book would be to help bring to wider attention the dangers of what I believe is the most widespread and invasive form of adverse energy on earth. I want to do this mostly to help save lives – both the quality of life and, possibly for some, life itself; but part of me also wants to write about this adverse energy because it is something of a crossing point between what science will address and the issues that people such as I know about.

The problem I want to bring out is that of geopathic stress, a state of energy that is local but which affects us personally and also interacts with universal energy. The name 'geopathic stress' may conjure up images of the physical or mental stress that so many of us fall victim to these days; in fact it can sometimes cause the same sort of symptoms – but it can also cause an awful lot more damage to your health. It is not only humans who can be drawn into its impact; geopathic stress also affects animals and plants including trees. Not all life forms are affected in the same way – some appear to be more tolerant than others and some creatures actively seek out affected places whenever they can. The causes of geopathic stress, its effects on us and simply its existence within the range of energies throughout the planet are not easy for anyone to take on board the first time they come across it, but everyone owes it to themselves to look at it seriously.

One of the most dramatic illustrations of its existence and the sicknesses it causes occurred with a young girl called Claire, who became a client of mine. She was a teenager at my children's secondary school around the time of their GCSEs and, it turned out, was suffering so badly from ME that she could only attend school for a small part of the week. My wife saw her on several of those occasions, coming out of school; she was so frail she would use a walking stick and support herself on the arm of her father, barely able to get to their car. It was always a distressing picture and my wife, knowing that ME is often related to geopathic stress, eventually decided to mention to the family the possibility that, as a healer, I might be able to offer some help. She had delayed approaching Claire and her father only because, as you will see, it is a difficult topic to raise and to get across to someone when you bring it up out of the blue. One day at the end of school when my wife saw Claire and her father again, however, she decided that the time had come to try to do something to help.

Not unexpectedly, when he was approached Claire's father admitted he knew nothing about healing – or geopathic stress – but to his credit was willing to listen to what my wife had to say. At the end of what must have been quite a puzzling exchange for Claire and her father my wife had been able to arrange for him to get in touch with me to see what I could do. I was very pleased when, true to his word, Claire's father rang me later that evening, though unfortunately it was too late for me to make a visit there and then. Now, here comes the dippy bit – so please bear with me! I knew I had to give immediate help for Claire the best way I could over the phone; nowadays I have other methods, but at that time the only way I knew of fending off geopathic stress in the home was to use black plastic bin liners as a shield. As crazy as I know it sounds, all I could do at that point was to offer Claire's father the suggestion that Claire used black bin liners under her mattress to prevent the unwanted energy affecting her for that night. As well as being a health issue in its own right, poor sleep is an indicator that geopathic stress may be present and I really wanted Claire to have any benefit I might be able to give immediately rather than 24 hours later.

If Claire's father privately thought I was some sort of new-age crank, he never showed it for a moment but readily agreed to try this highly unorthodox treatment. The following day I went to visit Claire, and was so relieved to be told that, once the bin liners were in place, she was immediately able to enjoy the best night's sleep she had been able to get for many, many months. It was such a relief to the family in itself, as well as opening up hope that things could get even better. I was as thrilled as Claire and her parents were to know that she had already managed so well thanks to the bin liners.

I followed up by giving Claire healing straightaway and then over a number of occasions afterwards I was gradually able to increase her strength and vitality by a combination of clearing the geopathic stress from her body by the healing, and protecting her from taking in any more thanks to the liners. Over a few weeks she had more and more gains in this way and in one never to be forgotten moment she greeted me excitedly by telling me that she had been jumping up and down in her room 'because now I can'. That statement alone gives a real flavour of the way in which geopathic stress, if unrecognised and unchecked, can rob us of our lives – both metaphorically and even literally. At the same time, for Claire, it was a statement of hope and even triumph.

In a relatively short time after that, from being unable to walk unaided she was able to reach the point where she was travelling on her own out of town to her first job in a building society. A few years ago she invited my wife and me to her wedding where she never stopped dancing all evening!

It feels wonderful to have been instrumental in helping someone overcome a condition that was ruining her life and for healing to give her the relief of normality. I say this not to be boastful but mainly to stress how essential it is for all of us to press orthodox medicine to catch up with the reality that is geopathic stress. Claire's doctors were never able to help her but healing and awareness of geopathic stress rescued her.

As a postscript to Claire's story, she told me that after she had made her gains she was strong enough to go on holiday with a group of friends. Unluckily her bed in the hotel also turned out to be affected by geopathic stress, which gradually weakened her again. This culminated in her collapsing in the street one day as she and her friends were out walking and Claire had started to struggle to keep up with them. The old familiar symptoms were returning and made her realise what the cause of her problem must be. To the amazement of the hotel staff she instructed them to bring black bin liners and to put them under her mattress – something that could not have been easy to achieve in a foreign language but Claire knew that it was essential. Not entirely willingly, but pressed to appease her, the staff did as she said and with the protective remedy back in place her health and strength soon returned. Fortunately it seems she had not been subjected to the stress long enough for it to bring back the ME.

I should emphasise that it is not necessarily the case that geopathic stress is the sole cause of ME but there is a lot of evidence that it plays a considerable part in very many cases. The last I heard was that there was debate about a viral connection to this condition and I have no idea whether this has yet been resolved. I can only say that geopathic stress has been involved in the few cases that I have personally dealt with and in many cases that Seka Nikolic has encountered; it is something that should always be taken into account.

Geopathic stress is not a condition in its own right but is what happens when energies conflict so that our body energy is being adversely affected by energy from outside. It happens when natural earth energy, connected to the planet's magnetic emissions, becomes distorted. It is as if the wavelength of the emissions is changed so that it is not compatible with our own natural energies – so much so that the body energy which is meant to keep us well is disturbed and then inhibited to such an extent that the health of countless individuals who happen to live in proximity to it begins to suffer in different ways.

My own introduction to all of this occurred shortly after we had taken Jenny to Seka for healing; Seka turned to me at the end of the session and puzzled me by asking if we lived near running water, or whether we were near to any underground mine workings. I said that we did live near, perhaps over, an area of former mine workings, though I was not aware of any running water nearby. In answer to a separate question I told her that we were not in the vicinity of electricity pylons or power lines. I was mystified by her questions and almost as mystified when Seka went on to explain that her aim in asking about where we lived was so that she could establish whether or not Jenny might have been affected by any negative energy, and particularly by geopathic stress. At that time I knew nothing about negative energies – and not all that much about positive ones; needless to say, I had never heard of geopathic stress either!

Seka briefly explained what it was all about and as I listened, much as I did when she first discussed healing with me, I found myself becoming committed to understanding as much as I could about another staggering feature of the planet on which we live. In addition to Seka's explanations and one or two books – and nowadays the internet – it has not been difficult to find out all that I wanted to know; I soon became concerned enough to pass on warnings of what I was learning about this astonishing topic to anyone willing to listen. To understand geopathic stress fully you would probably need a degree in physics – there is a whole lot of technical explanations involving gauss measures, waves and wavelengths and so on. At that level it is all beyond me but in broad terms the facts are easy enough to understand by anyone who has been introduced to the subject of interactive energies.

The simplest explanation is that the earth's natural magnetic 'rays' can become disturbed as they travel upwards from deep underground to the earth's surface and beyond. If they pass through certain features on their way – such as mine workings, certain types of rocks, or moving water - their wavelength changes and becomes much less compatible with our body energies. Natural earth rays are adversely affected in this way regardless of how deeply within the earth they passed through those underground features.

When it reaches the surface this continual flow of distorted energy acts as a permanent area of adverse energy interfering with our own body energy at the spot where it is arriving. That point can be in any location on earth and will therefore often affect homes, offices and other buildings. The bad energy might be generated as a 'line' of geopathic stress or as a 'pool' but either way it will have a weakening effect on people and animals who spend any length of time at, or over, that location.

It affects Buckingham Palace, and countless other properties, large and small, throughout the UK and the rest of the world; anyone who spends any length of time at a place where this distorted underground energy has surfaced will be affected, to a greater or lesser extent, by a magnetic field that is no longer in tune with their body energy. In the case of my client Claire this happened to be where she slept, which is why I was so keen to act quickly and why the protective bin liners worked so decisively. With this form of protection, the idea is to place the liners so that anyone sleeping, or otherwise spending long periods, over a source of geopathic stress is provided with a barrier. No one seems to know how or why bin liners help to give that protection, but some part of the plastic material is temporarily able to prevent the radiated field from reaching body energy and causing the health problems. If you believe your home or other location may be affected by geopathic

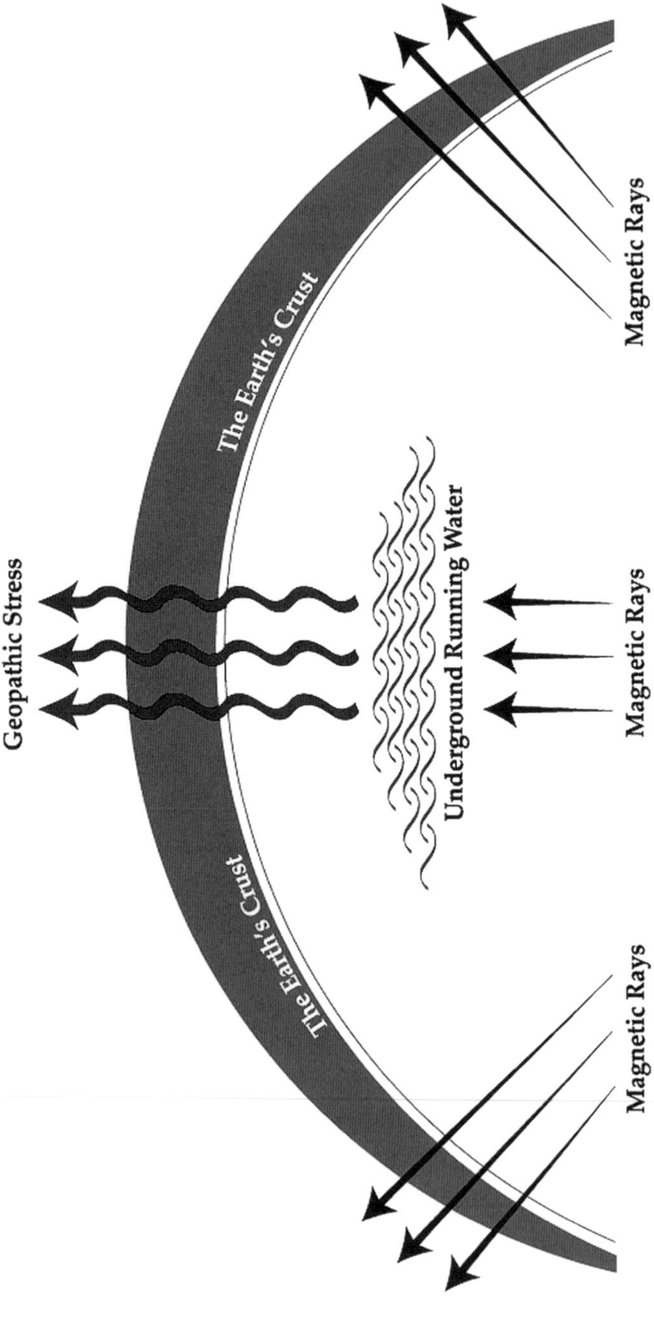
Geopathic Stress
The Earth's Crust
The Earth's Crust
Underground Running Water
Magnetic Rays
Magnetic Rays
Magnetic Rays

stress and you decide to use this technique for protection, *you need to know that the protection is indeed temporary and that the liners must be replaced with fresh ones after no more than a week.*

Not only is the earth's natural energy usually safe, it can sometimes be positively beneficial, even bringing us a form of its own healing, but once it is distorted on its way to the surface and reaches our energy its effect can be the total opposite of healing. During healing sessions the healer's energy combines with external fields to boost a patient's own body energy and to generate a beneficial impact on their clients' bodies. The adverse energy of geopathic stress is thought to have the opposite effect by creating disorder in the human field; once this happens a number of physical and other problems can follow which show up in the bodies, or minds, of those affected.

It is thought that geopathic stress principally impacts on the immune system to weaken our resistance; as a consequence any underlying health problem to which the person affected might be liable becomes much more likely to develop. It is also the case that treatment of any health condition, no matter what the cause, will be less successful if the patient also has to contend with the weakening effects of being in contact with geopathic stress. The whole issue of geopathic stress may be controversial, simply because it all hinges on the presence and interaction of energies which, of course, remain outside of science for now; but in my direct experience it is a very real influence which we must take seriously as a matter of urgency.

Geopathic stress will continue making us ill, in many cases seriously so, for as long as medical science has no awareness of its importance; until this changes our health professionals will never have the full story of our medical state before, during or after we are medically treated. Not to be able to allow for the possible presence of geopathic stress in patients is to be aware of only part of the contributory factors concerning their health. It is like not knowing about patients' weight, their medical history and background and their use of alcohol, cigarettes or other substances. No doctor would wish to diagnose or treat without knowing all the facts but that is what happens virtually every time any one of us seeks advice from our medics.

At best, time and money are wasted while treatment is being slowed or inhibited because geopathic stress continues to affect us; at worst, conditions will worsen and may prove fatal when they need not have done. Again, this is not an attack on our medical professionals who are never taught about geopathic stress any more than they are taught much about energies or healing generally. As a result they simply do not have the opportunity to address the actual or potential effects on their patients and are forced to give their help with insufficient resources.

The impact of geopathic stress on people is going to be much greater the more they are exposed to the source, which could be in their home or their place of work, or both. The impact on them will differ according to the strength of the distorted earth energy and this can vary enormously; for example, if two or more underground faults criss-cross each other at different levels beneath the earth's surface the strength of the geopathic stress will be multiplied. In addition, the length of time a person actually spends directly over the 'weak spot' is also important and is especially a problem if their bed is above a point at which the geopathic stress is affecting their home. Not only will they then be subjected to its influence for many hours, it will be concentrated on them while asleep at a time when they would be more vulnerable and should be benefiting from the healing power of a good night's rest. As I said, this is why I was so keen to get Claire immediate respite.

Although I cannot vouch for it personally, some research has suggested that at least 80 per cent of all cancers occur in those who are, or have been, subjected to geopathic stress. This is a serious claim for that research to have made and is something that ought to be investigated in earnest. Without wishing to be alarmist it is something that could also have a connection to other degenerative conditions such as multiple sclerosis or motor neurone disease – it is easy to imagine how body energy that is unable to do its job could lead us to such catastrophic failure. I am not for one moment claiming that this is definitely happening but neither can I, nor anyone else, safely say it is not so or that it could not be so. We owe it to sufferers and potential sufferers to take this possibility seriously as an area for research in order to find some definitive answers.

Apart from the onset of any specific illnesses or diseases there are certain classic indications that someone may be suffering the effects of geopathic stress that we should also try to recognise. These include:

- poor sleeping patterns, and particularly waking to feel that you have not had a proper night's sleep
- grinding of teeth during the night
- sleepwalking
- unexplained headaches
- displays of severe impatience and anger
- babies moving about their cot and finishing up pressed against the bars
- a grey 'unwashed' pallor and, often, very lifeless hair

It is claimed that buildings affected by geopathic stress can come across as properties that have a cold and unwelcoming atmosphere or with walls that make you feel as though they are closing in. In contrast, buildings that have been cleared of geopathic stress are often said to feel warmer and more inviting. Visitors often ask if the owner has decorated or what has been done differently as they pick up on the improved atmosphere.

Because I know the damage that geopathic stress can do in triggering health problems and in interfering with speedy healing, whenever I see a new client I automatically dowse for geopathic stress in their home and workplace. Dowsing is something I shall address in more detail later, but in essence it is a means by which information can be gathered in quite a strange way. The most familiar example is known as 'water divining' though divining is simply another word for dowsing – in that case for water. Another well-known form of the same art is being practised when a wedding ring is suspended from a length of cotton over the tummy of a woman who is, or may be, pregnant and used either to detect pregnancy or to indicate the gender of the baby. Although it seems impossible, the ring swings in response to questions about the pregnancy or to give 'yes' or 'no' responses to a much wider range of issues. I will explain the simple practical means by which this and water divining work in a later chapter; I need to draw on a few more experiences first.

Using a weight on a thread is known as pendulum dowsing and is how I mostly run those checks on my clients to detect whether or not they are suffering from geopathic stress. If I find that geopathic stress is an issue, then we discuss what this means and I can take steps to clear it. As I searched for, and found, patients and properties affected by geopathic stress I soon discovered, somewhat to my cost, that I had a particularly close affinity with this distorted energy. This was helpful in that I was quick to detect its presence but it also meant that whenever I did encounter it I was soon feeling unwanted physical effects – always a headache and aching limbs together with a sense of weakness similar to the sensations associated with flu. They are also not unlike the effects I get when my body energy has been inadvertently drawn from me in the ways I described earlier; with geopathic stress, however, the symptoms are stronger and seem to spread upwards until they reach my head. Thankfully these feelings do reduce and finally disappear after I have neutralised or left the area of the bad energy, although for some reason the headache I get can endure for quite a while longer.

The strong sensitivity that I have to geopathic stress may well stem from the fact that, without realising it at the time, I now know I have spent many years in houses that were affected by this problematic energy. An increased sensitivity is also one of the dangers of regularly dowsing for geopathic stress and connecting to it, as I had been doing for so much of my time as a healer. Apparently it is easy for the body to absorb it during the dowsing process and thus, over time, to become more and more susceptible to its effects. Now that I dowse for it a great deal less than I used to, and take better steps to protect myself, that high level of sensitivity has left me, though I can still pick up the signals quickly when I find myself positioned over a badly affected spot.

I often experience the effects of this interaction with geopathic stress unexpectedly and without ever consciously thinking about whether or not I may be in its vicinity. Although I admit to being ever ready to tell clients and others about it whenever the opportunity comes along, it is not something that I constantly think about. I am not convincing myself that something exists where it does not; I am never on the lookout for it, other than when I have a commission, but I find it always reveals itself to me whenever it is present.

The most obvious illustration of this for me was some months after I had started to work regularly to deal with geopathic stress and I met some friends at a local pub that I had used many times before without, on those earlier occasions, ever noticing anything untoward. This particular time I found myself at a crowded bar, concentrating on waiting my turn and trying to catch the attention of bar staff, so the last thing on my mind was geopathic stress and whether or not I was standing in a safe place. After all I was somewhere I had visited many times in the past before my sensitivity developed and all I really wanted to do at the time was order a drink. Nonetheless the familiar signals of headache, weakness and nausea soon began to make themselves known and put me in no doubt about what was happening – I was definitely standing over geopathic stress. Having known the area for many years, I was aware that the pub was built close to a former colliery site – one of the classic locations to find geopathic stress that Seka had first mentioned – but I had never consciously thought of any link between that local pub and mine workings until that evening when a dose of this incompatible energy struck me.

As soon as I realised I was standing in a bad spot I immediately moved away to find another part of the bar to get served. Geopathic stress is worst immediately over the fault beneath the earth's surface that is giving rise to the distorted energy, although it will seep wider than that to affect a bigger area. Fortunately on that occasion I had only been affected for a few minutes and moving away restored me quite quickly. The way I had been affected, however, shows that geopathic stress is real enough; it was not brought on simply by my convincing myself to find what I wanted, or expected, to find since the topic was not on my mind at the time.

Even on those occasions when I have set out to find

geopathic stress as a conscious exercise I have had many surprises when the stress didn't show up at all, or did so in a way I was not anticipating. For example, one time I was doing some dowsing in my friend's flat but was not yet skilled in the disciplines of dowsing or the features of geopathic stress. I picked up particular points in the room which revealed the presence of stress but I could not identify a pattern. Geopathic stress shows itself more often in lines than isolated 'pools' of bad energy and it took me some time to understand exactly what the signals meant. In fact the individual spots of geopathic stress that I was identifying as I tested different parts of the flat only showed a pattern when I sat myself down and plotted them on to a plan. It was then that I realised they actually lined up in an unexpected diagonal across the room rather than at a right angle to a wall as, for no good reason, I had been expecting.

I have detected geopathic stress not only while standing directly on the weak spot at ground level but also on one occasion when leaning over a sort of atrium, which allowed me to look down into the room below. I could therefore recognise the presence of geopathic stress in mid-air so to speak. This of course is not in any sense unlikely since the whole principle is based on energy rising to and beyond the earth's surface and probably continuing out into the atmosphere. No matter how tall a building might be, the geopathic stress will make its way through every storey.

A tale I heard quite early on concerns a block of flats in Dubrovnik in which a number of people on different floors developed cancer and caused the authorities to regard the block as unfit for habitation. I understand they demolished it and turned the site into a grassed area. As I said earlier, the material I have seen in articles, on the internet and in books does suggest that more is known on the continent and particularly in eastern Europe than in this country. I have to say that the example from Dubrovnik would seem to argue a very enlightened attitude from the authorities!

Nowadays there are less extreme methods than demolition available to deal with properties that suffer the impact of geopathic stress. There are machines you can buy for a few hundred pounds that neutralise its effects in offices and homes, or a feng shui practitioner can visit properties and should be able to deal with these energies as they would any other imbalance that needs attention. For some years now I have been using a more personalised method that works over distances, as when healers practise absent healing; this method, however, is much more than simply 'healing' the buildings in that it is necessary for me to use different energies in a different way. It is a means that is cheap and effective which I developed some years ago and first tried for real following a conversation with Chris, a friend of mine who was a headmaster in a stressful post.

One evening he happened to mention to me that he came home at the end of every day with a severe headache. You may say this is to be expected in someone who has a stressful time at work, but whenever I hear anyone refer to their health, especially headaches, my first instinct is to wonder if my healing could do any good, and my second instinct is to think about whether geopathic stress is involved. As soon as I could, I dowsed to check Chris's office for geopathic stress and found that it was indeed badly affected; I immediately put my new technique into effect, doing my best to clear his office for him and make it safe.

Some time afterwards I saw him again and was delighted when he told me that the headaches had stopped altogether, exactly as I had hoped. The job stress unfortunately continued, though he recently remarked to me that those office-related headaches had never returned from the day I had cleared his room; at the time we were speaking this had been about five or six years previously.

Although the method of clearing, or neutralising, geopathic stress that I adopted to help Chris is the one that I now use whenever I encounter a building that needs to be treated, let me say that as an emergency measure – or even as a permanent one – the bin liners are a genuine, cheap and quite effective solution. The main downside to that method of protection is the need to keep changing them each week because they definitely do lose their effectiveness after a while; if you do not remember to go to the trouble of putting fresh ones under your mattress you will most certainly lose their effect. My practice of neutralising geopathic stress for people from a distance is very inexpensive and works permanently – check out my website for details.

In my earlier years I had two graphic practical demonstrations that affected me personally and which proved just how the bin liners do work and how they do lose their effectiveness. The first happened soon after we had first established that our house did indeed have a problem; as we had been advised we quickly put bin liners under our mattress and, somewhat to our surprise, I must admit, both my wife and I found that the bed and the room immediately felt better and that there was no doubting our sleep was altogether deeper and richer. After a week, according to the theory, it was time to change the bin liners and so I gathered the used ones into a ball and, carrying them in my arms, went downstairs. By the time I had got to the bottom I was weak and aching – exactly as I am when geopathic stress affects me directly on site and just as I described that time in the pub.

I was shocked. Nobody had warned me of this reaction – and quite possibly nobody even knew about it. It seemed that the bin liners had actually absorbed the geopathic stress to saturation point, and were now releasing it back into my system in the most unexpected way. This was yet another example of the transferability of energy, which in this case had first contaminated the bin liners and then passed the negativity almost immediately straight into me. It had certainly never occurred to me that there would be any problem in handling bin liners in this way and the fact that they affected me so strongly when I clutched them to my chest as I handled them was another very clear demonstration that there is something very real about all of this. I became very much more careful when removing affected bin liners after that.

The second demonstration that bin liners work, and of how they have been able to surprise me, occurred during a most enjoyable holiday on the Isle of Wight – enjoyable, that is, apart from the shock of realising that the mobile home in which we were staying was quite badly affected by geopathic stress. It soon caused my legs to ache quite painfully so that during the day I was too uncomfortable to get the best out of the holiday; it was even worse at night, to the extent that I could not sleep and could not really even stay in bed. Of course I immediately tried putting bin liners under the mattress to try to gain relief from what was steadily escalating into a really debilitating ache in my limbs. I could not believe it when, for the first time, the method failed me – the liners gave me no help whatsoever. This failure was something I had definitely not expected and it left me in something of a panic with no options that I could immediately think of. Later I began to wonder whether perhaps these particular bags were too thin to give protection, or if they had maybe spent so much time already over a site of geopathic stress that they had become saturated before I bought them. To check this out I went and bought another pack of different, stronger liners and put them under the mattress. By then I had quite convinced myself that this time they would do the trick, but to my horror that night was no better than the previous ones and I found myself almost in despair, facing a ruined holiday.

By the next night I had started to worry that perhaps the geopathic stress where I was staying was simply too strong for this method of shielding me to be successful, but I had no alternatives. There was no machine I could call on and no handy feng shui expert, while the method that I now use to clear properties had not yet come to me. Then, prompted by the sort of thought from nowhere that was to become more familiar to me in later years, and would one day bring me that much-needed new way to neutralise these painful energies, I decided to see what would happen if I wrapped bin liners around each leg. To the understandable incredulity of my wife, before I went to bed, I did just that; for good measure I wrapped two around each leg and lay down again on the mattress. Within seconds the pain suddenly started to melt away and after a few minutes it had gone completely – it really was the most blessed relief. Although not a very dignified way to spend the remaining evenings of the holiday it certainly saved the day! I have to feel sorry for any other holidaymakers who might have been affected by the geopathic stress intruding into that mobile home, but who would have had no idea what was happening and no means to deal with it. It is one illustration of why it is time that we all discovered more about it.

A more serious case was that of a client who lived close to me in our area of former mine workings and who contacted me to say that he was experiencing virtually constant headaches;

what was worse was that he had also suffered some small brain haemorrhages. His doctors were increasingly concerned over the problem because the prognosis was that if he suffered another haemorrhage it was likely that it would prove fatal. My visit to see him at his home was enough to tell me that the house, and my new client, were affected by geopathic stress; when I asked, he also told me he had trouble sleeping. I told him all about the strange phenomenon that is geopathic stress and then gave him a session of healing before going home to clear his house from a short distance of no more than half a mile.

When I visited him a second time a day or so later he told me he felt much better, that the headaches were gone and he was now sleeping better. I carried on with a couple more healing sessions and when I stopped seeing him everything appeared to be fine; I hope it still is.

Another interesting illustration of the reality of geopathic stress is revealed whenever I clear it from a location secretly, removing the problem without the knowledge of the person affected. As a healer it is not often that I undertake healing on, or for, anyone without their being aware of it and only ever at the request of someone close to them who can reasonably be held to act on their behalf. As I recall this has only happened a few times since I started practising as a healer and includes the babies that I mentioned earlier. I generally take the view that people should have responsibility for their own health and that if they are determined to dismiss the healing that might help them, that is their business. I normally have the same approach to removing geopathic stress but there are times when I will step in if I feel I should.

One such treatment involved the husband of a friend of ours who constantly looked grey and 'washed out'. This gave him a somewhat unclean and ragged appearance, which is a common symptom of someone suffering from geopathic stress, whether or not the condition has manifested itself in any recognisable health disorder. I cleared their house at the request of his wife and, unknown to him, also sent him healing; when we bumped into him a few weeks later my wife and I noticed that his grey pallor had given way to a definite pink and that he looked much less tense and drawn. So far as I know he still has no idea that he received any help.

Another case concerned the nephew of a lady whose daughter I had healed. Healing her daughter had also included my dealing with the geopathic stress that was affecting their house and the lady was quick to spot a possible connection elsewhere in her family in the behaviour of her nephew in another house. I was told that he displayed particular behavioural problems associated with hyperactivity which were causing concern for those close to him. I was also warned that his father would not be willing to accept or countenance any 'nonsense' about healing or the like – a not unfamiliar story in respect of many men, and some women! Of course, for the sake of the child and the family, I worked on the geopathic stress in secret and without ever visiting the house or any of the people involved. When I checked back with my contact a few weeks later I was told that the child's behaviour had improved dramatically and that the household was much happier. Those in the know were extremely grateful.

One obvious question that these stories raise is why everyone is not affected in any readily identifiable way by the impact of geopathic stress; why we are not all feeling unmistakable symptoms or signs of suffering? There are a number of answers to this:

- We cannot easily see the extent to which people who are

exposed to geopathic stress are actually being affected. It causes few symptoms that we can point to other than the slightly subjective weak and 'grey-faced' appearance I mentioned earlier. There are the other indicators I referred to but again they offer little in the way of obvious signals that anyone else would notice; there are also very few people equipped to read the signals that might be apparent to those of us with more experience.

- Not everyone is equally affected because they may not actually be equally exposed; even people lying side by side in bed could find that one side of the bed is worse than the other according to where the line of geopathic stress actually runs. We are not all likely to be exposed in the same way for the same lengths of time, even if we are in the same location.
- Different people who are exposed to the same levels of geopathic stress can react to it differently – the impact of diet, smoking, other stresses, lifestyle or other external influences will change the mix and affect how well people can cope with the added burden of geopathic stress.
- It is also possible that people have different general levels of tolerance. People do have different degrees of strength and enjoy more robust constitutions and sounder general health than others; perhaps people can have more resistant body energy systems. All of these are likely to make a significant difference to how geopathic stress impacts.
- It is the nature of geopathic stress to inhibit health in different ways for different people; it seems to attach itself to existing or potential threats, which is probably because it seems to interfere with the immune system. Not every person affected by geopathic stress will therefore exhibit

the same illness or physical symptoms, so geopathic stress becomes a difficult factor to recognise.

In short, it does not present us with constant easily recognisable features and, without dowsing for it, its presence is difficult to identify. All of this helps keep it under the radar so far as the public and orthodox medicine are concerned.

As well as geopathic stress the current debate about mobile phones and the more long-standing one about electricity pylons and substations are likely to turn out to be variations on the same general theme. Not everyone who uses a mobile phone or lives close to electricity pylons and the like displays the same symptoms of any disorder; many show no detectable signs of any disorder at all. Maybe it is those who are also affected by geopathic stress who are the ones most likely to become troubled by what would be an added burden from mobile phones. Whether or not that is a factor, in such uncharted territory it is understandable that science has problems determining causes and effects or proving satisfactorily how magnetic fields can be harmful.

In the same way that scientists cannot yet grasp the nature of the energy mechanism that drives healing they cannot identify the physical means by which electromagnetic fields from any source could adversely affect our minds and bodies. Recognising that the body has an operational energy system, which plays an important part in the well-being of every individual, is the first step; the second is to accept that body energy enables us to be healed but can also be corrupted by outside fields and thus become harmful to us.

A good illustration of how different electromagnetic fields can clash with each other is to put a small radio near to your television with both sets switched on; the radio will scream and squeal once it is within the field of the television. The good health of our body and minds depends on energies being in harmony rather than in conflict; if you imagine your own body's energy field being similarly disturbed by unwelcome energy, it is easy to see in principle how things could go medically wrong for us when that happens. The more we expose ourselves to incompatible energy fields the more likely we are to suffer adverse reactions as our systems struggle to compete.

It is not only mobile phones that could potentially clash with our energy systems; as it happens I have never personally felt anything untoward when handling a mobile, but I do get a physical reaction of a burning sensation in the side of my face whenever I use a digital cordless landline phone. This reaction can only be happening through my body energy since there is no other realistic route for me to be affected. I have no evidence that these digital cordless phones are actually harmful, but the effect on me is so uncomfortable that I got rid of three different machines and handsets that I bought before I gave up on the system altogether.

Another interesting sideline on the impact of energies occurred when I began to develop toothache, which I put down to sensitivity. I noticed that it was worse after I had spent time at the computer and that over a short time the pain began to kick in sooner in the session on the computer than it had originally. My first thought was that working on the computer was actually causing the pain but a visit to the dentist and three sessions of root canal treatment soon solved the problem for me and made me think again; and yes, I have overcome my fear of dentists!

My second take on the effects of the computer was, I am sure, much nearer the mark – I realised that the computer's magnetic field was not the simple source of toothache but it was connecting to, or interacting with, my energy field at the weak point where the tooth problem was located. It is akin to what happens when we are affected by geopathic stress; again an incompatible electromagnetic field is bringing out – or worsening – an existing weakness in my own body energy system. In the case of my tooth, the electromagnetic field of my computer merely had the effect of increasing the pain I was already developing. Theoretically, in other circumstances mobile phones, computers and other electronic devices could be contributing to any number of apparently random and disconnected health conditions in those who, for whatever reason, are prone to this interference.

Many months after I had written this paragraph I discovered that something that is being labelled 'electric sensitivity' is now attracting a lot of attention and I am sure we are going to hear a lot more about it as time goes by. For now, those who are addressing it still seem to be arguing over whether an electromagnetic field that may not be of a high strength can affect the body. I am sure there are thresholds up to the point before incompatible energies will become unacceptably intrusive, but unless the researchers stop leaving the matter of body energy out of the equation the truth will remain harder to pin down.

In the meantime, my advice for everyone would be to take regular breaks from computers, as is generally recommended, and from any other devices that emit any sort of fields. But, equally importantly, I find it helps to rinse my hands under tepid running water at the same sort of intervals for three or four minutes while envisaging the unwanted energy flowing out of my system.

Because it is so important, and is a field in which I have had so much experience, I am keen to bring geopathic stress into the public arena if I can; geopathic stress really does need to be better known about, and better understood. While it is best to get a dowser to check whether your home – or your place of work – is affected by geopathic stress, most people can actually get an indication for themselves. This is done through a straightforward 'muscle test' that – because it ties into some other issues – I will describe in detail in a later chapter.

On the bigger scale there would be a lot of mileage in the authorities examining the possibility of geopathic stress being present in those instances where what appear to be clusters of cancer show up in some locations.

At the start of this chapter, I referred to geopathic stress as a crossing point between the knowledge of science and that of healers, dowsers and others who are active in related areas. Facing up to that would be a good opportunity for interested parties to join forces and share their work across different fields. The point about this is that geopathic stress is part of the real physical world that features earth energies and which different sciences should recognise and evaluate. Researchers should be designing easy-to-use low-cost devices that can measure this distorted energy for us and which would be easily available from shops, supermarkets and DIY stores – like smoke alarms. This will only be possible if those who have the capacity to bring it about respect, and consult with, the only people who currently can identify and explain the presence and the health effects of geopathic stress – the healers, dowsers and feng shui practitioners who are already dealing with it.

Geopathic stress is real enough; I know that for sure. I am not in a position to speak with the same authority about the possible levels of damage that it can do, but there are specific claims and research results that need to be taken seriously and properly investigated. I cannot express this better than the UK's Judge Pickles, who talked about it on television when he said something to the effect that if it were the health hazard that it is claimed to be then to understand it properly could be as important for public health as, for example, were the past discoveries about the effects of poor sanitation and hygiene. He was undoubtedly right – in our current relationship with this unwelcome, potentially lethal energy we are in a similar state to when we were dying of typhoid and cholera because people at the time thought there were no problems in letting sewage run through the streets. How long must we wait to make the modern-day equivalent of that leap in understanding?

6
THE SPIRIT
a matter of life and death

'Now he has departed from this strange world a little ahead of me. That means nothing. People like us, who believe in physics, know that the distinction between past, present, and future is only a stubbornly persistent illusion'

Albert Einstein

By this point in my journey, my life had changed dramatically. I had discovered healing as a genuine technique but also as a gift with which I had personally been blessed and through which I could help others. I had found geopathic stress, the ability to dowse for information about it and ultimately a new way to neutralise its potential effects. Above all I had found the freedom to rise above scepticism and beyond the limitations of orthodoxy; in our culture this is perhaps the greatest gift of all. I will return to this theme but it is worth mentioning now that, while alerting others to geopathic stress is the major direct way I can help improve lives; opening the door to encourage you to take the world of energies seriously is the most wide-reaching benefit of all in making the most of your life from this moment on.

From our initial consultation with Seka, it probably took me about two years to develop sufficiently as a healer to feel comfortable with my new ability and to understand properly the mechanics of healing and the techniques that worked best for me. As one step led to another my path drew me into more areas that challenge the orthodox take on life. Some of what I have encountered had been entirely unknown to me at the time; much else may have been new to me as an experience at first hand, but was well documented in principle, recorded and argued about for decades if not centuries. In time I encountered many unusual events directly and also absorbed the ideas and accounts given to me by others. Not all the people who were able to contribute to my growing awareness were practitioners in any of the alternative fields that relate to healing. Some did recognise they had a 'gift', an ability to operate outside the conventional world to some degree; others claimed no such talent, but still had a tale to tell, whether they were clients or friends. Some were familiar with psychic happenings of one sort or another and many were quick to admit how their own doubts or scepticism had been challenged by something they had found inexplicable.

Such accounts help make up more of those threads that I said I would bring out in order to illustrate the diversity of the immense energies that are at work; they reflect issues in our culture generally doubted by those who think they know best and which people are deterred from discussing for fear of seeming gullible or naive. I found the more I was prepared to talk about these issues the more others admitted their own experiences that led them too to doubt the certainties of science. I took all the instances I will describe on board only after much thought and on the strength of the evidence as I saw it; there were also other concepts that came my way but about which, for now at least, I am not so convinced. Even so, much was being added to what I did need to know.

One instance that really surprised me was the way in which the combination of interactive energies at the heart of my themes can actually leave imprints on objects that we gather around us. I am not sure when I first found myself personally involved in a specific case but I do recall being told during my early years of healing that such a thing could happen. The earliest general example I was given was the somewhat offbeat claim that food that had been prepared by chefs affected by negative energy of some sort might then easily carry 'bad vibes' on to some unfortunate diner – an interesting if somewhat disturbing thought!

It cannot be easy to prove any such connection but it is another claim that is very much in line with the way in which negative thoughts could impact on a person's body through their energy field. If food is capable of being affected by a chef's negatively charged body energy then that would certainly be a mechanism by which his 'vibes' would be transferred on to the diner. The same principle can be extended to explain interactions with items other than food; it would be entirely possible for body energies to leave imprints on any object that was 'charged' to receive them and for the effects of those imprints to be picked up by the body energy of anyone who later handled them. All solid matter is made from electrically charged atoms; for those electrical charges in every object to have links to energy is straightforward enough.

Although, so far as I am aware, I have not been affected by chefs carrying bad energies I have encountered other intrusive incidents of transferred distorted energy. On one occasion I had been asked to give healing to a young girl of about 15 or so who was having a bad time generally, but particularly at school. The teenager, who when she had been at her lowest ebb had actually seriously contemplated suicide, thankfully began to improve after a few healing sessions and eventually to recover. I was encouraged by our success, of course, but then, after the final session, something odd happened.

I always find it helpful for both healer and patient to have time after the healing to relax together and let the healing process subside. It gives time to reflect on the healing that has just taken place, to get feedback from the patient and to offer any advice that the healer feels able to give. On this particular day I had sat down with my young patient on the family's settee to round it all off; we had moved into another room after the session and the settee we were using was not one that I had sat on before. As we chatted I soon became aware of a dull headache and some nausea developing, similar to the sensation on those occasions I described earlier when someone close by is inadvertently draining my energy. Since I had just finished a healing session on my client, and she was the only other person present, I knew that it was not likely that the problem was anything to do with her stealing from my energy levels. I knew something else was happening. I immediately mentioned the growing sick headache I was getting, asking out loud, 'why am I getting a headache?' I don't know whether my actually saying it to nobody in particular helped but, between us, we soon tracked down that the only object nearby was a portfolio of artwork; some of it had been done by the girl while she was going through the worst of her health crisis and it was always kept out of sight behind the settee on which I was sitting. Retrieving the folder she opened it up for me so that I was able to examine the artwork inside. I could see nothing in it that that might have indicated a troubled soul – there were no heavy lines or blackness and no threatening or threatened images. As I handled it, however, I could tell from my headache and general sense of weakness that there was indeed much negative energy in the work; I immediately set about clearing the entire collection.

The process that I use for clearing objects of bad energy is a straightforward one – I simply point my hands in the manner of sending distant healing and concentrate for a minute or two on cleansing and revitalising the object. When the object is 'clear' I usually get a little shiver and a sensation of feeling lighter in my own spirit. It is a brief signal that the job has been completed successfully and the slight headache and discomfort I had noticed soon began to clear

There is no doubt that my client's body energy, affected by her bad feelings, transferred her negativity into the artwork she had been working on. It is worth remembering that this negative connection would have remained with her pieces of art permanently and would always be likely to affect anyone who came into contact with it. Any object you meet up with can have such unwelcome energy attached – the more so if it is second-hand or if it is something that has been handmade. If, after acquiring something different, you start to feel uncomfortable – perhaps get headaches or become unable to sleep so well or feel out of sorts in any way – consider the possibility that bad energy has been drawn into your life along with your latest possession.

If you experience such discomfort in unfamiliar surroundings the source will not be easy to pin down; it could be anything from a hotel bed to a library book. Thankfully, such instances are likely to be short-lived and you will soon recover;

the chances are you will not even notice. Personal possessions, however, can be more of a problem. A few years ago my son bought a new leather jacket which, although he very much liked it, he soon stopped wearing. At some point we noticed this and asked him about it; he told us that he did not like to wear it because it felt too heavy and made his arms ache. As I began to realise how uncomfortable he felt when wearing the coat, warning bells started to ring and I immediately checked the jacket for bad energy by dowsing with my pendulum in the same way that I do when I am looking for geopathic stress. Sure enough, in response to my probing, the dowsing on this occasion showed that the jacket was indeed carrying bad energy, which I immediately set about clearing. I actually did this by my method of distant healing since he did not have the jacket with him at the time; clearing bad energy from objects is a process that can be done 'absently' as well as by 'contact' treatment.

Once I had cleared my son's jacket I was happy when, a week or so later, he was able to confirm that he no longer had a problem; the jacket did not now feel heavy or cause his arm to ache and he was able to wear it without any further trouble. On reflection I thought it was most likely that the sense of heaviness he had been experiencing was nothing to do with the actual, physical weight of the jacket; it was more likely to be a 'dragging' sensation triggered by the effect of its bad energy interacting adversely with his own body energy to set up a physical problem.

Subsequent to this incident, I have found other leather goods to be particularly prone to holding that sort of negative energy; this is not surprising when you think about the circumstances in which we get the material! I remember too his partner being similarly troubled by a cardigan and on another occasion by an identity badge she had to wear at work; in that case the problem proved to be with the chain rather than the badge itself. The sensations she felt were of a dull ache, this time in her neck and shoulder. The discomfort was very draining for her but had no obvious medical cause and it would have been difficult for any GP to treat. Fortunately I was able to clear the bad energy from the cardigan and the chain so that neither caused any discomfort afterwards.

Of course, these feelings of discomfort did not happen with every new possession of my son or his partner; neither of them generally expected, or looked for, untoward sensations but on those occasions they happened and I was able to deal with them swiftly and successfully.

On another occasion, my wife and I were visiting a friend when I again experienced that easily recognisable dull headache and feelings of weakness. The couple were musicians and had a large number of old instruments as well as other artefacts decorating the walls of the room we were in. There were also a number of pictures and other ornaments around, any one of which could have been giving off the bad energy I had recognised.

Having so many objects around meant that I had very many possibilities to examine if I were going to be able to pinpoint the cause. All I could do was to go systematically around the whole room with my dowsing pendulum, checking every single piece I could see. I did this carefully but could not pick up on any specific object as the source of the problem. I was not happy to have failed and was not at all sure what to say to our host. My wife continued to chat to our friend as I wrestled with the problem, even trying all the objects for a second time but, again, I had no success. With such an array of musical instruments which must have been used many times by different people over years and even decades I felt sure one of them was holding the bad energy – but which one?

The second pass around the room proved no more effective than the first; I was left at a complete loss, very frustrated by having so much difficulty in being able to pin down the source. Eventually, and mainly in order to give myself some more thinking time before I admitted defeat, I tried the only item in the room that I had ignored – a pair of new-looking curtains hanging at the window behind me. I was amazed to find that the dowsing immediately signalled to me that the new curtains were, in fact, the cause of the problem. I was really puzzled, and not at all sure I could be right to be sensing new curtains to be the source in a room full of so many objects that seemed to be far more likely candidates. Eventually I had no choice but to admit defeat and announce, 'the only thing I can connect to any bad energy in this room are the curtains'. Instantly, and pretty much conversationally, our friend simply said, 'you would not believe how much hurt and anger I have put into those curtains, I made them myself when I was going through a terrible and lonely time'.

While sympathetic to our friend for the experiences she had suffered, I must confess that I took a measure of selfish pride both in eventually getting it right and in the dowsing technique that had been able to come up with the answer. There was no way I could know of the bad time that had happened before we met her, or that she herself had made the curtains; I had been led to the source of the bad energy by the systems that I work with all the time as a healer and as a dowser. Dowsing alone had connected me to the specific object whose energy had absorbed another form of negative energy, apparently based on 'hurt and anger', and which had affected me physically before I went looking for it with my pendulum.

What I also found intriguing about this incident was our friend's use of the phrase about what she had 'put into' the curtains. It is as though at some level we know – or have an instinct – about the way in which energy transfers do take place. There are other similar phrases that we regularly use in the UK which suggest the same sort of connotations, such as 'I don't know what got into him', or 'I don't know what came over her', or 'whatever possessed you to do that?' and so on. These are all familiar figures of speech, which only make sense in respect of a reference to someone being taken over or otherwise affected by influential energies of some description.

A case similar to the one involving the curtains happened to me when my wife and I went to see some more friends following the birth of their new baby. Once again, very quickly after we had been greeted and had settled down, I felt the familiar intrusive signals and asked our friends what might be causing them. As usual, my first instinct was mentally to assume that someone in the room was not well, perhaps with a headache, and I was picking up that sympathy pain that I get sometimes. Nobody thought they were suffering anything that might register with me so I glanced around the room, which of course was full of new baby stuff including many greeting cards on the walls and surfaces. They provided me with another treasure trove of possible candidates for bringing bad energy into the house and so, after getting permission from our friends, I dowsed the room carefully, checking every item to look for the cause.

Eventually I identified two of the new baby cards that were both giving off their own bad energy and pointed them out to our friend. She immediately confirmed that I was on to something, telling me that I had picked the only two cards in the room she could think of which could be carrying negative energy – one of the senders was quite ill, and the other was going through a divorce. I cleared the negative energy from both of the cards and very quickly the signals I had been picking up disappeared.

If this is an area that you wish to look into, there is much that is recorded about instances in which energy from events or circumstances is translated into personal items; clairvoyants like to handle personal possessions as part of a reading for their clients in order to pick up clues on facts and stories that the energy has stored. Psychics with this ability, known as telemetry, do much more than I as a healer can; I only recognise the disturbed energy patterns emanating from objects whereas others can connect to facts including names and incidents, which they can recount in detail. While I cannot personally vouch for that ability I have seen it demonstrated many times. I am perfectly comfortable with the principle that if everything is made from energy, then so are thoughts, experiences and emotions. It is not a big jump for that to mean that the energy that comes from thoughts or experiences, generated by electrical impulses in our brains as they happen, connects to the energy of our possessions.

One other reason from personal experience that makes the concept easy for me to accept is that more than thirty years ago, when my wife and I were first married and long before I was aware of the realities that I have since discovered, she would tell me of the many occasions when one of her fellow secretaries had taken over my wife's typewriter while my wife was at lunch. In the days before computers and even electric typewriters it would be more convenient for someone to use another empty machine for a short piece of work than to take a half completed paper and carbons out of their own typewriter.

Whenever this happened on my wife's machine she would know, not because anything obvious had been disturbed but because her machine itself felt different – she would say it felt somehow more 'sticky' and 'sluggish'. My wife was sensitive enough to be able to feel that effect on her machine, making it different from how it normally felt. At the time this intrigued me but I could not understand or explain to myself how it could be happening. Thanks to the concept of interactive energies, now I can – and I also know about taking steps to sort it out. If you have any suspicions that incompatible energies are present or are affecting you, members of the dowsing or healing fraternities would also be happy to help you deal with it.

The effects and properties of energies also account for the success of treatments such as reflexology and acupuncture as well as Bach flower remedies and homeopathy; all are controversial for some and indispensable to others. In each case, however, the fact that makes them controversial is that they can only be explained by reference to energies. When it comes to good old-fashioned prejudice none of them struggles more than homeopathy. The problem is that homeopathy is a healing process in which the active healing agent in a remedy is repeatedly diluted until, for practical purposes, there is no trace left of the original substance. Paradoxically, the more the mixture is diluted, the stronger it is said to become; this is an impossibility when set against modern instincts and enough to suggest to many that there can be no way that homeopathy could ever be considered a serious treatment.

I am afraid I cannot totally validate the use of homeopathy myself though I have benefitted from treatment by a homeopath who used additional techniques as well - which made it difficult to be certain about just what was helping me.

To make matters worse I was also using my own healing to boost the homeopathic treatment so I cannot vouch for what my homeopath actually contributed. However, between us we did make considerable gains for me beyond what had been achieved by orthodox medicine – of that there is no doubt.

Unfortunately clinical trials on homeopathic treatments do seem to contradict themselves, though there have been successes with animals (as well as humans) in test conditions, which suggests that perhaps there are failings in the application of homeopathy or in the tests rather than with homeopathy itself. Tests of any kind can throw up contradictions, of course, but it is hard to escape the fact that the biggest hurdle for homeopathy remains the riddle of how a substance can be physically diluted in order to make it more powerful. However, if we bring energy transfers into the equation then it does open up the way for a perfectly reasonable theory to explain how that happens.

The broad concept with homeopathy is that health conditions can be treated by giving the patient a dose of a substance that would actually cause the condition; in principle, it is not unlike the way we build up immunity generally and also how we guard against infections through medical 'immunisation'. With homeopathy the remedy to be applied is diluted in a particular way during a process which involves shaking the dilution before each next dilution is made and then repeating this method time after time so that the original concentration gradually weakens to zero while the liquid that has been used to dilute the remedy appears to do the opposite – it increases its power to heal with each dilution.

The laws of physics only recognise the dilution that has taken place and therefore that the mixture must have been weakened. We naturally expect the original substance to be the most potent aspect of the preparation and assume that every subsequent dilution reduces its strength. Homeopaths, on the other hand, believe that each physical dilution of their preparation enhances its power and claim that this effect is brought about because the 'memory' of water is able to concentrate the potency more and more as the water is added. For me, this brief explanation actually hinders more than it helps because those to whom it is addressed are not likely to believe that water can have a 'memory' and are hardly likely to give it much credibility as a reasoned argument. In fact, it is not bad shorthand to describe what could be going on through the power of energies. I have a theory about the mechanics that I want to share.

Let's say that, at the start of the homeopathic process we hold 100 cc of 'original' pure water, but that every single cubic centimetre of the water actually carries the energy imprint of the whole 100 cc. For every part to carry the imprint of the whole is not controversial – it is certainly accepted as the property of every cell of an organism to carry all the information for the whole being through its DNA. It also occurs with holograms. If a hologram which is laser-created is broken, each tiny piece when viewed again through a laser will clearly show the entire, unbroken original image. Based on this familiar principle it is easily possible that every part of the 100 cc of water does carry the energy impression of the whole; from this it is easily possible to build up a model of how homeopathic remedies could be developed.

When the homeopath adds 10 cc of a base liquid homeopathic remedy to our 100 cc of 'original' water, three things happen physically:

1. The volume of total liquid increases to 110 cc.
2. The base liquid remedy is diluted – shared among the

whole 110 cc.

3. The original 100 cc of water gains 10 cc of base remedy, to create a new, and weak, remedy mixture.

However, at the energy level an energy rush takes place in which the whole of the energy information in the 10 cc base liquid substance races into the whole 110 cc of the weak mixture; more than that, thanks to the principle of every part carrying the imprint of the whole, each cc of this new liquid mixture is receiving the *energy potency* of the whole 110 cc – each single cc of the new joint liquid has gained the energy power of the entire 110 cc. The energy power of the first 10 cc is now that of 110.

The homeopathic, energy potency of that new liquid has therefore been multiplied, but if 10 cc of that more powerful remedy is then taken out and added to another 100 cc of pure water, the energy potency will be multiplied yet again in exactly the same way to 110 x 110. Of course by adding it to the new water the remaining *physical* level of the original remedy will also have been diluted yet again.

I am not a homeopath but I am sure that a version of that energy process does take place when homeopathic medicines are prepared; it definitely shows that when we take energy into consideration it is not at all certain that sceptics are right to be quite so scathing about the homeopathic principle.

I have concentrated so far on invisible energies that are able to interact and create an effect that we can recognise. In our culture, however, there are many other claims that are made with great sincerity by those who have had encounters or experiences which are very much out of the ordinary; in this respect angels must come high on the list. Of course angel stories date back thousands of years, mostly within a religious setting. In the present day they are often seen as more personal and many devotees insist that they can be contacted at will in the right circumstances; it is also claimed that we all have at least one who will look out for us.

I do not have any certainty about the nature of angelic presences, although I have a strong feeling that I may have had two visits in my life. Unfortunately both took place around a dream state which makes it difficult to be sure what was going on. I do recall both instances vividly, however; I can picture both events now with great clarity – far clearer than any actual dream I have ever had and much more like a strong memory. For this reason I believe them to be real events, though I have to admit the evidence is harder to pin down than it is with my known real-life influences. From the perspective of issues that are readily dismissed by conventional opinion, however, there is no doubt that if you consider them within the framework of interactive energies they do become much more credible.

They crop up in different guises on different occasions although aspects of their appearance are repeated; it is usually reported that they are tall and that they appear from nowhere and, after giving some essential assistance, they disappear just as mysteriously. On the other hand one of my personal, less distinct cases, involved only the name 'Angel Mary' printed on a newspaper in a dream which was accompanied by the most powerful explosive healing sensations actually happening to me. The sensations continued well after I awoke and once they subsided I felt especially well and greatly relaxed; there is no doubt I enjoyed something more than a good night's sleep but I cannot be certain that angel activity took place.

My second encounter happened when I awoke one night as a teenager to find an angel figure praying by my bed. I was alarmed at seeing this and in some shock I covered my eyes with the bedsheet; when I judged it safe I peered out to find that the vision had gone. Was that really an angel? Well, it was a stereotypical winged figure in translucent blue – similar to pictures of the Madonna but with the wings. As with my other 'meeting' I believe that I was in the company of an angel because of the vividness of what was happening and because I still recall both events with absolute clarity.

The other reason I believe, of course, is the one I mentioned in introducing this chapter: that once we apply some knowledge of how energies work then we can be much more open-minded about matters which people tend to dismiss without further thought. A more interesting angel story was told to me when, with my wife, I was in a chiropractor's waiting room and had got talking to a lady who I would guess was in her sixties. I had mentioned healing and this, as it often does with people, prompted her to tell me of her experiences in related fields – on this occasion, an angel experience. She was, I think, German by birth and told me that she had been brought up by carers, not I think her natural parents, who were very strict with her. As a teenager she had to return home early if she went out and was told that she would be locked out if she did not arrive back by the due time. On one occasion she got home after the curfew to find the doors locked; despite her tears and pleas her home remained tightly shut against her. In distress she walked a short way from the house and lay down on a bench for the night. She couldn't sleep for her panic and upset but as she lay there she became conscious of a figure watching over her. She saw the figure as an angel and, unlike me, was not terrified by her meeting. The angel told her not to worry, that she would look after her until morning and that there was nothing to fear.

The angel also said, 'Do not cry any more, it is upsetting your brother in heaven – he does not want you to be so sad'.

The lady told me she replied, 'I have no brother in heaven', but she was told again that she did have a brother in heaven and that he loved her and was troubled that she was so upset. The lady said she then went on to spend the night comforted, if not comfortable, but at least in safety, and next morning returned home where she was allowed in. When she was able to tell her story of the angel she was shocked to learn that, unknown to her, she did have an older brother who had died before she was born, just as the angel had said.

When information which is not known to the person receiving it is given out and verified, then it is difficult to argue seriously that nothing of significance is actually happening. The only position for those who do not wish to accept it as evidence is to argue either that the whole story is false or that subconsciously the person did know the information but had forgotten it. I very much doubt that the lady I met was likely to be recalling forgotten facts through an invented angel in the midst of an evening of some considerable trauma!

There is quite a thriving industry concerning angels and you can easily find opportunities to learn about them for yourself if you are interested. For me they seem to make contact in many different guises and it is difficult to pin them down to a particular form that I could comfortably define. I do believe there are grounds to accept that something genuine takes place on these occasions but I cannot give any other insight; decide for yourself and if you choose to investigate be satisfied that you are taking advice from a reliable source.

Other 'physical' encounters are also regularly reported which do not carry any implication of there being angels at work. A friend and colleague of mine, most definitely not the fanciful type, told me of a strange experience he once had when he met an old friend while in London on the evening before an annual dinner of an organisation to which they both belonged. They chatted for a while and my friend was surprised to find that his colleague had not been formally invited to the dinner. They agreed that they would both go together anyway, and arranged to meet the following evening; my friend went to some trouble to arrange for a place and an invitation to be sorted out for his friend at short notice. Unfortunately, the dinner came and went but his colleague did not arrive.

This did not go down well with my friend who does not just moan about such things as many of us might; typically he decided to complain direct and rang the best contact he had, the man's father, to get a telephone number. Telling the father of his disappointment he said he was particularly annoyed that he had gone to so much trouble to fix a seat at the dinner and had so enjoyed his reacquaintance with his colleague that previous evening when he had been able to learn that his long-time friend had moved to South Africa, married and had three children.

The father agreed that his son had done this but the only thing wrong was that his son had actually died five years previously! Both my friend and the father were, as you can imagine, totally taken aback by the experience and the ramifications not only of the meeting but, as with the German girl, of gaining access to unknown details from beyond the grave that were subsequently verified. Whatever it is and however it may work, something went on there that does demonstrate a very different dimension from that of our daily lives. It would be easy to dismiss my friend's story as fanciful, or to argue that he imagined the whole thing and nothing 'real' happened at all; the problem remains that, like the German lady, he was given accurate information he had not previously known.

As a healer I found many 'paranormal' stories opening up to me which, along with the various events that were happening around me, continued to shape my thinking. My background in management stood me in good stead as I analysed in detail everything that came my way; I was determined that not only would I learn *of* new realities – I would learn *from* them. Finding tantalising pieces on a regular basis I set about fitting everything I could gather into an overall picture. My friend's encounter with his ex-colleague who was actually deceased at the time pointed up a new link to be explored: 'what happens to our body energies at, and after, our death?'

Our energies orchestrate our development and contribute to our whole lives but since, so far as we know, they require no bodily sustenance, none of the essentials that our bodies require, they need not necessarily expire when we do. They could come in time to guide our life cycle and depart intact at the end; we can therefore see them almost as a system that is governed separately from our physical bodies despite being wholly essential to us throughout our lives. How and when our energies do arrive is perhaps of some academic interest – spiritualists have theories about it that are beyond the scope of this book – but the matter of what happens at the end of our lives seems highly relevant to us all. One of life's greatest fears and taboos is the matter of death; what we believe happens after our passing must affect, and can therefore also change, how we live our lives.

Since living beings are indeed a combination of 'two systems', the physical and the energy systems, then it becomes perfectly feasible for energy to survive the neurological death of our brain. There is no reason to be certain that the energies cannot continue in some form; maybe even that they do so to take part in some other purpose. Spiritualists believe that the further purpose is more learning for the soul – or spirit – and that this includes possibly connecting to another incarnate life at some point in the future. This belief, of course, is what we know as reincarnation and there are many accounts told through personal stories of past lives; it is a concept which has many adherents, particularly through eastern religions, but also increasingly so among westerners.

Much of what I have heard about this topic I do find thought-provoking, but real proof is hard to pin down; the possibility of hoax, exaggeration and that catch-all possibility 'coincidence' cannot be ruled out altogether. Nonetheless, if pushed, my own inclination would lean towards our having many lives – though I cannot find a way to demonstrate the probability in the same way that I believe I can for other arguments I am presenting. Many stories about reincarnation do include factors that are verifiable; locations, names, living relatives and businesses have cropped up in a number of instances that I have heard of but unmistakable proof – as opposed to intriguing evidence – has not so far been accepted scientifically.

Whatever the evidence for reincarnation we are still left with the vitally important and inescapable fact that the human energy system does exist. Once we accept that, there is no question that the energies could, theoretically at least, survive the death of the body that they have spent a lifetime sustaining. This totally destroys the standard assertion that no part of the biological system is capable of continuing on to another dimension after death. Without doubt there is an active part of the body that might be able to do that; the energy system does exist, and belief about what happens to it is only one of the 'paranormal' matters that deserve more respect.

Aside from reincarnation, my own belief is that our energy

does survive death; it is a view that is formed by some direct experiences and other indirect ones. I am a big follower of three particular television psychic mediums: the UK's Colin Fry and Sally Morgan and the American John Edward. If you are not familiar with their work they simply do what you might expect of mediums – they talk to people, most often drawn from a studio audience, and make connections between them and their family or friends who have passed over. Much plausible information emerges via these mediums and is almost always totally verified by the person for whom the messages are intended.

In this short passage, which is only intended to connect my concept of the role of energies to the wider issue of an enduring life force, I cannot possibly do justice to the many stories that have been unfolded on their programmes or to the manner in which they conduct themselves. I do find it hard to believe that what they do is not genuine; all three mediums, and some others, are so accurate and so determined to stand by the information they receive from what they call the spirit world that it is easy to be convinced. They are especially impressive on the many occasions when their 'sitter', or client, cannot at first verify what the psychic is picking up but does eventually get there – sometimes by asking other members of their circle who are better placed to know. On the face of it there seems little likelihood for the process, and the information they receive and pass on, to be anything other than the genuine communication from the departed that mediums claim it to be.

I can see only two ways for there to be explanations other than the one that direct links to those who have passed on do actually exist – these would be that either there is complete fraud and/or collusion on the part of mediums or that the messages are received telepathically from the member of the audience lucky enough to have been chosen. Theoretically, there could be a direct connection between the energies of the psychic and their sitter; alternatively information could be channelled through an interactive process, similar to the one that passes on information and awareness during healing. This would mean that the messages would come not directly from a 'conscious' and surviving spirit but rather through the medium gaining access to the universal energies system. This would still be another remarkable feature of the world of interactive energies, but not proof that we survive death.

However, what I do notice is that the information passed on by mediums to the sitter is almost always given in the form of direct, conversational messages as if received from the deceased. Presenting the information as conversation, rather than giving the sitter a series of general facts gathered from a universal store of knowledge, suggests that those messages are reaching the medium in that personal format. Otherwise, it would suggest that deliberate fraud is being practised by the pretence that real dialogue was taking place between medium and departed spirit.

Why then do I rule out fraud? As sceptics will be quick to point out, there is no doubt that there are people clever enough to be convincing about all manner of trickery and deception whether honestly for entertainment or dishonestly to take advantage of the trusting public. Nonetheless, so far as I am concerned, I do rule out fraud as the explanation, partly because I accept the integrity of those TV mediums I have mentioned, partly because I can see interactive energies as a clear mechanism by which it can genuinely happen and partly also because of my personal dealings with one particular medium – a lady by the name of Pat Baker.

I first met Pat Baker when I visited the Mind Body Spirit exhibition in London. I was wandering among the many stands, browsing as you do, when I was approached by one of the exhibitors and asked if I wanted to 'come in'. When invited like that I almost never do; the sales resistance of mine that I mentioned always kicks in first and I decide that if I had wanted to 'come in' I would have made the first move so, with varying politeness, the answer is almost always 'no'. This, however, was one of those occasions when a decision seems somehow to be taken out of my hands. I have found that all the key decisions in my life, the ones that looking back I had to get right, never posed any doubts for me; no other move was ever seriously contemplated, a door opens and I am through before I know it. This is what happened again that day at the exhibition.

I had no idea even what the stall at the exhibition was when that exhibitor invited me to take a closer look, so in response to him I asked why I should go in; the slightly matter-of-fact answer was, 'it might just change your life'. Again, in normal circumstances that sort of explanation would have got short shrift and I would have been on my way! This time, for some reason it seemed to be enough and in I went – indeed, as it turned out, to 'change my life' once more. Inside was Pat, one of those kindly, sunny, matronly people – everyone's favourite aunt, friendly, relaxed and easily approachable. Jenny was with me at the time as we were in London on one of our trips to see Seka, and this in turn meant that Jenny had to join us inside the exhibition stand. She sat next to Pat who put her arms around her as I sat opposite and waited for whatever was in store.

I don't remember how Pat began, but we were soon getting messages from familiar sources from my wife's side of the family who had passed over although nothing dramatic was revealed. As I have come to know from the TV mediums' programmes I have since seen, the messages that come over on these occasions are mostly about maintaining contact and proving to those who are in the physical world that there is indeed an existence after death. It seems to be particularly important for the 'spirit world' to be able to assure us of the continuing relationship that those whom we have lost can still share with us. Given what I have already said about how much we have misled ourselves over the true nature of existence, it is small wonder that those who have passed over are so keen to share enlightenment with us. Their desire to do so actually gives added credibility to the whole exercise.

Unfortunately the cynics take the opposite view. The mundane nature of the dialogue which often takes place in these sittings and the information that is passed on is sometimes cited as a reason to doubt the validity of what is happening. If a departed spirit only wants to talk to the living about the new wallpaper or last week's barbecue then, the argument seems to be, messages from beyond the grave somehow lack quality and should be discounted. Unless a spirit weighs in with a cure for cancer, or next week's lottery numbers, it seems to the critics that it must follow that communication with the departed must be a myth or a confidence trick. Well, it goes without saying that it would be good to get a cure for cancer in a reading by a medium but we have to acknowledge the very real possibility that if the person being contacted had no such cure when they were on this side of life, they are no more likely to have a cure just because they have crossed over. Incidentally this is just one of the many examples of how those who do not accept the existence of psychic abilities like to tell the rest of us how they should work.

In any event, critics have no reason to condemn the process simply because the nature of the messages is usually personal. To condemn beliefs that have been around for centuries just because spirits concentrate on matters that are familiar only to those whom they are trying to contact seems a pretty desperate argument. I certainly prefer the merits of the counter argument that the uncertainty in most people's minds about whether there is some form of continuity after death is the reason that the spirits are so keen to prove that they really were surviving. Being determined to reassure their loved ones about immortality and the future for all of us would make them keen to demonstrate that it was indeed they who had come through. The best way to do that would be to talk about those things that did have some personal significance – even if, in the grand scheme of things, they don't mean much to the rest of us.

Getting back to that first sitting that I had with a medium, it was not long after Pat had started to concentrate that she made contact with a figure which she told me she could see behind me. The figure, she said, was hovering and hesitating in a way she had never seen happen before. Pat continued to encourage him to stay and give her his message – it was a male, she told me, dressed in a brown suit. He continued to wait, apparently uncertain and reluctant to commit himself. Gradually Pat was able to tell me, 'He is saying something about a ring'. I nodded but it meant nothing to me. Pat continued to probe the spirit and somehow we were able to recognise that it was that of my father who had joined us. Certainly his last suit was a brown one and I thought so were other ones; my wife, who has a better memory than I for such things, said afterwards that he usually did wear brown.

Pat confirmed again that he was talking about a ring, a gold ring, she added. It meant nothing to me still. Pat said other things in a more general vein as if to give her or my father more time to sort out the message. She soon returned to the theme of the ring; it is definitely a gold ring, she said – you will either give or receive a gold ring. I still couldn't connect. I told Pat that my wife and I had occasionally talked about an eternity ring for her, or getting round to buying a wedding ring for me. When we were married wedding rings for men were not quite so common as now, and we probably had a better use for our cash than to get one for me. Certainly I didn't have one and this was the best interpretation I could put on what Pat was saying.

I have already mentioned how good mediums will persevere to get the message right and, on this occasion, Pat was very keen to stick at it because she knew that she had not fully understood. Suddenly, that perseverance paid off. 'I know what he is saying,' she exclaimed excitedly, 'it is "why are you not wearing *my* ring?"' To say I was amazed puts it far too mildly. With a shock, the whole truth and proof about life after death was there before me – or rather standing behind me. I was the only living person in London and out of about six in the whole world who knew that I possessed my late father's signet ring. I had given Pat no clues, just the opposite – if anything I had misled her because I had not thought about that ring at all. It had never occurred to me until she worked her way through the very difficult communication process to get that vital question to me.

Note again the personal nature of what she said – it was not 'why are you not wearing your father's ring?' She simply repeated what she had heard as if she were an interpreter: 'why are you not wearing my ring?'

For Pat to be able to refer to my late father's ring meant she had been given information about it, and the only possible way for that must have been from Dad in spirit form. Obviously I was not wearing a ring and, as I keep out of the sun and never tan much at all, there were no signs from my skin colour that could have tipped her off that I ever wore a ring. More tellingly, she could never have known that any ring I might have owned had come to me from my father. It might seem that a possible way for Pat to have gleaned information about this may still have been through inadvertent telepathy on my part. This, however, is pretty unlikely since I was struggling so much to make any conscious sense of the message that I cannot accept that I was simultaneously engaged in passing on the correct information to her subconsciously. The other possibility would be that she was tapping into the universal energy and universal knowledge for the information, again as I suggested earlier. However, what happened next blew away any possibility that we were not dealing with the actual appearance of my father.

'He is going to touch you,' said Pat, perhaps as much to Dad as to me. 'He will touch you gently on the shoulder and you will feel the warmth.' Nothing happened. 'He is still hesitating,' said Pat, 'he will come forward and touch you.' I have to admit that my side of the family has always been independent and in some ways a bit reserved, not the sort who had a lot to say or to be demonstrably tactile. It was no surprise to me that it was not happening quickly, if anything were going to happen at all.

I sat and waited, for some reason expecting to feel a warm sensation towards the tip of my right shoulder by the top of the arm – that, after all, is my 'shoulder'. I also remember being ready for the gentle warmth associated with healing and to which I had by now become accustomed. I was wrong on three counts: instead of my right shoulder a sensation began to grow in my left one; instead of the area around the top of my arm it was further along my shoulder at its junction with my neck

– when I thought about it later, a much more likely place to touch someone with affection than the top of the arm. Third, the warmth was much, much sharper than I had thought – just like sunburn, hot and a bit spiky rather than just the gentle warmth I had been preparing myself for.

I regret that I did not have the presence of mind to say anything out loud to my father; I just took in as much as I could of what it all meant. More than ten years after his death I was in direct contact with him, probably more so and at a much deeper level than during his life. No possibility of any trickery, or of self-delusion. I was not vulnerable or still grieving as I had long since got over the loss I had felt. I did not go in to meet Pat expecting anything; until she began I had no notion of what I had gone into that exhibition stand for!

On that day in London when so much opened up to me it was Pat who was the emotional one as she picked up the significance of what had happened. She had totally broken down in tears as she said, 'I think that was something that had been a long time coming.' She didn't mean a long time within the session, of course, but a long time in my relationship with my father; she was right, in life we had never had the equivalent of that moment that I can remember. As it sunk in with me in the weeks that followed I too understood its importance. I still feel closer to him now than in most of our adult time. I still feel aware of him, and often dream about him – now more than thirty years after his death. For me this experience was all the proof that I could need about the existence of a form of continued life after death – the truth that spiritualist mediums have been telling us for years.

In Victorian times there was great interest in the concept of spirit communication and many public figures were enthusiastic believers, famously including Sir Arthur Conan

Doyle. There was no shortage of mediums ready to meet the needs of those who were keen to contact departed loved ones and other spirit entities. Unfortunately there was also no shortage of clever people willing and able to take advantage and so there are many documented cases of trickery and fraud. Information about genuine contacts by mediums is less easy to find, and would probably be overwhelmed at the time by all those cases associated with the fraud. Then, as now, there was plenty of enthusiasm for devaluing and 'debunking' psychic claims and it often seems to me that the high profile given to these fraudulent mediums still affects attitudes today.

We should also take into account evidence from what are now called near-death experiences. These reports are virtually identical; all involve a person travelling down a tunnel towards a bright light that could be a version of the experience of birth. Those who 'return' from these experiences usually tell of being met by those they knew in life but who had passed and saying that 'this is not your time' and to return to their physical lives. The frequency with which this particular phrase is repeated in these circumstances almost proves in itself that there has been a real encounter with an afterlife.

There are a small number of instances in which those who 'return' report chilling and horrific encounters and do not recall meeting up with former loved ones. There is no known reason why some experiences are so terrifying rather than joyous and they do put a different complexion on events that are difficult to pin down. However, no matter what is really happening, the common link between them is that the person involved returns to life and does so with a new, far more spiritual, outlook. Establishing such a new, or renewed, awareness might be the main point of the near-death event regardless of whether or not the experience itself is alarming or supportive.

Although these stories are now well documented and some research has been undertaken, none of it can yet be accepted as definite proof of life after death. The nature of science is such that there will probably never be an acceptance in that no one who had a near-death experience has, by definition, remained dead; they cannot therefore claim to have gone the whole way, whatever and wherever that may be. Understandably recovery from the brink of death, though cause for celebration personally, taints the whole process in terms of pure research.

Moreover, researchers often also claim that they can create similar experiences through sensory deprivation and oxygen starvation – factors that could indeed be affecting someone close to death. Of course, the fact that similar brain conditions can be recreated artificially doesn't mean that in a near-death state the subject has not made genuine contact with departed loved ones, or even with unsavoury entities. Mediums make preparations for their work by getting themselves into a highly sensitive state – including through meditation. It is quite possible that the experiments echo that preparatory work and come close to turning the scientists' 'guinea pigs' into receptive communicators with that other world. It is equally possible that the scientists' experiments create a version of near death that simply allows brain activity to register in a particular way, totally unconnected with 'real' near-death experiences.

To be able to invoke similar reactions in the brain artificially does not mean that there is no natural version that really does work in the way described by those who do survive the encounters, descriptions that, in a sense, chime with the contacts made by mediums such as Pat Baker, Colin Fry and John Edward. In addition, I may be wrong, but I do not recall anyone reporting that they heard those words 'it is not your time' when they are taking part in the artificial experiences. Either way, of course, the real driving force behind the insistence of scientists that near-death experiences are not valid is that they have yet to view the claims from the perspective of understanding the role of energies; that of course is the underlying theme of this chapter.

Whatever the truth may be, near-death experiences in themselves do not have to be the sole indicator of the survival of the spirit. For me the proof of life after death is the meeting I was privileged to enjoy with my father thanks to Pat Baker. If you add to that the work of those other mediums that I have encountered both live and on television and the fact that our body energies can survive death, at least in theory, then the odds seem to me to weigh significantly in favour of real survival.

Related to all of this also are the stories of 'out of body' experiences in which people, usually in traumatic situations and often in hospitals, find themselves watching their physical body from outside themselves. They frequently go on to describe the medical treatment it is receiving and from a 'viewpoint' looking down from above. The accuracy of information that is revealed is sometimes verified by those who confirm details that the subject could not have obtained any other way. There have been so many of these events that an experiment is being set up in one hospital to see if those who do claim to have had the experience can identify specific information that has been specially prepared and put in place in the treatment room.

So, has all this given definite proof of the reality of reincarnation, the powers of mediums, the presence of angels or any other matters that lie beyond what we normally understand? No, of course I have not quite managed that; but I have made links with some of those threads that I mentioned which confirm something of the breadth of energies that have been part of our culture for thousands of years. They have been dismissed because scientists cannot fit them into their model – any more than they can accommodate the reality of hands-on healing.

Building on the facts of healing, I have shown that we should not let our lives be limited by what others believe to be possible or 'appropriate'. There is much to explore for ourselves and it is to the advantage of everyone to do so; it really is a whole new world when we see it properly and I want to show more of it in the next chapter.

7

HOW CAN I BE LONELY WHEN I AM CONNECTED TO THE UNIVERSE?

'A human being is a part of a whole, called by us universe, a part limited in time and space'

Albert Einstein

No matter how and where you begin to learn about the energies that make such a huge contribution to our universe, once you are on board and see them for what they are, the more obvious it becomes that we are touching a dimension of infinite possibilities. The implications that flow from a world based on energies continued to pile up for me. It began to be as important for me to make sense of the energies and their role as it was to continue the healing work that I still loved to do. As I dwelt on the opportunities that came along I started to realise that this interest was meant to be more than academic. I was in a growing process that would teach me practical lessons about our healing universe – about the way it works, just what it can do for all of us and what we can do in return. Not for the first time the pieces that were needed to make sense of all of this suddenly started to fit together when I least expected.

Wandering around a Mind Body Spirit exhibition on another occasion I overheard someone observe to one of the exhibitors, who happened not to be busy at that moment, that he must be finding it a lonely experience with no customers around. His reply of 'how can I be lonely when I am connected to the universe?', delivered not as a put-down but in a gentle, relaxed tone, nicely gets to grips with the bigger implications of the world of energies that I have been heading towards.

Over the years that I had been gaining experience, knowledge and understanding of the world that I had discovered after our first visit to Seka, I had been led towards insights and into finding pieces of a picture that certainly made it easy for me to endorse that very perceptive observation from that unknown exhibitor. All around me was ever-growing proof that the entire universe is totally based on energies – our personal energies and energy fields that are part of my healing work and part of the way in which I gather information when I dowse. Universal energies are 'out there' just as gravity is 'out there', as are radio waves, microwaves, solar wind or the earth's magnetic field – the difference is that the latter are familiar while the energies are not.

The different forms of energy can easily be seen to be compatible with each other. External energies of the universe that fill all the space around us interact with our body energies; body energies will connect to each other, to earth energies and to the atoms that make up everyday objects. They enable living beings as well as departed spirits to interact in different ways – in the right circumstances. Indeed it is even possible to regard interacting energies as different wavelengths of mighty forces that contribute to every aspect of the universe. We, and every living thing in creation, every form of energy, can be seen as united with each other, linked by particles of energy that are all as one.

The healing energy is nearby, sufficiently so for us to connect easily with it each time we carry out healing; but then it is also sufficiently widespread to reach any corner of the planet as it channels its healing properties. There is no reason to believe that this force is confined to the earth – our solar system is typical of billions of others, so is our galaxy, and since the healing energy exists here, it will interact everywhere.

It is very evident that healing energy is truly universal, always ready to channel a healing input which can only become effective through its contact with body energy – both the healer's and the client's. But it does not end there, a similar widespread energy system also interacts to channel information to us in various forms such as: dowsing, telemetry, telepathy, the added prompts that can come through during a healing session and so on. It is not clear whether this means there is one, universal, energy force that does several jobs or more than one force with each variant having specialist functions, but to know the answer to that would not change the picture by much. Either way the energies have truly remarkable powers; whatever their precise place in the hierarchy of a 'solid' universe, at one level they can be regarded as a unified structure of subatomic particles, upon or around which everything is built. It is another way of defining that universal energy field within which everything exists that I described earlier when I was explaining the detail of the healing mechanism.

Having worked on the family pet to give healing, using exactly the same method as I use for human clients, I know that animals too must possess the energy centres and energy flows with which healers and healing interact to bring the same benefits as when we treat humans. In dealing with animals, most healers have reported successes similar to those I have enjoyed; some even specialise in healing only animals, of all types and sizes. Apart from underlining that healing is a genuine phenomenon because animals cannot fake or misinterpret their gains, we can also use such case studies to show there is no difference between humans and animals within the healing process. There is no difference in the mechanics that make it happen for each, which means we must all share a fundamental energy system as the basis for life and well-being; this may help explain our rapport and shared background with all forms of life.

There are grounds also to argue that we enjoy a similar rapport with the plant world. We have all heard the expression 'green fingers' applied to someone who seems particularly adept at growing plants and it is logical to believe that the body energy fields of those unusually successful gardeners are also somehow in especially close harmony with the energy of plants. Harmony in this sense may mean that some form of healing or 'plant care' is being passed on, or 'channelled', by those lucky enough to have the gift – even if they do not realise it. Certainly there are many reported instances of acknowledged healers improving the growth of plants through their attention.

Many successful gardeners are also known to talk to their plants, something which amuses sceptics because plants have no system with which to hear sound. However, through the medium of energy, words mirror thoughts, and as we can experience through those experiments I described earlier, thoughts influence energy which can then affect the physical plane. Gardeners' thoughts – verbally expressed or not – can just as easily affect plants through links between energies.

There are arguably aspects of pagan and similar beliefs in

some of this, beliefs that pre-date modern religion and science but which resonate with what I am saying about energies. The pagan way of life was to work with nature as a form of living entity that drew forth spirits that had to be kept bountiful. It has to be said that this relationship included sacrificing human lives as well as offering other gifts to the forces that pagans acknowledged. In their own way those who lived within this interpretation did at least know something about respect for the natural universe; the rapport they had with nature included something of the spiritual level, embracing reverence for their ancestors and a desire for the wisdom of the elders to remain with the community after death and burial. Indigenous tribes throughout the world followed similar codes and many still honour that way of life. Whatever our culture makes of the fine detail of it, we are the worse for having let it slip from our understanding.

I am not recommending pagan practices as any firm working model for twenty-first-century life; I am pointing out that they represent conscious connections at an energy level that would perhaps be supported by those present-day people who have enthusiastic environmentally 'green' credentials. I am not alone in thinking that the earth and the environment would benefit from some measure of ancient 'pagan' attention and harmony at the present time. Such conscious connections with the universal energies able to benefit all of us – as well as the world and its biodiversity at large – are as valuable in the present day as they have always been. We can make connections in a variety of ways; these include sympathetic synergy with plants and nature and overtly psychic encounters as well as more direct practices as in healing, dowsing and many other mind–body–spirit techniques.

The most common way in which we link to a wider power

is by practising religion – another of those issues that doubters often confidently dismiss but which can be seen differently if we apply the principle of universal energy. To follow any of the world's religions is to recognise that they are founded in claims for the existence of a universal power that is all-knowing and with which the religious have communicated for thousands of years. They do this according to a variety of practices and doctrines which can differ in detail but are broadly similar and aimed at making a contact that will improve their lives. There is little difference in principle between a universal force that I know transmits healing and one that believers see as a divine creator and protector around which holy books have been written. It is for theologians or 'the Church' to debate the principles involved but the fact that I can show the role of the universal forces with which I work means that the power worshipped as 'God' cannot be dismissed on practical or so-called scientific grounds. I will take a closer look at this later.

Over time I began to be very comfortable with my broad understanding of the nature of energies. I believed I knew about the mechanics of healing and a great deal about the theories. I knew what happened, what everything did and pretty much how it all hung together; at least I thought so, but in fact I was missing one staggering, life-changing piece that hurtled into my mind one day quite out of the blue. I was reflecting on the implications of exactly how we tap into that external healing power and the way it linked to my clients and their health conditions when I suddenly realised a stunning fact – in order to carry out healing we actually have to communicate our intentions directly to the energies, and, astonishingly, they react and respond to what we ask. I suddenly realised with a shock that to be able to work through the energies in the way I did, for them to respond to my promptings as a healer and for that to translate into the right and specific help for the benefit of every one of my clients, could only mean one thing: *the energies were actually engaging in direct intelligent communication with me!*

This interpretation went much further than recognising the existence of external energies that transmit healing. I had reached that stage much earlier – what I now realised was that the energies had to be aware that I was asking them for help, verbally and sometimes mentally; for them to respond they in turn had to 'hear' and react to my requests!

As soon as this different way of looking at the healing process struck home it made total sense; I had never seen it expressed this way in any of the material I had read but it was all so obvious that this was the source of all healing. More incredible still, it must also be the essence of the real nature of the universe!

The more I thought about it, the more I realised that the evidence was to be found in much of what I have been saying throughout this book – and of course in any number of conversations I had been having with friends and clients over the years. From the beginning I must always have been transmitting healing through intelligent forces that were 'listening' and responding. As I have shown, healers always have to channel the energy from an external source rather than simply emitting it from their own 'supply'; for this to be possible means that something has to attract the outside energy into the human healing event at the moment it is required. Intelligent communication with the healing force is the only way it can reciprocate and deliver the healing. Healers directly ask for that power to be channelled through them before they begin each healing session. Without that dialogue, spoken or unspoken, the healing does not happen; it only flows from that outside source after we healers ask for the healing to be given. We have to make contact with the healing force in order for it to respond.

This always has to happen; it is always the case whether the healing is carried out by contact or from a distance. I have already shown how our ability to give distant healing enhances the argument for the existence of universal energies and adds even more to our understanding of the sheer power that makes up this force. For years, from time to time, my wife and I would remind each other about how remarkable was the power of healing – even if constantly putting it into practice did breed a certain amount of familiarity that sometimes bordered on taking it for granted. I found myself now remembering the times I had sent healing across the UK with great accuracy to clients I might only know as 'George' in Glasgow or just to 'Barbara'. It made me appreciate even more the power and complexity of the forces with which I was interacting. It is quite staggering to recognise that the healing power is capable of helping patients at all, that it is able to discern what and where the problem is within the client and then, based on that awareness, to take the correct steps to help. It is an amazing process even when healer and client are in the same room, but to be able to do that, just as effectively, over the thousands of miles that can sometimes separate me from my patient really does change everything.

If I do not know what is wrong with a patient or, in the instances of distant healing, if I do not know where a patient lives and yet I can still switch on a system that brings physical healing to the right person (sometimes persons) at the right time and place, it means that I, along with every other healer, am dependent on an intelligent accomplice consciously co-operating through the energy fields on a literally cosmic scale.

It proves the words of that unknown exhibitor at the healing exhibition – we are indeed all connected to the universe.

As the enormity of this continued to grow in my mind I looked at it all again many times, considering whether there was a different explanation. Was it perhaps possible that I could be sending healing to my clients without there being a power that had to 'listen' to what I wanted, and was able to know who was waiting for it and then to respond on behalf of healer and client? Any mechanism that brings successful healing to us is still absolutely awesome but it might not necessarily require the, literally, intelligent co-operation about which I had now become convinced. I had the advantage of knowing for certain that the healing could indeed be channelled to those in need but, even to me, this new twist was an enormous leap and difficult to take in. I had to be sure.

I recalled that there is nothing new in healers representing themselves as 'transmitters' and their patients as 'receivers'. If I took that analogy almost literally, especially in distant healing, I wondered if the healing energy simply left me and crossed the world exactly like radio signals; was it just powered out randomly to connect to anyone out there who was in the way of this invisible 'beam' of healing power? If that were how it worked then the healing would not have to be guided to its target by a 'knowing' co-operative intelligent power; I would just have to be able to 'pump it along' more or less indiscriminately for my clients to somehow latch on to. But no, the fact is that on most occasions when distant healing is sent, the patient is not alone, there are usually others in the same room, even sitting immediately alongside, and no one other than the person for whom it is intended ever picks up on the healing. It only ever works for the client intended to receive it – unless I have deliberately sent it to two people at the same time and then both do feel it; in her experiment Seka sent simultaneous healing to some fifty patients in different parts of the UK. In all cases of absent healing that I know of, mine and Seka's, all the patients to whom we send the healing pick up the physical sensations and enjoy the improvement in their health. No person for whom healing was not intended has ever noticed anything happening for them. Nobody benefits from a random beam of healing that crosses their path and is intended for someone else.

Was that itself a clue? Do we perhaps send out general healing that the designated client has to capture for themselves by somehow switching on their own receiver? I soon realised that this could not be the answer either because animals and babies will receive healing even though they are not aware that healing is being given or sent. Remember the baby Daniel who received distant healing with no knowledge of what was supposed to happen yet he clearly received what had been meant for him with no possibility of helping himself to draw it in.

On a related tack, remember also Margaret whose absent healing did not connect at the appointed time because, unknown to her, I had not then sent it; yet it worked in the usual way a short time later. Margaret could not connect to the healing force until I sent it to her; Daniel connected while knowing nothing about it. Taken together, these instances illustrate slightly different features of the fact that distant healing cannot rely on clients just switching on their own receiver to tap into a general, beneficial force for themselves. I also realised that even if the healing power itself were able to switch on a receiver in each individual patient whenever it was sent to them, the energy still has to 'do' that. It would have to *know* that the healing has been requested and then find the client at the right moment, wherever they are in the world. However it works, the interactions that make up the techniques of healing must be conscious and deliberate.

Transmitting healing over an area as widespread as the whole planet, as opposed to the intimacy of a treatment room, demands an accurate, wide-ranging and super-powerful network. It requires an energy mechanism with which we can communicate intelligently in respect of millions of healers and their patients throughout the world, even if they are all active at the very same moment. It is a system that requires the immense power and awareness to diagnose every client's healing need, in response to every healer's request for assistance – instantly. It must always be ready to work appropriately with every healer to channel the healing energy that will help deal with their clients' individual medical problems, whether nearby or on the other side of the world. Remember again the case of Barbara and the tumour behind her eye that was known through the healing force before anyone else was aware of it, including Barbara. Although Barbara did not receive her healing from a distance, if we had used that method the force would have reacted in exactly the same way, having exactly the same impact immediately.

The few examples I have just given from my cases in order to illustrate this mechanism may seem isolated instances; however they were part of a healing pattern with which I was totally familiar, even if I was now seeing it from a new angle. It was enough for me to define, in my own mind at least, the true nature and concentration of this energy and to describe it exactly; the forces undoubtedly are 'Intelligent Energies'. Now that I had recognised them I had to validate their presence and their role properly, by examining my experiences against the background of such a universal force.

'Intelligent Energies' is more than just a label; it describes, though very much understates, the nature of the force that healers and others have used for many thousands of years, bringing 'knowledge', 'action' and 'communication' across the cosmos. For Intelligent Energies to have the power to bring individual healings to every part of the earth – and arguably every part of creation – is breathtaking; the more so when you add in those insightful prompts I keep mentioning that make treatment more effective. However, the energies are not limited to the role of delivering healing to the sick; remember I also argue that the same energies, or perhaps another version or wavelength of them, also interact one to one with every dowser in the world to pass on detailed knowledge immediately to those people who are skilled and plugged in to the dowsing methods.

I have already referred briefly to dowsing as the means I use to obtain knowledge when I investigate and then deal with the problem of geopathic stress and said that I would explain exactly how it works. Dowsing is a truly remarkable technique and dowsers constantly demonstrate their skills in finding not only geopathic stress and underground running water but the whereabouts of pipes and cables as well as information about the health of individuals or the location of precious metals and even lost objects. Obtaining accurate information by dowsing is something that can be done outdoors, directly on site if you are looking for something specific but, surprisingly, it also works at a distance; as with absent healing, dowsing can be done equally effectively from anywhere in the world. It can be done in order to establish detailed information about any item, fact, person or site from across the planet. You could dowse for information about a site on the other side of the world from where you are now sitting!

The complexity of a force that can enable virtually anyone in the world to practise both healing and dowsing, even across a tiny planet like ours, can hardly be imagined. When we extend the concept to recognise how the same power must also be able to cover the rest of the universe as well as our small part of it, we open up a dimension that is truly colossal – yet paradoxically simple. For this to work it just takes two main components:

- a universal energy force that is interconnected with everything – every thought and action, every object, event and all matter that has ever existed anywhere
- a series of questions asked by a dowser that can elicit 'yes' or 'no' responses from the universal force.

Dowsing, like healing, is just a means of interacting through energies but is entirely concerned with accessing information. There is no attempt to generate the same direct intervention on the part of the energies as when we channel healing to our clients but we are making contact in a similar verbal way as we ask for information that can be signalled to us as 'yes' or 'no'.

Water divining remains the most well-known example of dowsing, and there can be few who are not broadly familiar with the stereotype of someone with a Y-shaped hazel twig marching steadfastly through fields until sooner or later the hazel dowsing rod suddenly dips or shoots upwards to signify the presence of underground water; the movement of the rod is a 'yes'. The alternative method of water divining in which the dowser holds a rod in each hand pointing directly out in front is equally familiar to most of us. With two rods the signal that something has been found is when they swing to cross over each other.

Whether directly on site or from miles away, dowsing is often accomplished with the aid of a map or plan to pinpoint whatever the dowser is looking for. Uri Geller has apparently made himself very wealthy by hiring out his ability in this field, searching for minerals all over the globe from a comfortable office vast distances away from the location of the site he is surveying. I use the same approach when I check for geopathic stress and when I check objects for 'bad energy'. The modest, convenient tool when dowsing from indoors is the pendulum to which I referred to earlier. The weight on the end of a piece of thread is held so that it will swing when dangled between finger and thumb and allows skilled dowsers to interpret exact information that they can record using the plan.

The principle with using a pendulum is that we can obtain facts by allowing it to swing in different ways that can similarly be interpreted to show positive or negative (or 'yes' and 'no') replies to the questions that we ask. It is something that is easy to try and most people can get reactions relatively quickly. The object on the end of the thread usually swings backwards and forwards or side to side or will rotate clockwise or anti-clockwise. For some reason dowsing produces these slight individual variants in the way the pendulum behaves to create a small range of slightly different responses, which occur in their own particular way for different people.

If you wish to try dowsing for yourself the pendulum is the best way to begin. To do so you first need to identify how it will swing to signify 'yes' for you and how it will swing to represent 'no'; as I said, this is not identical for everybody. The easiest way to find your own reaction is to ask, mentally or out loud, a question to which you know the answer. For example, say 'is my name John?' and see what happens. If your name is indeed John, then of course the way the pendulum moves will show you how you are identifying a 'yes' or, in other words, getting a positive reaction for your particular dowsing. If your real name is not the one that you used for the test, then the movement of the pendulum will mean that you have identified your 'no', or your negative response.

Whichever is the case, then, of course, you check for your opposite reaction, establishing a 'yes' or 'no' by using another name. Whatever swings you get from your pendulum will always remain your way of identifying your own 'yes' or 'no' for as long as you practise dowsing.

Once the pendulum movement has shown how you personally interpret 'yes' and 'no' reactions, you can then use it to tackle other questions that can have a positive or a negative answer. The more you practise the more skilled you become though there appear to be grounds to suggest that the process works on different wavelengths for different applications and may be in tune differently with different people. For instance, I have had no success in finding lost objects but considerable sympathy in other areas, particularly of course with geopathic stress; some dowsers specialise in matters regarding health. In theory perhaps, all dowsers should be equally adept whatever the field and this may well be so in some cases, but to be gifted in all areas of dowsing does seem to be unusual. This means that if you do try it for yourself, you would be wise to attempt to do it for different objectives in order to identify your own forte.

There are further sophistications to this simplified description of how to go about dowsing that will only matter if you become much more advanced in the art. For instance, dowsers vary the weight of pendulums they use and the length of the thread from which they hang; this is to help them 'tune in' more efficiently to the information they wish to establish. Many dowsers also like to use what they call a 'witness' – that is, some material or substance related to the object of their enquiry such as a photograph, lock of hair or a piece of precious metal, depending on what they are trying to ascertain.

An extra feature also is that a pendulum will sometimes swing in an elliptical orbit rather than a circular one and at an angle. This is said to mean a qualified 'yes but' or 'no but' rather than a total 'yes' or 'no'. In other words you are being told that you are on the right lines but you need more information that is not possible to pass on by either 'yes' or 'no' to the question you have actually put. You then need either to ask supplementary questions or rephrase your original one until you get an unequivocal 'yes' or 'no'.

In this particular exchange, the force that is getting the answers to you seems to have a wider sense of what you need and wants to help you get there – something which suggests a high degree of sophisticated interaction that makes the Intelligent Energies especially worthy of the name!

The missing ingredient in everything I have just explained about dowsing, the obvious question that must be answered, of course, becomes 'what exactly is happening to generate the responsive movements of the rods or pendulum?' This actually breaks down into two questions:

1. What physically or physiologically is taking place – that is, why does the pendulum or the dowsing rod move at all, let alone in an informed and disciplined way?
2. How does it access the actual answers to the questions we ask?

It is plain that the pendulum itself, made up of thread and a weight, does not know anything; the pendulums, like the various dowsing rods, simply react to, and exaggerate, involuntary muscle movements being made by the dowser. Physically, although it is not happening consciously, it is the dowser's own muscles that cause the movement of the dowsing tool. Our hands are moving in response to the answers to the questions we are asking and the role of the rods or pendulums is to exaggerate and draw attention to this muscle movement so that we can more easily read what our body is telling us during the process.

From experience of how Intelligent Energies communicate in order to put healing into practice, it is easy to see how a similar interaction between energies will allow information to be channelled to those who dowse. When healing is taking place, Intelligent Energies pass healing energy into the body energy of the healer, which in turn is channelled on to the client. I have also shown that the energies are able to pass practical advice on to the healer at the same time – Seka Nikolic is able to use this in order to be 'told' what is medically wrong with clients and I often get guidance about where to concentrate my healing for it to be of most benefit to my clients. All of that, plus the way in which Intelligent Energies transmit healing across the miles to named patients, confirms that healers are taking part in a comprehensible 'dialogue' through this interaction between energies. It is a similar interaction between energies which channels responses through rods and pendulums when dowsers ask for information; the fact that both healing and dowsing respond to our thoughts, as well as to the words we may say out loud, underlines yet again the awesome forces that are in play across our world.

In order to be able to interact, the Intelligent Energies have to be a part of everything that exists – they are connected to unlimited data in the form of facts, thoughts, words, deeds and medical conditions as well as all matter such as subterranean minerals and other features. In principle that means absolutely everything that exists and has any possible connection at an energy level; Intelligent Energies have to be constantly accessing this as up-to-date information every second of every day. When I use my technique to clear a property of geopathic stress Intelligent Energies register it; within seconds a dowser who is sensitive to geopathic stress would be able to use their skill to connect to Intelligent Energies to confirm that the property was now clear. Intelligent Energies even remember when the property still had the geopathic stress, allowing a dowser actually to check back that before I had taken the action the property was indeed stressed! How well this understanding of the power of energy impulses chimes with the concept of a God who is instantly aware whenever 'a sparrow falls'.

As I said earlier, the key to it is for everything that exists or has existed to have its own 'imprint' at an energy level. Objects, food and artwork can have an energy imprint as I have shown, imprints that can be passed on by, and also recognised through, our body energies. This 'imprint' is accessible to the universal forces that will pass the information into the body energy of dowsers who are sensitive enough to be able to capture and understand it as reactions to the questions they ask. In our test experiment it was 'is my name John?' The Intelligent Energies respond to the question with a 'yes' or 'no' answer which the dowser's body energy passes on to the subconscious brain. Our subconscious triggers corresponding reactions in the dowser's muscles, making them twitch to give exaggerated movement to the pendulum or to the dowsing rods which we can then interpret as 'yes' or 'no' answers from the Intelligent Energies.

A more sophisticated technique that dowsers often use is to measure the scale of something on a range of 0–100, either as absolute amounts or as percentages. To do this it is necessary to prepare a scale based on a semi-circle drawn on paper and used in exactly the same way that a protractor is used to measure angles. Using a pendulum held over the semi-circle you find that, as Intelligent Energies connect to the dowser's appropriate questions the pendulum will start to swing at an angle away from the baseline so that the line of its swing can be read as a measure against the 'degrees' of the arc on the semi-circle scale. Dowsers can use this technique to make comparisons or to ascribe values in any appropriate enquiries, for example speed and depth of underground running water, the relative strength of geopathic stress lines, the 'freshness' of food and so on. These are not 'yes' or 'no' responses, of course; they are, however, a variation of the motion of the subconscious muscle movement – this time going at an angle to convey 'proportions'.

Although the use of rods or a pendulum is the most familiar way to tap into facts that can be revealed by dowsing, the Intelligent Energies have another trick, almost literally, 'up their sleeve' for us. This, even more surprising, method of interpreting the universal energies takes two people to carry out; it works by testing variations in someone who is asking the questions and receiving the answers. In the same way that responses from the Intelligent Energies reach a dowser via their body energy to generate the involuntary muscle movements, we can also interpret the signals our body energies are receiving by looking for changes in the *strength* of someone's muscle. For this reason this type of dowsing is colloquially termed 'muscle-testing' but the more correct name is kinesiology.

In essence it is possible for two people to work together to ask questions that will invoke the yes/no or positive/negative answers from Intelligent Energies. One person, in a way, acts as the dowsing rod as they ask the questions, while the partner tests the changes in the questioner's muscle strength. In the hands of a professional it can be a highly effective way to identify and treat medical problems.

The process operates on the basis that 'no' or negative answers to the questions are recognised by way of a detectable weakness in the muscle strength of the patient while 'yes' or positive responses yield appreciably stronger muscle resistance.

When I adopt it, my basic technique is to stand behind the person I am using to perform the test (I will call them 'the subject') and ask them to raise their stronger arm at right angles to their body, straight out from the shoulder and pointing sideways with their palm downwards. Once they are comfortable, and with their permission, I can then test the normal or natural strength of their resistance by my pressing down on their outstretched wrist with one hand, while putting my other hand on their opposite shoulder for balance.

Having gauged how firmly they are able to push against my downward pressure in this way, we then ask our question to elicit a yes/no response, which I interpret according to whether the strength of their resistance changes. If the resistance of the subject weakens, this is equivalent to negative and 'no'; if the subject's arm retains the same strength, it is positive and 'yes'.

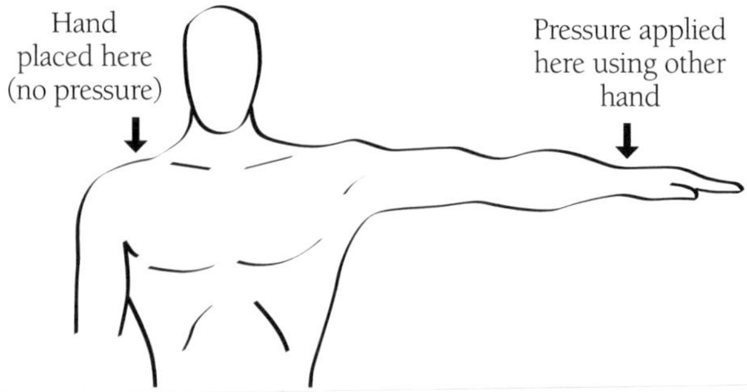

For example, you might be working with your subject to see if they are intolerant to chocolate. To get at this information, having tested the muscle strength of the subject, you invite them to ask an appropriate question: 'I am looking for intolerance to food, is it safe for me to eat chocolate?' The dowser then retests the strength of the subject's arm muscle by pressing downwards as before. If the response is positive and your subject has no intolerance to chocolate the arm will be as difficult to press down as when you first tested it. If the response is 'no', that your subject does have a chocolate intolerance and it is not good for them to eat it, then both of you will realise that the arm is much weaker and easier to press down.

The fact that the subject cannot resist your pressure usually comes as a shock and many will often demand a retest. This is particularly so if they fancy their strength to be much greater than yours; a rugby player once kept trying to do this, to no avail, when my wife was testing him for something. You may of course also get the same demand for a retest from someone who is keen to be able to keep eating chocolate!

Another way for the layperson to use the muscle test is to check for geopathic stress. I said earlier that I would explain how you could test a building for yourself, and this is how to do it. The technique is the same as I have just described, but – as with any dowsing – the secret of success lies in how the question is framed. I always use the phrase 'I am looking for geopathic stress, is this a safe place to be?' Be clear what you mean by the word 'this'; substitute the name of a location if you wish – a house or other building, a named room in it or the spot where you are standing. As long as the person whose muscle is being tested understands clearly what is the focus and location of the site they wish to know about, the dowsing by the muscle test is properly set up.

The muscle test will also allow you to check for yourself whether an object is carrying bad energy such as was the case with my son's jacket that I talked about earlier when I used a pendulum to get at the same information. With a partner to press down on your extended arm, ask whether the object has any form of bad or negative energy attached to it. If the answer suggests that there is a problem with the object, consider having your result checked by a dowser and then get it cleared, perhaps by a healer.

Remember you can also use the same muscle-test procedure to ascertain in advance whether an object, or any site you think may be affected by geopathic stress, will be safe after it has been treated. I believe it would also be possible to establish whether an object or a location would be safe if it were to be treated by the specific person or method through which you intend to tackle the problem. Do not necessarily rely on the muscle test alone for that – it is always wise to have recommendations from satisfied clients and to use dowsers that you can contact through the British Dowsing Society. Nonetheless, the muscle test would be a way to satisfy yourself as well. Do not be afraid to name that person while you check their abilities through the muscle test.

Muscle tests will also allow you to address health and other issues but be warned of three things:

1. First, you should use it only as an indicator of what you wish to know; all your health concerns or questions must be referred to your physician. It would be foolish and dangerous to rely only or mainly on dowsing over matters of health, even though trained professionals do use the same system in a very sophisticated way to deal with health issues.
2. Second, my purpose in offering this brief explanation is to address the matter of energies by illustrating ways in which you can access information that is available from these fields of energy – all dowsing relies on the

open subconscious mind if it is to be accurate. It is all too easy for your conscious mind to overcome the subconscious if the result for which you are dowsing has any personal significance for you. To be able to understand kinesiology and use it properly it is also essential to study it in some depth, perhaps beginning with one of the many books which carry full references to it and are intended to set it out in proper detail.

3. Finally, as is the case with dowsing for any form of bad energy, if you find that you have identified any negative issues always finish the session by asking a question which leaves you with both a positive answer and a strong resistance to the pressure on your subject's arm. There is no doubt that frequent exposure by testing for geopathic stress without undertaking proper 'cleansing' causes problems, including increasing susceptibility to its effects, and this must be either avoided or controlled.

I have only given the briefest outline of what dowsing and kinesiology are about; it is outside the scope of the book to do more. There are many books on these subjects, as well as much material on the internet, of course, but if you are interested in learning more about dowsing get in touch with the British Society of Dowsers. It is a fascinating field of human abilities; just to search the Society's website illustrates the range of categories in which dowsers work to access information that they could not find purely by the five basic human senses. It is another of those topics that people do not readily take on board, but which can be easily demonstrated to an open mind.

When I first began to have my own success with dowsing I talked about the topic to a very sceptical colleague of mine who, to my surprise, came back with a dowsing story of his own. He told me of his neighbour who had found he had a blocked or collapsed drain somewhere on his property and had called in the local plumber to deal with it. To his amazement, when the plumber arrived he immediately began pacing round the garden with dowsing rods; he soon found a spot where he said the underground problem was located and announced that this was the spot he had to investigate. The plumber then dug down, found the source exactly where he had predicted and carried out the necessary repairs.

For me, the most interesting fact about this story is not so much a tale from a sceptical colleague that had made him reconsider his thinking, but more that the plumber had the confidence simply to set about dowsing as part of his daily trade. He must have known that he would successfully find the right spot – it could hardly be coincidence or a one-off. In some ways indeed it might even be said to be not entirely in the plumber's interest to find the pipe so easily, as a couple of hours extra 'searching' in the wrong place might have been more profitable from a crude financial perspective.

Dowsing also has more 'official' blessing than you would think. Apparently until the 1960s it was a recognised and accepted technique used by engineers in the British Army to track underground features. It was also used in identifying underground facilities connected to First World War trenches at Flanders that were being opened up in 2008. You will be in good company if you too find that you are able to tune into Intelligent Energies in this way!

As I have been saying, to accept the presence of energy, in all its forms, is to open up realities that move us outside what we see as normal and of course there is much more evidence out there among others who have had similar experiences in healing, dowsing and psychic and related matters. Considering the amount of evidence I have presented so far, the question to which I keep coming back is: why does science find it so difficult to accept our experiences? Why have we not included – or more accurately retained – an understanding of such matters in our culture? I want to take a closer look at that next.

8

...IF DARWIN HAD SENT HEALING TO GEORGE IN GLASGOW!

'Science without religion is lame. Religion without science is blind'

Albert Einstein

From the events and experiences I have been describing, it is pretty obvious that the evidence to support the existence of an interactive dimension to the universe will never go away; it dates back centuries and reappears, in particular, every time successful healings take place. Some still dismiss the concept out of hand; they are mainly those who have not tested healing directly for themselves or who have not seriously explored the facts. Conversely, anyone who is prepared to draw closer and examine the subject soon realises how much it has to offer.

I always respect the views of anyone who doubts my work. I do my best to explain the facts about healing and to debate and demonstrate the reasons for my beliefs. I have little interest in those who refuse to listen or who do not want to test the powers of the healing force; that is their business. Everyone is entitled to their opinion, of course, but uninformed opinion is of no value and ultimately there is little point in challenging the views of anyone who chooses to remain uninformed. It is always surprising, however, to see that, as a generalisation, scientists still assume that the interactive energy dimension at the heart of everything I have to say does not exist. They seem to treat the concept as a myth that belongs to ancient history, as something which lost credibility centuries ago and was finally destroyed somewhere between the inputs of Newton and Darwin. The problem for such an assumption is that it is only partially informed. I sometimes allow myself the flight of fancy to consider the possibility that if, like me, Darwin had found he could send healing to George in Glasgow, he might have dared to find room within his theory for its implications. Had that happened the grand debates in the decades that followed would have been very different from the ones we have actually had, and continue to have. What to me is a simple, if breathtaking, universal healing interaction reverberates throughout the universe, something that could have informed the philosophical and scientific analyses long ago but has barely even been noticed.

As a healer I took a modest interest in the scientific perspective as soon as I found myself repeatedly coming across claims in healing circles that discoveries in quantum physics were chiming with some of the realities that I have been showing. I wanted to understand exactly what that meant; in truth, I think I was hoping that I would find that science was indeed getting closer to recognising and taking on board some of the evidence that I have been writing about. Sadly all I could really establish was that although scientists ought to be able to connect with what we are saying, in the main no discernible steps are being taken towards building the necessary bridges.

There is no obvious enthusiasm to take our experiences seriously because the scientific model that took hold some 150 to 300 years ago is still considered good enough.

Despite the excitement of hoping that healing and quantum physics were starting to match up, I found it was mostly based on physicists proposing, and to some extent confirming, the existence of a growing number of particles and fields throughout the universe. This attracted healers because we could see that these discoveries lined up very neatly with the energies that we have been talking about for centuries. Our collective excitement was strengthened when we picked up on the growing realisation that subatomic physics shows behaviour that is entirely different from the historic laws of physics on which general science has been based. It hasn't happened yet but I still hope that this realisation might soon tempt scientists into recognising that the unconventional world of healers and others might not be as far-fetched as they think. There is little or no difference in principle between the universal energies that I have been referring to and the modern advances in particle physics or, for that matter, the more long-standing discoveries, such as radio waves, magnetic fields, X-rays or 'solar wind'. We have all recognised how matter that we know to be invisible can be interactive and often makes its presence known by its effects; we say exactly the same about healing and other energies.

Among scientific theorists, a proposition known as string theory argues that everything rests upon subatomic particles known as strings that might act as the foundations of the universe. In this theory we, along with everything else in the universe, are all made of 'string' moving in something that has been called string space–time. This seems to me to be another way of saying that we are at one with the universe exactly as my unknown exhibitor said when he pointed out that he, like the rest of us, was 'connected to the universe'. Certainly, it is a more or less exact reference to that concept of 'beings of energy in a sea of energy' that I have long argued is the broad basis for healing.

If string theory were to include the possibility that the strings can resonate throughout the whole of existence, communicating – or aiding communication – with all the other strings, we would have a scientific version of interactive Intelligent Energies! This is all it takes for science to accept what they have spent the last couple of centuries denying – 'paranormal' transfer of information on which the psychic perception depends can indeed be reconciled with science. String theory does not yet go that far, of course, but it remains an uncanny reflection of most of what I have been saying. I was also delighted to hear one physicist reminding us that just because the string particles are too tiny to be seen would not stop them having an immense effect on our lives – another truth that corresponds with the whole new world I have come to know.

There is even one specific connection that has already shown up, first as an unlikely sounding theory and later as a successful if highly challenging experiment – challenging, that is, to those who have not yet come across interactive energies. The idea was that certain particles have the property of being aware of what is happening to a separate but related particle instantly regardless of the distance between them. The proof came in 1997 when two particles seven miles apart were made to spin in opposite directions to each other but at the same speed; as soon as one of them was manipulated the other one immediately revolved in exactly the same way. So far as the scientists were concerned there was nothing to create a link between the two but both acted in an identical way; what actually connected them, of course, was universal Intelligent Energies. So far the scientific experiment has still not been explained; no one knows how the information about the direction taken by one particle can reach its twin apparently faster than the speed of light. As an experiment, however, it is very like the mechanics of healing – particularly those of distant healing – whereby we can affect our clients' body energy over any distance, as my earlier case studies illustrate.

So far, none of this seems to help; science continues to avoid any validation of the work of psychics even while making their own claims that often make little obvious sense to the layperson. For instance, there are many theories about the elusive dimension of 'time'; they include the notion that it may be 'granular' and that it is not necessarily a straight line as we commonly experience it to be. A growing number of scientists are now even arguing that time travel may one day actually be a serious possibility, once they sort out wormholes and the right technology. This is at the same time as they generally reject the gift of foretelling the future – the ability to look ahead into 'time' that clairvoyants have been claiming for centuries.

If those who do take time travel seriously are right, they must equally accept that when people do go back into the past, they would be meeting others while they themselves were actually alive in that past. These characters from history would be meeting travellers who had been living in their future! This must mean that on some plane that future exists now, along with the present and the distant past, a difficulty for laypersons to grasp. Imagine a time-traveller arriving back in 'history', let's say to this present moment of time, having said goodbye to their living future family and turning up in the here and now. They would arrive possessing all the knowledge of everything that had happened (was to happen?) between our present and their future times. They could only come to us now either if they are alive somewhere now, or if the proposed wormhole technology would completely change everything about time once it was in operation. Both options raise the possibility that the future plane would always have been available to anyone with the ability to access it. The energies that are accessible to psychics are a strong candidate to be able to conduct such an exchange across time, yet the ability to foretell that future, as with beliefs in 'fate' and 'destiny', seems to make no sense to the same community that will discuss time machines seriously.

On 8 April 1996 a clairvoyant told me I would write a book; he said he could 'see' me researching and writing it. Nothing was further from my mind at the time, and it seemed an unlikely prediction; nonetheless, 16 years later, here it is. Sceptics will say that the thought was put into my mind and I therefore went ahead and fulfilled the prophecy because I had come to expect that I would. They would claim that without that trigger, it would never have happened.

I can see why that would be said; there may even be some truth in it, though the fact is that in 1996 I had nothing new to say in a book. I had never tried to become a novelist and I had never set out to find a topic for non-fiction. Crudely, I suppose the prediction had a 50/50 chance of proving to be accurate; either I would or I would not write the book. It is also true that, many years later when I had developed something entirely new, I remembered that prediction; it is equally true that I remembered the prediction before I began to work on the book. At the time the prediction was made, however, the real odds for or against it happening were much greater than 50/50 – in any realistic sense the concept was so unlikely as to be totally off the radar!

Another clairvoyant once told me that, one day, I would find myself experiencing a feeling something like champagne bubbles coming out of my head! No time frame was given for this and I neglected to ask what would be the purpose of the event if it were to happen – what, if anything, it would signify. Despite that mysterious background, the prediction itself was clear enough – champagne bubbles were due to come my way! I had almost forgotten about it until one morning, months later, I was relaxing at home when I felt a pitter-patter across the top of my head. It was a sensation I had never experienced before or since and heavier than I would describe a feeling of champagne bubbles popping, though that was not a bad attempt on the part of the psychic. In practice, it was more like soft, slow rainfall or the bubbles and craters that appear in something like thick soup as it starts to boil. Once it happened the popping sensation lasted for probably a couple of minutes and I am still uncertain what it did for me, but whatever its purpose I rate the prediction as totally accurate and an unlikely experience for anyone to predict; maybe that is all it was meant to be!

Unfortunately, although healers and others may be able to see the connections in all of this, it seems that science is unable to accept anything that does not fit the present view of the universe. For all practical purposes psychics and scientists may now be headed vaguely in a similar general direction but, for the present, the best we can believe is that we may be on parallel lines rather than converging paths. I am not sure whether or not to draw any comfort from the fact that scientific reluctance to accept new ideas is not limited to a mistrust of people from my background; science is littered with examples of derision being heaped on any of their own kind who dared to challenge orthodoxy and push new ideas too far, too soon.

They are welcome to that, of course, but we should not let that hold the rest of us back!

The pieces that I have been putting forward to demonstrate the range and roles of energies seem to me to speak for themselves; they come from a combination of my direct experiences, including case studies, alongside some experiments, plus what I regard as sound interpretations about what it all must mean. All the things that led me to recognise Intelligent Energies as the ultimate force of the universe – and in particular as the only means to explain the realities of healing and dowsing – are as plain as day! Intelligent Energies not only explain a great deal but, by their presence, they also help prove the other energies that we know to be around. If Intelligent Energies are to achieve anything they only make sense if there are other energies with which they can interact; without a corresponding force with which to connect they would just be 'one hand clapping'. Because they are able to show their effect, Intelligent Energies also help prove the contribution of other forms of energy.

Although all of this seems a long way from the familiar science of today, if you look more closely it resonates quite well. Theoretical physicists tell us that energies from the Big Bang turned into matter in the form of subatomic particles. Particles and energies preceded the creation of matter by constantly switching their identity from energy to particle and back again, alternating back and forth between the two states before the atoms emerged. The link between energy, subatomic particles and matter is therefore at the heart of scientific understanding and at the heart of healing.

Atoms from which all matter is constructed are a combination of protons, neutrons and electrons; everything in the universe therefore comprises nothing more 'solid' than electrical charges. In 1910 Rutherford established that the arrangement of particles in atoms was such that they are mainly empty space; to a layman this is not an awfully robust arrangement to make up a universe, but at the common knowledge level we have all come to recognise that this is how it is. The atoms hold together and so our 'solid' universe is created.

We are living in a universe that we know abounds with subatomic particles and physicists are constantly proposing and finding ever more. It is easy enough, therefore, to propose that the energies that I am describing, our body energies and those external universal energies, are comparable to – and compatible with – 'acceptable' subatomic theory.

From my healing case studies and those experiments which allow us to feel our body energy fields as they are being affected and changed, I have shown the case that we are indeed made from energy; or at least that we have those energy fields and flows as an integral and essential part of our physiology. It is not in fact particularly controversial to claim that the body does have its own energy fields; electrical impulses from our brains power us both physically and mentally and, nowadays, our electromagnetic fields are commonly referred to in scientific circles. Similar electromagnetic fields are known to exist in animals too, and are often cited as the means by which predators are sometimes guided to their prey. The role of human and animal electromagnetic fields may not be fully understood within science, but it does seem that their presence is. In addition, cosmic rays reaching earth from outside the solar system have been known to science for almost a hundred years while something called 'energy waves' are thought to have played a part in the formation of particles during the early development of the universe.

We can now also point to a much more specific and exciting scientific discovery that adds some weight to the concept of widespread universal energies. For quite a long time scientists have been telling of their reckoning that the recognisable mass which makes up the universe is as little as 10 per cent of the amount that, by their calculations, should be evident. In other words, 90 per cent of the mass that scientists know must be around somewhere in the universe is invisible and unaccounted for, apparently doing nothing! The calculations are based on the fact that stars on the outer edges of galaxies are captured in orbit around a mass which is actually insufficient to hold them; the outer stars are travelling too fast to be held by the gravitational pull that would be available solely from the visible galaxy. This anomaly can only be explained if there is a greater mass within galaxies than science can identify – or in other words if some form of undetectable energy is spread throughout the universe.

Considering how much energy and power would be required for Intelligent Energies to work forever with every organism throughout the universe it would not be too surprising if their whole force did amount to many times the known mass of all creation, a huge interactive power fundamental to the development of the entire universe, hidden but making its presence known in different ways. It cannot surprise any of us that hitherto it has been undetectable to scientific measure and left entirely out of the reckoning by physicists and cosmologists. Indeed, the scientific discovery of this discrepancy in the known mass of the universe is an acknowledgement that has generated the occasional newspaper headline asking whether this confirms the existence of 'God'.

Perhaps as a response to such occasional media references, scientific talk now seems to have shifted towards claims that 'dark energy' and 'dark matter' exist within and between galaxies respectively. It seems to me that both those names are unfortunate, almost sinister, choices that perhaps deliberately try to position these energy fields further away from any ideas about finding God, or any other positive force; never mind, they are labels that still reinforce what I am saying. As I understand these new discoveries, dark energy is now thought to provide the superstructure for galaxies – a sort of framework holding each galaxy together; dark matter may keep the galaxies individual and apart as the universe expands. There is a further theory that the escalating speed of the universe's expansion will ultimately lead to its being separated and collapsing, possibly to be born again through another Big Bang, endlessly renewing and repeating the whole process.

Present debate about all of this includes the proposition that something called the Higgs field permeates the vacuum of the cosmos, raising the hopes of finding yet more subatomic particles, including a Higgs boson. Such fields have been given more credibility by physicists who have measured how light from stars is 'bent' around them and the theories have even been refined further with the development of a 'map' showing the shape of the universe with countless galaxies sitting within the outline of the energy field. Seeing it represented visually like this does make it hard for me to avoid the obvious hope that this map really does reflect Intelligent Energies – especially as scientists across the world are now racing to prove that the universal fields are indeed present.

It is said that the prize at the end of this race will be a discovery claimed by some scientists to match any of the great discoveries the world has known! Well, I maintain the real discovery has already been made; not only do such fields exist, some exist as Intelligent Energies – communicating and interacting at the energy level with each other and with us as they organise the universe.

—— The scientific framework ——

These new masses that are now part of the scientists' vocabulary, along with many other particles and fields, strengthen the prospect that all the energies I write about are also simply waiting their turn to be recognised. Professor Alvaro de Rújula of the European Council for Nuclear Research in Geneva, who is also Professor of Physics at Boston University, has said, 'complete lack of understanding often precedes a scientific revolution'. I find this genuinely encouraging and hope it means the time is now ripe for such a gigantic leap to bring science closer to the healing nature of the universe.

For now, mainstream scientists continue to work within the bounds that our planet, and the complicated structure which brings order, must have arisen spontaneously on the back of random incremental steps of fortune. They are still caught up in the notion of a mechanical universe where everything is rooted in coincidence from which the consequences then go on to develop naturally. Scientific conviction rules out any question of intervention by a wider force and few individuals seem prepared to challenge that conviction which has become equally firmly fixed in the collective western mind. The present model is held there by the many scientific discoveries that are valid in their own right and have led to all that we have achieved in the modern world, progress that encourages us to dismiss past beliefs just as we have overtaken outdated technology. As I said from the outset, before I met up with Seka I shared that view. When I became a healer I knew the view was wrong; eventually, I knew how it was wrong and why.

Human advances through to the twenty-first century have

been rapid and widespread. They have been built in stages on the foundation of proven successes that led to rich insights and major leaps in understanding. New inventions and fresh ideas caught on; Darwin and before him Newton were both heavily instrumental in demonstrating a credible 'technical' universe as opposed to a divine one. Between them they drove the most telling wedge between the 'new' scientific discoveries and the beliefs of the past. It is difficult for anyone to step outside of the framework that this has produced without seeming to be returning to the dark ages of ignorance and superstition. Darwin's theory of evolution is the most familiar factor of the debate about scientific or religious explanations for the universe – these still remain the two main views on offer even now. Darwin did a lot more than to present an alternative workable model to replace 'God'; his explanation was so telling that there could be no room for both views. You believe the Bible or you believe Darwin – science and its framework or holy books. The ground was staked out 150 years ago and we are free to choose; regrettably, the two choices on offer then and now are still not the right ones!

There are many who, as a matter of principle, do not entirely accept the scientific line. They often simply argue that the universe and life within it are both too complex to have arisen by chance or coincidence and claim that some other influence had to be involved. It is a tempting argument and even scientists have found sympathy with it despite the fact that it is a sentiment that in particular does not really do justice to Darwin's theory of the rise of life. Darwin did not argue that major, complicated genetic mutations occurred 'overnight', driving species along to the sophisticated perfection and variety that we now see. Instead he showed that minor genetic mutations, happening by chance, can build limitless complexity as long as each change conveys a sufficient advantage to any of the species. Once that simple single advantage occurs, that life form is able to use the genetic gain to outperform its competitors. Those without the mutation suffer and eventually disappear while the better-adapted members continue to pass that gene on; the new gene, along with a new version of the species, survives and continues. Eventually more chance mutations follow and the better-adapted, again, move upwards through the so-called tree of life spreading gains and increasing diversity. There are no all-singing, all-dancing dramatic creations, merely tiny but critical changes that evolve step by step.

Scientists are generally content with the theory that all the complexities of life on earth arose in this gradual way based on chance but, critically, also on the benefits that were triggered by those random gains. I do not quarrel with the notion that gradual gains through genetic mutations led to the intricacies of all life. I am not supporting the alternative of divine creation and I am not nailing my colours to the belief that everything in the universe is too complex to rest on coincidence – though I repeat the conviction that it probably is! My continued argument is that it is much more credible that Intelligent Energies, known to be active and responsive, were there to stimulate every crucial mutation and development that peppered and promoted the universe and everything that grows within it.

—— Religion and science ——

Religion argues the case for creation though, increasingly, it is straying into acceptance of Darwinism as the mechanism for 'God's plan'. 'Intelligent design' is an alternative label that has appeared in recent years to mean much the same thing but without identifying a divine designer. Science takes issue with either or both concepts on the same grounds – that in each case there has to be a designer or a master planner to trigger the process and, for scientists, no such architect exists.

One hundred and fifty years ago Darwin chose to eliminate the idea of a plan or a planner in favour of random chance mutations and natural selection as the 'origin of species'; he was convinced that such mutations were statistically possible and in keeping with his research. Darwin himself originally had a strong religious background; he studied theology as well as science but lost his faith after his daughter Annie sadly died at the age of ten. Although his research and recognition of the principles of evolution were well established before Annie died from tuberculosis, it is thought that his grief further encouraged him to doubt the presence of God; in any event, he abandoned his faith and become an agnostic.

Darwin knew that the biblical concept of 'creation' individually designing every living organism as a finished product could not be literally correct; this meant that 'God the Creator' had no credibility so far as Darwin the scientist was concerned. By the time he published his work, his science and his agnosticism could leave no room in his theory for his former God and so the only candidate that could be seen as the trigger for the gradual genetic mutations on which evolution depended was random chance. Though the factor of chance has never been exactly proven (how could it be?), it remains pretty much unchallenged as the only option available to the scientifically minded.

To my understanding, the best-known scientific argument against the presence of God is based on the theme that Darwin was correct about the whole mechanism of life. His explanation of chance genetic mutations does not require there to be a God and shows also that the process of fully formed design described in the Bible did not happen. For the biblical accounts to be so at odds with scientific evidence is used as the convincing argument to support science over religion. However, the present debates on the existence of God now go beyond Darwin's theory and on to criticise God's apparent failure to meet the expectations that are raised by His followers. These failures embrace the harm, not to mention the wars, tyrannies, fears and oppression that have been allowed to happen in the name of religion, as well as all the other instances of tragedies that God must allow, or cause. These include the sad event which led to Darwin's own loss of faith after God had apparently failed to save his young daughter's life. Darwinian science, added to the philosophical conviction that no just God would either permit, or require, innocent suffering, is seen as pretty conclusive proof that religious believers are mistaken about their faith.

Science also poses the further philosophical problem that if a creator did exist, then who or what could have created the creator? According to scientists, to have the creator appearing first would be at odds with their conviction that any natural process of development must have the most complex, sophisticated form at the end of it rather than at the start. Any power that emerged as the force of all creation would be the most complex force we know or could imagine – but natural selection requires that evolution must work upwards to any ultimate 'design'; it cannot start with the ultimate and go on to build lesser beings.

Professor Sir Richard Dawkins explains the broad scientific case in his book 'The God Delusion' and I admit that reading his account helped improve my own thinking but has not altered it. The scientific framework does not permit the existence of any force with the sophistication to influence the development of life. Scientists do not see how this barrier might rather mean their own model is in fact flawed and in need of refinement. Instead they defend the role they say is played by chance and refute any other option, including those they know little about. This is despite, as I said, of having no proof that the genetic mutations of evolution do happen by chance and despite the fact that they are left with no model at all for the development of the physical universe.

My book is not about the existence of God – it is about the existence of Intelligent Energies based on my experiences as a healer; however, my theme does give me the background to point out a couple of possibilities that are highly relevant to those who are pursuing the 'God' debate. To begin with, a creator need not necessarily have arisen at the end of one single process of developing life on earth; nor does a creative force have to arise only after the complexities of the physical universe have been formed. It is perfectly realistic to see how the most sophisticated power in the universe came into being as the culmination of a process in which forces developed and escalated to unlimited complexity and power as a universal energy. That way a field, or fields, could reach perfection through an entirely separate process completed before they formed every other element of our universe.

Second, the logic of denying the existence of God because of His apparent failures is misplaced. The argument can only be applied to religion or to the Church which has taken the decisions, created the doctrines and made the interpretations about what God can do. God, religion and the Church are three separate elements and it is the latter two, not the presence of God, on which sceptics have actually based much of their case. God is the name given to a universal force; religion is the interpretation of the force of God and has been made and modified by man for centuries; the Church is made up of the people who are in control of that interpretation at any time. It is the Church that, throughout history, has waged war and condemned friend and foe in all manner of ways. Doubters cannot blame God for that or cite it as proof that no God exists; all it suggests is that God does not act in quite the way that religion and religious believers have led us to expect from their scriptures. Scientists should use their existing logic to explore religious interpretations, not to challenge the power that religions define.

As I mentioned earlier, Intelligent Energies offer a different way for us to consider and experience the presence of God. This is not intended in any way to be disrespectful to any religions or their followers; I am not seeking to detract from the beauty or wonder that historically belongs to the connection anyone has with their God. I am saying I have found my own practical examples of interactions with universal energies that I see as evidence of influential powers across the cosmos and across the millennia. We can all relate to that according to our own beliefs; the only mistake is to believe we are alone.

—— The world of energies ——

Humankind has had access to Intelligent Energies since we arrived on earth; it is arguable that connections were clearer in earlier times and that messages received through the links with the energies were given greater credibility than they receive today. At some point our ancestors took a detour away from the direct links they had formed with universal energies and established their concepts of multiple gods and, alternatively, the existence of one single holy power. I think it most likely that, in keeping with their culture, men interpreted messages that emerged from the energies as instructions or advice from a divine God and acted accordingly. Religions would be built from the stories and beliefs that ensued and from demonstrations such as healing events that came in their wake. Religions would gradually strengthen their own concepts of God; they would do it slightly differently through their individual forms of worship and doctrines and through interacting with the universal energies to build genuine and effective communication that persists today.

I have dwelt on the attitude of science towards religion because it is better documented and justified than any scientific case against healing, or against the world of energies generally. The scientific framework, however, means that religious beliefs and psychic experiences are treated with similar disregard even if the case for psychic interventions is not challenged in the same detail as religion.

I have been telling my own detailed story that is based on an analysis of personal experience over more than twenty years. Psychics and other practitioners such as healers display our respective individual gifts every day, mostly for the benefit of others. If you visit any of the Mind Body Spirit exhibitions anywhere in the world you can easily detect a family of like-minded people around you, both exhibitors and visitors; you will be aware of some sense of connectivity between it all. There will be a huge range of techniques, topics and interests that all fall within one general theme, that of spirituality. Science has long since generally dismissed this theme and its individual strands as little more than folklore, superstition, dreams for the gullible, and opportunities for charlatans. Despite the evidence and even though ideas about energies in all their forms have been around for centuries, science still cannot recognise their existence as present-day interactive forces.

The result of all this is a distance between the three traditional perspectives that leaves scientists unable or unwilling to build bridges between them. As I said in my Introduction: 'We therefore have a modern society which separates out our understanding of one universe into three often conflicting cultures; none of them can claim to be complete until science, religion and the psychics join forces. That is until we all recognise the fully joined up story that shapes what I describe as a Fourth Perspective; a picture that 'makes room for all three previous perspectives – and then adds something more besides'.

- Religion looks at the bigger picture; it sees the universe and recognises an intelligent force at work that followers define as God. Individuals connect to God through their prayer and worship.
- Science examines the universe almost literally through the microscope. Theirs is a clever understanding of the fine detail – it is all about atoms, gravity, quantum physics, biology and many other fields. They add it all together to describe the big picture but fail to see any intelligent force at work and are generally uncomfortable with the whole idea that such a force exists.
- Healers and others who recognise a role for energies concentrate mainly on direct action – they use their individual gifts and can usually see a spiritual connection to a bigger picture. Unfortunately, unlike science and religion, our practitioners do not usually spend their time exploring that bigger picture as I have done.

Although the Church often has an uneasy view of the activities of healers, clairvoyants and – particularly – mediums, there is a degree of overlap in what we might call these spiritual realms. Our scientific perspective is much further adrift because scientists can never acknowledge what is known outside of their general framework. When they form their theories, make their assertions and give us their contribution, scientists ignore the presence of healing energy and the interactive way it can travel the world to help the sick; they also take no account of the energy which will work with dowsers to reveal anything that is knowable. They cannot therefore easily ask themselves what else such forces might have contributed; nor can they allow any other aspect of the energies into their reckoning – not least the effects of geopathic stress and of other incompatible energies.

They keep the new world that I found for myself seriously off limits; so much so that each time I have seen any attempt to study it the investigation soon becomes more a matter of how to disprove the claims that we make rather than how to understand them. The scientific model lets us down because it prevents scientists from seeing a factor within the universe that is as vital as anything they know about, a factor that has far wider implications than, for example, whether or not an individual clairvoyant is genuine.

The consequences of a weak scientific model hold back the potential for even greater progress that could be made in health and academia because both of these areas are limited, reined in by an incomplete picture. This affects all of us – including those who are deterred from practical treatments or techniques only because scientists seem to dismiss them as not valid. I know because I was facing that position before I found Seka and tested out her reputation and her skills for myself. As a result of all my experiences then and since, it is easy for me to consider the whole range of non-scientific activities and to judge the effectiveness of practices and practitioners for myself. It has therefore become important to me that I help others to become free to do the same and so help themselves.

Genuine self-help and advancement via many energy-related means is a practical option. There will be false claims and misunderstandings out there and people must not be taken in; there are many weird and wonderful possibilities to investigate – but be on your guard. Everything genuine will prove itself, from acupuncture to yoga; treat the opportunities you find with due scepticism and an open mind. Do not be put off by the fact that science has not caught up but do not be sucked into something just because it is new, or you are told it is good for you. Investigate credibility and credentials thoroughly and be satisfied before you get involved that your interests are being looked after properly.

In the next chapter I want to start to show some of the implications that follow when we do grasp that the universe is based on the existence of the Intelligent Energies.

9

THE ENERGIES OF SPECIES and natural selection

'That deep emotional conviction of the presence of a superior reasoning power, which is revealed in the incomprehensible universe, forms my idea of God'

Albert Einstein

Intelligent Energies spreading throughout a healing universe may sound like science fiction but the energies are undoubtedly real; they are a scientific fact just as radio waves that cross the galaxies were a 'scientific' fact before, and while, dinosaurs dominated the planet. Because scientists have not yet signed up to the full picture does not change the picture; it simply means that it is not yet visible to everyone. A healing universe based on interactive energies makes good sense – it is there to be explored carefully by all of us as we seek to understand and to find our own ways to enhance our lives. It is a concept that has much to teach us and much to offer us and over the remaining chapters I am going to show something of what that means.

I am convinced that Intelligent Energies are the product of the mechanics I referred to in the last chapter – those of interaction, reaction and problem-solving that assembled a universal force. The force that emerged was then critical to the formation of a living universe that, in turn, developed life on earth and almost certainly on other planets across the cosmos. I argue that all of this – the universal force, the physical cosmos and the spread of life – have all been achieved through the same principles of incremental growth that Darwin identified in his theory of natural selection. The only adjustment to Darwin's theory that I propose is that the universal energies intelligently interacted throughout the entire process he described – there is no need to rely on chance or coincidence at any point. The interactive forces did not act through godlike creation; instead they formed mechanisms and rules that built up everything that happens in nature, and everything that needed to happen across the cosmos. They responded to needs and opportunities, strengths and weaknesses as they communicated back and forth through their own world of energies.

Intelligent Energies must have been able to connect with, and influence, the energy of any aspect of the universe at any time since they formed, influencing other energies and affecting electronic particles, atoms and physical mass. It is this feature, to affect other energies around them, that becomes the key factor to explain how the universe and life on earth really did emerge as an organised structure. Indeed it may help build a bridge towards scientific respectability if we regard this act of creating a living universe not as the work of a separate power that 'looked in', 'planned' and 'created' from somewhere outside but rather as a force that is itself a part of a burgeoning, evolving universe. The universe, like the energies and life on earth, follow the same evolutionary pattern – a universe intelligently assembling itself, neatly in line with Darwin and with the ideas of Einstein and others who can recognise a more complete and dynamic universe than is popularly accepted.

If this were the process by which they did develop, Intelligent Energies would meet the scientific requirement that in order to be credible they have to come at the end of an evolutionary trail. This is exactly what Intelligent Energies would have been able to do – emerge from an interactive chain of ever-increasing complexity and sophistication to reach the top of their own pyramid, one that is mainly, or exclusively, devoted to the development of subatomic interactive energies.

These powerful energies may have formed before, during or immediately after the Big Bang, but that does not affect the fact of their presence or the nature of their role. For Intelligent Energies to have emerged around this time is no more spectacular or unlikely than it is for the rest of creation to have developed. Either the whole universe, including Intelligent Energies, starts from nothing, or it starts from some pre-existing form that evolves into all that we know. Intelligent Energies are no less likely to feature in this than is time, space or thermonuclear laws.

In a sense scientists have the most to gain from coming to terms with the effects of these energies; there is no doubt that science would be much better equipped if its theorists, researchers and practitioners were willing to take Intelligent Energies – and other forms of energy – into their calculations. I have spent the greater part of this book showing how and why my experiences, and those of millions of others, make it clear that communicable and interactive energies genuinely are the major element throughout the universe. As a healer I know they are around us and part of us; they are no less practical a proposition than anything else we know of. I also know we cannot yet put any limits on their power because we know so little detail about them.

I have shown how Intelligent Energies are able to transmit information to and from other forms of energy; that they have access to knowledge; and that they are able to identify, diagnose and co-operate to help us deal with illness, disease and so many of the other troubles that come our way throughout life. Long before any life was formed, however, they had already been around long enough to have accumulated all the building blocks of the physical universe. Although Darwin has shown the broad mechanism for how life has been able to evolve across the planet there is no equivalent formula in science for how the universe was able to grow as an equally sophisticated working entity. It is not at all far-fetched for interactive Intelligent Energies to have emerged from their own process of evolution to formulate and apply what we now know as the physical laws of the universe.

The energies can interact with anything that has an energy component, across every aspect of the universe, to calculate and put in place all that is needed to create the balanced presence that the universe had to have in order to be viable. Intelligent Energies can be regarded as the one mechanism that is capable of interactively orchestrating first itself and then the physical universe, prior to establishing the evolution of the natural world. None of this is at odds with anything that science has demonstrated; it is only at odds with what scientists believe.

The fact remains that, for many, to rely on chance and coincidences to explain the order of the universe is still an unconvincing proposition. Whether we are trying to fathom how the stars and planets assembled within the laws of physics or how life has blossomed on earth, for everything to depend on one lucky break after another persistently seems not to be enough. It actually seems to be unscientific insofar as the notion of coincidence lacks structure which everything about the universe has in abundance. It has gained credibility only because scientists keep using it as the same explanation for events they cannot otherwise unravel but it is almost no explanation at all; a scientific experiment that relied on chance or coincidence for it to work would be considered a failure – but not for developing a universe and life within it.

The late Professor Sir Fred Hoyle is one of those scientists who famously had sympathy with the instinct that other forces might be at work. He is credited with observing that the possibilities for life on earth being driven by random chance are equivalent to believing it to be possible for a hurricane sweeping through a scrapyard to have the good fortune to build a Boeing 747 – at the everyday level such an event is obviously impossible to conceive. Although the professor seemed to enjoy making opportunities to exasperate some of his contemporaries with his ideas, he speaks for many in having made his famous comments. For there to be Intelligent Energies readily interacting across the universe removes the weakness he was referring to – that forlorn dependency on chance and randomness as the foundation for how everything came to be. He even claimed to be 'aesthetically' biased against the Big Bang theory, which is a nice approach to take; I suspect he would have preferred that, too, to have been triggered by Intelligent Energies – something which is entirely possible, neater and far more likely.

What is common ground for most of science is that at the point of the bang a tiny amount of matter was created that grew into everything that was to make up the universe; material was created and thrown out from the source of the bang across the whole of space. Incidentally, in order to receive this matter space itself had to be coincidentally created at that same moment, as indeed was time. We humans, along with every living organism, are made from the same materials that went on to construct the stars and the planets. How simple it is to consider that the energies that also appeared at the same time could equally have found their way into our physiology as readily as any of the other material that makes up our bodies.

This massive explosion with its tiny start grew into an expanding universe of billions and billions of galaxies with billions and billions of stars and planets. It created, unaided and more or less at the very same instant, all the other essential ingredients that were to be needed and without which the whole affair would be doomed to a mass of rock and gases hurtling through space to no good purpose. It has been estimated that the success of this working universe depended, and continues to depend, on at least six numbers – or values – turning up as exactly the right 'frequencies'. Funnily enough this is the same number of digits used in the UK weekly lottery jackpot, a prize nobody seriously expects to win. The numbers recognised by science represent values of essential aspects of the universe such as the force of gravity and the rates for thermonuclear activity, which allows the sun to hold together, and so on. These scientific numbers even exist down to decimal points – they are not all whole numbers such as we have with 'real' lotteries! I have even seen other arguments claiming that in fact there are as many as twenty numbers which could be regarded as essential to the successful formation of the universe – in other words another 14 key factors would also have to hit precisely for the basic rules of the universe to come together by chance.

Just to put some flesh on some of this, one instance behind

the figures is that hydrogen has to be converted to helium at an exact rate that is less than 1 per cent; if this rate had varied by as little as 0.1 per cent then this critical conversion could not happen. Depending on whether the variation had been upwards or downwards we would either have a universe consisting only of hydrogen or one that had consumed all the hydrogen long ago. These are very precarious values in respect of hydrogen conversion alone. If you add the other essential numbers that the universe needed in order to exist then we really are into super lottery odds against being here as we are today, alive in a universe of precise mathematical rules that govern everything. The laws apply to the formation of every star in every galaxy and to every planet in orbit around every star. Against the odds, the rules create patterns that make the formation of galaxies inevitable – rules and mathematical patterns that are stable throughout the vastness of the cosmos, some of which are mirrored in nature as well as in physics.

In all other circumstances you would expect scientists to treat arguments in support of hitting between six and twenty values by chance as a pretty weak explanation of anything. It certainly persuades many of us that science is lacking proper answers – a view that, in fairness, is also shared by a significant number of scientists, academics and philosophers.

For me the fact remains that if the numbers that 'control the universe' do have specific values then they could have had other values instead. To take one example, if the force of gravity had simply kicked in naturally and randomly, it could have been stronger than it has turned out to be – or it could have been weaker; for that matter it might never have kicked in at all. Either way, gravity has to work exactly as it does according to the individual mass of different objects – too strong and everything crashes together, too weak and nothing holds together. For gravity to be any different from its precise value would have doomed the universe; it could never have come together.

For me, Professor Michael Green of Cambridge University added something to this mix when he said on television that gravity actually weakened after the Big Bang and that this may be due to the appearance of as many as six extra dimensions to the universe, in addition to the dimensions that we commonly accept. I take this to mean that the value of gravity is only precisely the power it needs to be because the universe happens to have nine dimensions; had gravity remained at its initial strength following the Big Bang it would have failed and there would have been no coherent universe at all. Then again, perhaps there are only eight – or even ten – dimensions to the universe; either way the actual number of dimensions and their combined impact in weakening gravity are critical to its eventual and essential value. I find it enthralling to think that this weakening might so easily have been the work of Intelligent Energies adjusting the laws of physics at the critical point in the birth of the universe – so elegant, so simple and so easy to understand as a mechanism.

Particle physicists think that gravity appeared within trillionths of a second into creation followed immediately by electromagnetism. I am happy to believe that Intelligent Energies were in there somewhere and conceivably ahead of both by the same sort of unimaginably tiny time span, even if that would delay gravity by a millionth of a trillionth of a second or so! So far as I am aware we do not know how long the ingredients of the Big Bang may have been gestating – a process that could have given rise to Intelligent Energies – so we cannot be certain about how and when the energies were able to impact on the developing universe. If Intelligent Energies did not precede the Big Bang but came into being after that first act of existence they would probably need to have been the first effect of creation in order to shape what happened from then on. Such fortunate timing would have made for yet another coincidence – if Intelligent Energies had not arrived early they would not have had the maximum impact on everything that followed; it seems more likely to me therefore that the Energies did appear prior to the Big Bang. Whatever, if anything, science does make of a role for Intelligent Energies, I am more comfortable as a layman with the idea that they did appear at the earliest point, and helped to form the universe, than I am with the notion of random chance having the key role at every stage of proceedings.

That, however, is not the whole story. As well as forming the laws that lie behind the development and the order of the universe, nature had to construct the atom which is so complicated that it is still not fully understood; slightly earlier, the even more complicated deluge of subatomic particles came into being. These particles are still being discovered, taxing our finest minds in establishing exactly what they all are and how they fit into the smooth mathematical precision that runs the cosmos.

Without Intelligent Energies, the physical universe has no helping hand to make the millions of pieces come into being in any organised pattern. There is no cosmic equivalent of Darwinian natural selection that now explains the process that advanced life on earth, a process that even with Darwin's theory still depends on the argument that every stage of incremental change in each species requires pure luck in order for the mutations to occur. In a survey of the public as many as 50 per cent of those approached did not accept random chance as the only possible way that the initial mutations could happen.

It is not the idea of progress through natural selection that troubles people; what keeps getting in the way is that business of 'chance' genetic mutations being the starting point for every critical improvement.

Possibly the development which causes people to have the strongest doubts about every aspect of life being dependent on chance is the complexity of a focusing eyeball, an organ that is capable of operating through a system of nerves and lenses connected to a brain capable of making three-dimensional sense of the images along with eyelids and tears for protection. The facility of sight is the feature that is most commonly regarded as the real proof of the need for a creator by those who assume that vision appeared in full one day by one of those lucky breaks; after all, what use is the chance arrival of part of a vision system? It is a question that nicely illustrates the dilemma – but it is misplaced.

Darwinists are happy to explain that, for the faculty of sight, along with every other sophistication throughout the whole of creation, the route of unaided natural selection is all that is needed. The theory seems to be that, in order to develop the eye, a cell which recognises light appears one day by chance and gives an advantage to the recipient – perhaps to pick up the shadowed movement of a potential predator and so gain an advantage by being able to avoid it. The facility was subsequently made a tiny, but critical, degree more effective by another spontaneous improvement maybe thousands of years later, as the cell that recognises light starts to focus and forms a cup that becomes an eyeball; part of this hardens into a lens, optic nerves are connected to the brain, and so on up the scale to 20/20 vision in humans, and something unimaginably better in other species.

This same principle is repeated for every feature of every

living organism – random mutation upon random mutation, time and time again hitting every rudimentary system and constantly improving it with no ability for the mutating genes to have foreseen any possible advantage. Science is happy with the statistical probabilities and holds to its argument that over a timescale of millions of years such things are feasible.

There will be different takes on why some of us do feel resistance to the issue of whether random coincidences really are a feasible theory to account for 'the tree of life'. My principal reason, of course, is that interactive Intelligent Energies would do a far better job, but there is something else that also makes me personally uncomfortable with random chance. To me it seems odd that this whole concept crucially depends on mutations occurring because of the sudden failure of DNA; it has to fail in its singular purpose which is normally to pass repeat information accurately on down the line so that successors continue to have exactly the same genes as their ancestors. For the random mutation theory to work, the consistency of DNA has to break down in order for a better gene to turn up by accident and be passed on. In other words, a piece of kit which is the 'essential' for life to pass on a copy of itself only works within evolutionary theory when it doesn't pass on its information properly; evolution only works when the DNA process accidentally corrupts!

I understand that everything actually possesses a gene that is somehow more likely to cause mutations and create a slightly different successor. Given the extraordinary properties and 'nature' of DNA it seems to me that this rogue tendency to mutate, so critical to natural selection, is itself far more likely to have been introduced by Intelligent Energies from the start than for it too to have subsequently arisen by chance.

To acknowledge the possibility of Intelligent Energies

being active in creation, as they are in healing our bodies, is justifiable as a theory – a theory that is realistic and altogether more complete than that preferred by science. The natural beauty of the heavens and life on earth shows elegance – as does mathematics for those who can see it; we should expect the natural features that brought everything into being to be equally certain and equally elegant rather than hit-or-miss randomness.

The most usual convention for our starting point, however, seems to be that life as we know it began on earth as some sort of primeval soup that emerged on its own and was accidentally struck by lightning to kick-start the process that eventually led to humanity. At about the same time as life emerges it would also have to build for itself those principles of genetics that need to be captured in DNA to enable the genes to survive and for each species to pass on their natural information for the development of the next generation. Only now are scientists beginning to realise how complicated DNA actually is and they are a long way from fully understanding it. Along with all the other miraculous aspects of life, this hugely complex and essential feature must have appeared very early as another product of chance. On another day it would not have appeared, because chance is like that, and life would have remained at the primeval soup level. In order for life to progress the primeval soup had to consist of molecules capable of renewing themselves and building chains that diversified into 'life as we know it'. They might never have had that property on another day, in which case life as we know it would not be as we know it – probably not capable of knowing anything at all; but it seems chance always did intervene.

If so, the primeval soup required two lucky breaks – first to appear initially in a spectacularly constructed complex physical universe and, second, to have at least the rudiments of the ability to pass on information to its successor molecules. If it is true that lightning did play a part in kick-starting life, through the primeval soup, that would amount to a third lucky break. Even though there was a lot of lightning around the earth in those early days, that does not get away from chance because it would have been entirely possible that there may not have been! This really is how the whole concept is played out but it is ultimately all about whether chance alone, or an existing interactive force acting as a catalyst, is the more likely. The same question can be asked of all the advances made by the mutating genes that Darwin showed were the mechanism for evolution. Did they fall or were they pushed? Was it chance or Intelligent Energies?

I mentioned how people have long regarded the function of sight, the development of the eyeball, as the single biggest problem they have with accepting random chance as the foundation for life; there are many other issues that will give the same trouble once you start to look more closely. While I accept the principle that, in theory, the most sophisticated complexity can arise by chance, it is still the case that the billions of improvements and subtleties that have managed to emerge do make the theory quite breathtaking. Conversely, the application of Intelligent Energies makes a perfectly straightforward means for nature to achieve its complexities.

As an illustration, take the blue butterfly whose grubs produce chemicals, as well as sounds, that fool ants into nurturing them for two years, even to the extent of concentrating on that task rather than looking after their own grubs. After two years the blue butterfly emerges to start the whole process over again. Again, if we think about this we must consider what is the more likely – whether Intelligent

Energies or an unaided random sequence led to the blue butterfly hijacking the ants' nurturing instinct, passing this tendency on to all future blue butterflies before expanding the trick into producing particularly effective chemicals and sounds to enhance the whole routine.

In principle, the story of the blue butterfly is very similar to that of the cuckoo. Evolution has developed the cuckoo's well-known ability to get away with leaving its eggs in the nests of other birds, so that they will rear its chick from the moment it hatches. For this to be possible requires the adult cuckoo to have produced an egg that is sufficiently similar to the host bird's to be accepted as the host's own, the egg has to be laid at the right time in the cycle of the host so as not to arouse suspicion, and the cuckoo chick – literally from day one – has to join in by throwing any of its host's chicks or eggs out of the nest. The cuckoo chick has even become blessed with a concave area at its shoulders which greatly eases this process; but that's not all – in order to be fed sufficient amounts by the hosts, the chick comes prepared with natural begging calls recognised by the hosts as a cry for food to which their instinct is constantly to respond. They are genetically obliged tirelessly to bring enough food for the huge cuckoo – and far more than they would have to find for any of their own babies – until it finally leaves their nest. The tactics of the cuckoo are not so complicated as the function of an eyeball but they do require a succession of subtle variations in behaviour to develop and insert themselves into the birds' DNA to enable them to establish the successful pattern.

No doubt the scientists can tell us how the cuckoos formed the habit of abandoning their eggs to the care of other birds. Did they never look after their young? Was there always an absence of maternal instinct? I can see why foster care might become an easy option but why would it be quite so advantageous that it took over the species? I cannot explain why or how Intelligent Energies helped the cuckoo down this path but it seems to me that Intelligent Energies stepping in to help deal with whatever made fostering an option makes more sense than the notion that a peculiar chance genetic quirk in a dysfunctional cuckoo became a blueprint for survival.

An interesting twist on how problems encountered by animals can be solved for them concerns the hippopotamus. This creature has managed to secrete a natural sunscreen to protect it from the effects of the sun's rays – sunburn – to which it is sensitive. What this amounts to is that the animal had a need for such protection; that need was met at some point in its evolution by a process which somehow was driven to deliver a solution. Although it is a remarkable solution, it is not exactly a hugely complex one – but is it more likely to have happened by chance, or by the cognitive intervention of something like a universal healing force?

I realise that we all have protective features of one sort or another, from fingernails to armoured shells, not to mention the range of animal strategies that have emerged; it's just that for sunscreen to develop seems too weird to be put down to chance but would underline yet again the responsive nature of interactive energies.

For more subtle protection what about the mosquito? It is made immeasurably more efficient at taking our blood and getting away intact because it has developed an anaesthetic which it injects so that we are less likely to feel its bite. Supremely useful and a definite candidate for the argument about natural selection – that the family of the first one to acquire that advantage would be able to survive way better than its competitors; but can coincidence really be the best that science can offer for such a useful facility to turn up and improve fitness for purpose so dramatically?

Some years ago I was struck by a TV programme showing how scientists had produced the optimum shape for a device to collect dew in the baking desert. They had simply copied the shape of, and more importantly the grooves etched on to, the back of a beetle capable of living in the desert with no access to any source of water other than that which it could collect from the pattern on its shell. Science could not improve on the beetle's complicated pattern for collecting moisture and yet would have us believe that this specific design emerged from nature as a result of nothing more than random good luck. First of all a set of grooves that presumably had no known purpose formed themselves as a feature of the beetle's shell. Random chance continued to enhance a meaningless pattern until it was perfect for providing moisture for the beetle, sufficient to keep it alive in the most inhospitable environment.

Just as staggering in terms of 'design' is the fact that there are turtles and beetles with a facility that enables them to right themselves should they fall backwards on to their shells. Instead of being doomed, they are rescued by the shaping of the shells that makes it impossible for these huge turtles and tiny beetles to stay upside down – they automatically turn themselves the right way up! Apparently mathematicians have been able to design something they call a 'gomboc' which has the same property to self-right. To get there they spent time looking at shapes in nature before fixing on the design which, in order to work properly, has to be accurate to within fractions of a millimetre. Not something very likely to happen by chance, you would think – but somehow nature invented it. By complete contrast this is the totally opposite development to that of the eggs of cliff-dwelling birds which have taken on a shape which stops them rolling about and tumbling to destruction from their cliff-top ledges.

There is an even wider issue to all of this. Darwin concentrated on genetic mutations that improved and extended all of the world's species. Although these individual gains secured advantages and constant progress, life depends on many other twists and turns. Once the foothold on life has been secured other techniques have emerged for which the involvement of interactive energies is also a better argument than chance. For example:

- Ants, bees and other creatures that depend on a community approach to existence have formed themselves into complicated, interdependent, working structures. In order to achieve this, the arrangements necessary to set up and develop that community co-operation, all the shared tasks and specialisms had to assemble and run through the colony.
- The bee dance is by any standards a complicated system of understanding and passing on to other bees the exact location of a pollen supply. It is a clever piece of natural ingenuity but did one brilliant bee invent it and one brilliant bee interpret it so that the whole colony could eventually receive the skill genetically over time, to allow their offspring to come to dominate the bee world?
- Nature has come up with the hexagon as the shape to use in the construction of honeycombs which just happens to be a remarkably efficient shape for storage space in a nest for honey – and quite separately also for wasp grubs.
- Wood ants build their nests from pine needles laid on top of each other, uniformly pointing downwards in the

manner of a thatched roof so that rain runs off rather than penetrating the structure. Apparently unaided, they hit upon a design which recognises that pine needles come to a point and there is a 'right way round' construction for their nests.

- The same wood ants have also managed to establish, co-ordinate and get into their DNA the ability to choose together how and when to open and close openings they have designed into the nest in order to aid ventilation. Termites have even more elaborate techniques to construct and organise mammoth structures that they call 'home'.

There are many instances too of creatures modifying their habits or practices more or less simultaneously but having had no opportunity to learn from each other by copying from an example. In the UK blue tits, for instance, began pecking through the tops of milk bottles in different and unconnected parts of the country in a remarkably short time. Monkeys on different islands from each other are known to have 'telepathically' begun dipping food in the sea to 'wash' it after the practice began on the first island. Something similar is also said to occur in the laboratory where I believe it is a recognised phenomenon among research scientists that animals in behavioural experiments solve the same problem more quickly once a method has been established by animals who can have had no physical connection with those doing the same task at a later time elsewhere. Interactive energies, of course, require no obvious physical links in order to influence behaviour or to communicate.

At the time I was dwelling on all this, I also found myself wondering about the general balances and interdependencies that are equally essential to the planet's ordered ecological system. They also had to begin and to prosper but where too did they come from? There are physical elements that are essential though we are so used to them that they are easy to take for granted such as the facility that we call osmosis, which enables water to be drawn through plants. It is one element of nature without which we could not prosper, along with the properties of soil to support plant life and bring the richness that we see. Yes, there are plants that survive in the desert, and others that take their chance to appear and fulfil their life's purpose immediately the rains fall, or only after a forest fire. They seem to be miracles of adaptability in themselves, but would that sort of life at the extreme create an earth that has reached the potential that it has achieved? In order to flourish as it has, surely the earth needed to develop more hospitable and less extreme conditions, and mechanisms. Even those successes that we do see at the extremes seem to argue for a role for Intelligent Energies to develop the tolerance that enables those life forms to have adapted to harsh environments.

With the life cycles of plants that are more familiar, we also often overlook the vital properties that growing matter has to be organic. Where would we be if nothing died, if nothing ever rotted away? And what if there were no process by which creatures live off each other and on dead material that would otherwise be left behind. Without this the world, or at least the evolution into sophisticated life, would probably have collapsed relatively quickly. Our experience on earth is that life helps itself, helps fellow organisms, permits order and enables the whole process to remain sustainable.

Like so many creatures in nature, we humans have enjoyed fruit and vegetables in our diet for as long as we have been here. Thanks to science we know nowadays that we should eat five portions each day in order to stay healthy. Without the nutrients, minerals and vitamins that fruit, vegetables, grains and the sun provide, our health would be drastically impaired; how could our lives have ever been established without that essential supply to nurture us? Life has grown up to require – not just to use but to *require* – those essentials that happen to be found in the natural resources we have at our disposal.

Scarcely a month goes by without an announcement that a new super-food has been found – blueberries, cranberries, blackcurrants, rhubarb, beetroot, holy basil are just a few – in addition to all the green vegetables that children have been urged to eat for decades. Television regularly illustrates versions of 'bush tucker' in every country in the world that will sustain us, as well as the more familiar sources we find more conveniently in the supermarkets. Is it most likely that coincidences alone brought all those vital essentials together for us? Was it chance that assembled both the dependence of creatures on health-giving food, containing particular nutritious 'goodness', and the plentiful supply of it all around.

Of course life has grown incrementally into that pattern but it is still a pattern of essential ingredients that are far more likely to emerge with the aid of Intelligent Energies than without!

We also know that many, many plants can be used as medicines or are beneficial in other specific ways, such as to ease pain, reduce stress, lower blood pressure and so on. The properties of aloe vera to heal in a number of ways are now recognised; the soothing effects of dock leaves that counter the discomfort of stinging nettles have been generally known for much longer. Are these remedies too nothing more than a matter of chance and coincidence? Is it not more probable that the world is better structured than that, maybe even that every malady or 'condition' we have faced, or will ever face, is curable by the plant world either by a single plant or in combination with others – a plant world we are destroying at a terrifying rate?

It is also the case, of course, that there are many plants that are harmful to us, which at first sight might suggest that Intelligent Energies are somewhat perverse in the way that they have structured the planet for us. But therein lies the answer – I do not believe that the planet has been structured for humans nor, as I said earlier, has it necessarily been 'designed' in fine detail from, or towards, a precise plan. I believe it far more likely that everything has evolved opportunistically within the rules set by Intelligent Energies. At different times and in different ways problems have been solved and opportunities developed that confer some advantage on to each and every individual species. This includes those plants that turn out to be poisonous to humans though not harmful to other forms of life; some of them may do no more than fulfil their own existence, others may fit into a wider purpose.

The relative barrenness of the planets in our own solar system compared to the rich life that has developed on earth might at first seem out of keeping with an intelligent force that has succeeded in populating our planet but not the others nearby. Every cosmic body across the entire universe must be subject to the same laws of physics and nature, yet Intelligent Energies have not formed 'successful' planets everywhere. Does that mean that the idea of an intelligent force guiding evolution becomes flawed by the many times that, in our own solar system alone, the vast majority of planets and moons have failed to begin the process that generates life? Not at all; as I have said, Intelligent Energies do not construct to a design, they adapt and evolve to make the best of the entire process – they set the rules which apply everywhere in a way that allows planets to form around suns as the best home for the growth of stable intelligent life. Those rules have structured the universe and brought a degree of order that allows life to grow in the right circumstances; many times it fails but sometimes it will succeed and our planet is our best example.

In this, and not for the only time, the universe reflects nature which often provides species with offspring in great numbers to make up for the colossal losses when only a few survive. Saturn has not developed in order to be barren, or to be beautiful which it undoubtedly is; it has developed from the laws of the universe to have the opportunity for it to blossom into fruitfulness like the earth – but it was not to be. It is not surprising that Intelligent Energies have guided solar systems to be like frogspawn. There is one universe, one set of rules – the many increasing the chances for the few whether in ponds or settling life across the cosmos.

Although I have referred to it a number of times throughout this chapter let me stress again that my argument against chance and coincidence being the foundation for everything is not simply because we live in a universe which is too complicated to have been formed without 'help'. I am basing it on the obvious notion that Intelligent Energies do exist and are able to interact and this makes them a far better candidate as a foundation than pure chance.

Previously I mentioned that the presence of a universal interactive energy actually confirms the existence of other energies (and most importantly the living-body energies) with which they do interact. As I said, if there is no other energy field with which they can communicate then the universal Intelligent Energies are just 'one hand clapping'; they can serve no purpose. Let me end this chapter by taking this argument a critical stage further to show why the three energy aspects of all sentient life – the energy mass, the energy centres and the energy flows must have been formed through the universal field, as part of the development of life from the outset.

Our energy fields exist as an interactive aspect of living beings and this requires that Darwin's theory of evolution through natural selection needs to allow for their presence. If species developed and progressed through chance genetic mutations then that must include our body energies. Somehow they too have emerged as part of a sophisticated system, an integral part of our mind, body and spirit combination; this raises very interesting issues.

To begin with, does Darwinian Theory mean that at some point a random chance genetic quirk led to an energy centre or an energy flow or an energy mass appearing somewhere in the life chain and from that point changing forever the way our systems operate? It is possible (or indeed quite likely) that, once it had appeared, interactive body energy could have evolved into more sophisticated patterns. Over time the patterns could have extended into the complex patterns of energy mass, energy flows and energy centres that we use today.

However, for me, it is very difficult to see how that initial interactive energy could have been introduced into a living system in the form of a chance genetic mutation. Interactive body energy seems too advanced and complicated a feature to arrive as a random minor adjustment to a gene. It is equally difficult to accept that such a mutation could also be coincidentally equipped to resonate with the universal energy field, unless they came from the same source.

I also find it impossible to accept that, once they had landed by some means, body energies could have worked backwards in order to be the creator of the external and universal Intelligent Energies field. I am sure scientists would not quarrel with me there!

If body energies cannot reasonably have created the universal energies the only convincing explanation is that the universal force pre-existed our body energies and gave rise to them at some stage of the cycle of life on our planet.

Once again we are led back to the inevitability that the Intelligent Energies orchestrated not only the existence and role of body energies but, by more or less the same consistent mechanism, orchestrated the growth of the universe and all aspects of the development of life through the process we know as evolution.

These reflections are the foundation for the whole new world I promised in the title of my book; they illustrate the general implications for science, in particular, that follow when we do recognise that the universe is based on the existence of Intelligent Energies. In the next chapter I want to explore the more specific and exciting personal opportunities to which this also leads.

10

IT'S GONE HOT ... should it?

'There comes a time when the mind takes a higher plane of knowledge but can never prove how it got there'
'The only real valuable thing is intuition'

Albert Einstein

Interactive energies are not only effective at the grand scale. They are not confined to setting the universal laws, sustaining the natural evolutionary process, developing particles and delivering healing for everyone throughout the globe. They can also be seen to be active at the personal level, playing a major role with each one of us as individuals in a way that has always been important to human progress on earth – and continues to be so.

I have talked already about those who use energies – those who claim to be overtly psychic and those with other gifts that are special in themselves but not always regarded as metaphysical. Interaction with the energies may be seen as conscious, deliberate events to help a practitioner's clients or they may appear as unexplained 'strange' incidents that happen occasionally in people's lives. No matter how they arise, the very personal and focused nature of all these experiences means that it is rare for anyone to take them further and connect them to the broader picture of how the universe has come together. Once you see the connection, however, it is easy to detect a common denominator at work in quite surprising settings.

A good illustration of this is arguably the most common example of our connections with interactive energies. When it is consciously used by psychics it is described as being 'clairsentient' but it is also encountered by most of us almost every day. Clairsentient simply means the ability to 'know' something – to understand without consciously being made aware of it by any usual or apparent means. It is a skill that is similar to clairvoyance in which psychics 'see' information that they interpret, or clairaudience in which the information is heard via 'voices'. Clairsentient messages are less distinct than either of those; they appear as thoughts, that is to say ideas or inspirations that usually strike without any indication that they might have occurred from outside of us. Such messages have been received over the centuries and have shown themselves to be highly revealing, not just sent to those who realised they had a psychic gift. Psychics may be more aware of the moments and the source of their sudden insights than others but there is nothing to say that people need such a level of awareness, or to carry the claim 'I am psychic', before they can pick up these vital messages through the energies.

The effect is often described as having a 'sixth sense' or a 'nose' for something – an instinct; it may turn up as a feeling that something is especially good or definitely wrong or even construed as a premonition. If we think about it and know what we are looking for, most, if not all of us, will recognise occasions when these energies have been at work – those times when we may have said 'someone was looking after me' or I had 'a feeling' as well as 'something told me' or I rely on 'gut reaction'. We can see communication through energies when twins 'know' about each other in ways that seem telepathic and also when people think of someone moments before they telephone. These and many, many more instances can be explained as what happens when we naturally and unconsciously interact with the energies.

Interestingly I can pick out quite a number of examples of what I see as clairsentient information being passed to those engaged in scientific work and who are then quite rightly regarded as making great scientific breakthroughs. Perhaps it can be applied to most, if not all, of those men and women who have moved life along in a giant leap in science, literature, art and other fields. Einstein had every faith in what he called intuition – as well he might. Bill Bryson records that the conclusions in one of Einstein's famous papers were described by C. P. Snow as having been largely 'reached by pure thought'. It seems there were practically no mathematics and no evidence of any structured identifiable route by which he had achieved his results.

We are also told by Bill Bryson in his book *A Short History of Nearly Everything* that astrophysicist Fritz Zwicky is reported never to have had sufficient knowledge of the laws of physics to have been able to understand why his revolutionary theories about neutron stars could actually be correct. Just dwell on that thought for a minute; if it wasn't hard knowledge or scientific skill that led Zwicky to his conclusions in such a specialised field, where did they come from? If he lacked the technical education and had insufficient ability to come up with the theories then the source of his breakthrough had to lie somewhere else; for this to be the gift of having encountered a clairsentient input is the only known candidate. The influence of Intelligent Energies, passing information on to someone capable of receiving it, explains the inexplicable.

Is it not likely that the world's great visionaries, Sir Isaac Newton included, had something more going for them than their physical and mental skills or even plain good fortune? Surely people who made such extreme and apparently random leaps in understanding towards very precise conclusions are very strong candidates to have had the advantage of being given a helping hand by the forces that built the universe! This is not to diminish their greatness or the dedication of their efforts; it is to say that such intuition may well have a source upon which those who received that initial guidance used their skills to build. There is a saying about success being 10 per cent inspiration and 90 per cent perspiration; to be inspired is to receive an input upon which to work, begging the question 'from where exactly does inspiration arise?'

That Intelligent Energies and the clairsentient process underpin at least some, and maybe all, of mankind's leaps in understanding might also apply to Swiss scientist Johann Friedrich Miescher who is also mentioned by Bill Bryson. Twenty years after examining used bandages under a microscope and identifying something in our physiology which he termed 'nuclein', Miescher suggested that what he had discovered might be the driving force of heredity. From nowhere, and for no known reason, he had effectively come up with the first recognition of what became known as DNA. The notion that DNA might exist at all, and that it was in the substance he had examined, was a fantastic leap, so far ahead of its time as to be virtually ignored within the scientific community – and therefore, of course, everywhere else as well. It was a claim that he appears to have had no basis to make; there was no research that he might have used as a vehicle – he simply articulated his idea out of the blue. The power of Intelligent Energies offers the most credible explanation as to how he was prompted to do that.

Another man connected to science, the Reverend Robert Evans, has the amazing gift of being able to spot the death of stars by recognising the explosion of a supernova – to us no more than a tiny pinprick of light in the gaps between the stars in a sky teeming with stars. Bill Bryson has included Evans in his book as a man who has this amazing talent to such a degree that it has been likened to that of an autistic savant. Certainly Reverend Evans is not autistic and does not believe he is savant either. He has no explanation for his unique ability to spot immediately the infinitesimal change in the night sky that reveals these stellar explosions, a feat which Bill Bryson likens to spotting a single specific grain of salt against a black background on a dining table two miles long!

Let me stress that Bill Bryson does not allude in any way that I can see to the points I am making anywhere in my book; it is simply that his fascinating work furnishes scientific detail some of which then rang bells in my mind. I urge everyone to read or to reread *A Short History of Nearly Everything* against the background of Intelligent Energies as an example of how such forces could have intervened.

It is my experiences that allow me to point the finger towards Intelligent Energies as my own explanation for such events as Mr Bryson describes, though I am conscious that I will be accused by many of providing only inferences and deductions rather than presenting irrefutable proof. The point at which evidence becomes proof is a debatable one but any doubts that I might personally have had about there being a genuine clairsentient mechanism at work within the universe were removed long ago. In perhaps the most startling impact of the work that I had been doing I was to encounter very real demonstrations of the way in which inspiration would work for me!

By the time it happened for certain, I knew the potential role of Intelligent Energies to be important at many levels but, at the same time, I had no means to pursue the concept of these forces in any practical sense. Day by day I was still very active in healing and also particularly committed to passing on what I knew about the perils of geopathic stress. I did not want to lose sight of this work and had generally expected to continue in that vein for as long as I retained the power and the will to do so. However, despite all the advances I had been able to make to my belief system – and the useful work I thought I was doing as a healer – I was to discover that my journey was not nearly complete. I was not to be allowed to drift along as a healer for very long before the new and unexpected dimension began to open up to me. I suddenly found myself 'inspired' to step up my dowsing techniques in different ways that extended my knowledge and furthered my potential.

As usual with me there was nothing obvious about the way I was tempted to make changes to my methods; I was simply working on different issues, still connected to healing, when I suddenly found myself coming up with a number of thoughts and concepts that began to intrigue me. I now see them as insights, more examples of prompts that I had to follow and which were soon adding up to something far beyond my own conscious research up to that point. I had begun to pick up on suggestions that were too far adrift of anything that could be described as my rational thoughts, or any logical next steps based on my own levels of knowledge. Although I did not recognise it immediately, I realise I had begun channelling specific inputs from the universal energies – but through a different route from how information normally arrived when I was dowsing.

As I have said, when we dowse it is to find 'yes' or 'no' answers to direct questions that we ask about the topics we are investigating; we have to decide what we wish to learn and then structure our enquiries in order to receive the guidance or data we are specifically seeking. Now, instead of this deliberate technique, I found that suddenly and for no reason that I could see, I was beginning to be inspired into themes that were totally 'outside the box'! It seems the Intelligent Energies had even more to contribute as, unbidden, they started gently pushing me to fresh horizons. Somehow I was absorbed into an interactive connection that was similar to those psychic 'nudges' that occasionally and unexpectedly guided me during healing sessions; connections that make their own contribution regardless of what I might be seeking and pointed me in the right direction on behalf of my clients. This time something similar had started to help my thought processes as I struggled to make rational sense of what my work meant and the direction it needed to take.

At some point I came across that word 'clairsentient' and was able to recognise that this nicely defined what had started to happen. I had indeed found myself with a new psychic gift; I was sometimes able to 'know' things by means of some form of raw information, snippets of inspired fresh ideas, coming straight into my brain. I was getting the hints which I previously suggested had come to the aid of some of the world's great scientists! Sadly I cannot claim to stand comparison with them but I believe the same interactive energy was helping me as it can help anyone.

As I had found years earlier, when I had reflected back on the sudden appearance of my healing gift, it was difficult to be sure whether I had always had this clairsentient facility or whether it was something that had just started to develop naturally as the next stage of my progress. What I am clear about in my own mind is that if this were not an entirely new gift then, at the very least, any ability I might previously have had was making itself better known; it was becoming altogether stronger and more focused.

Typically of this whole dimension, to be clairsentient does not necessarily mean I can tap into this intelligence whenever I wish. I do not receive with crystal clear accuracy and do not always catch on immediately to the fact that an inspiration has accumulated; at present for me it is an intermittent facility, subject to its own rules and with no easy user's guide. It is especially unfortunate that I cannot always be sure when I am registering genuine and trustworthy insights from links to the Intelligent Energies rather than simply coming up with something from my own imagination in the usual prosaic way – something that has no special value and is not at all promoted by the universal power.

For instance, if tomorrow I unexpectedly decide to go into a shop and buy a newspaper or magazine there would be no way for me to know whether that was a random impulse of my own or if I were being guided by external forces towards an important piece that would help me along my learning path. That is something I do now believe was happening to me all those years ago when I picked up that copy of the *Guardian* on the holiday campsite. I had no intention of doing that when I walked into the shop – I simply gave in to a sudden temptation that proved to be the start of a life-changing chain of events. Looking back over my life, there have been a number of instances when I have been given that sort of push – which perhaps does suggest that I have always been in tune with the energies to some degree. Scientists would call it coincidence and see it as something that is statistically bound to happen sometimes in our lives but then science uses words like 'coincidence' or 'chance' to describe quite a lot of events that I see differently!

Because my decision to buy that newspaper did turn out to be one that led me to Seka and everything beyond – and also knowing now that psychic help via Intelligent Energies is a reality – I do believe that buying the *Guardian* on that particular day was something into which I was guided. There was no way for me to have recognised this at the time; if my gift were to hear voices or to see visions then I would be much better placed always to know for sure what was the source of the impulses and inspirations that I get. Having said that, I know I am not ready to start hearing voices or seeing visions and so by saving me from what I regard as that unwelcome experience, I can see that the external power seems to have got that right for me at the present time as well!

Even so, it is frustrating and often seems a bit inefficient not to be clear whether or not I am actually in communication with the power. Perhaps if I had the discipline to meditate deeply and frequently I would be able to establish clearer links. However, having said that, I know I am not alone in having some difficulty recognising the best paths to take. The gifted American medium John Edward has clear access to all kinds of information by psychic means but in his book *Crossing Over* – named after his TV show – he makes it plain that when it comes to his own life decisions it is not always clear to him what his guides want him to do, or why. Eventually he gets there and only later understands the reasons. We all just have to accept that this is the way the system works; we have to trade the rigour and regularity we are used to in the dimension of our daily lives for the less tangible fluidity of interactive energies.

Because the information passed through Intelligent Energies does not signal any automatic clues that the energies are indeed the source of any prompts I get, the only thing I can do for certain is to test out all 'messages' – or ignore them! Now that I am a bit more experienced I find I can sometimes detect certain indications that the energies are at work. There are times when I mentally try to check the validity of what I think might be a message from 'outside' and immediately get a physical sensation in my tummy – not unlike the one you would get on a fairground ride when it suddenly plunges downwards. This seems to be a signal confirming that whatever 'thought' I am addressing is indeed accurate. Mostly the truth of this is then borne out by later events and only rarely proves false; the odd failure probably happens when I have forced the pace too much or have been ambivalent in the way I checked back and have somehow distorted my connection.

[I often wonder if this tickling sensation in the tummy is the origin of the saying 'gut reaction' to describe a feeling about something being right or wrong when there is no other real evidence.]

Once I had noticed the intermittent 'tummy-signal' I was able to find this strange feeling cropping up more and more, especially when I eventually did redirect my efforts in order to spend more time and effort deliberately opening myself up to the wider influence of Intelligent Energies. I also soon noticed other signals that suggested the energies were in touch with me – sometimes I realised that random ideas would keep returning like an obsession and would only stop when I examined them seriously; alternatively I would have a sudden conscious thought that maybe something or other had indeed come from the energies.

Sometimes the hints I get seem to work the wrong way round when it occurs to me that something hasn't happened – and then it does! As an example, after we had lived in our house for about seven years and enjoyed attracting and feeding a wide variety of wild birds I was struck by the thought that it was surprising that, in an area so rich in birds, we had never seen a sparrowhawk. Just two days later one hurtled in like a missile and narrowly missed taking one of our visitors; I had been alerted within a two-day window in over seven years!

Unfortunately I do not always get my 'tummy-tickle', or any other obvious signs, to alert me to energy messages, and in the early days I had no real grasp of what was going on. It was only subsequently that I have been able to spot that I was getting some outside help. I know that a sceptic will now be asking how I can be so certain that messages are arriving from Intelligent Energies if the process is so tenuous – how I could possibly know that they are ever anything other than my own random thoughts. The answer to that is partly that such a gift is widely recognised and is entirely in keeping with the properties of the energies that I have been close to for more than twenty years. It is partly also to do with the way in which very special insights have moved me along through experiences and outcomes that are far more telling and dramatic than 'my own prosaic imagination' I referred to earlier.

The first clear insight started to form one evening when I was working on geopathic stress. *[and let me remind you now of what I said earlier: geopathic stress is not a medical condition it is a description of what appears to happen to magnetic earth rays]* I was tinkering with the plan of someone's house that I was dowsing with the pendulum; I was trying to identify where geopathic stress lines lay when suddenly the simple thought entered my head that there ought to be a natural way to deal with geopathic stress – something other than the 'electronic' devices that are available but which are not necessarily cheap or convenient.

I remember that feeling coming to me not in the form of a question 'could there be a natural way?' but as a more positive mental observation on my part that 'there ought to be' another way. Later I realised that this was almost certainly a clairsentient message because, as well as the way this prompt was phrased, I instinctively acted on it immediately. I was compelled to address the idea seriously straightaway and equally quickly began to get some clues. I was not given the finished article by any means but words and concepts started to fill my head and I just had to try to make sense of what was coming through. I have always had a close affinity with geopathic stress as I have said; I can sense its presence in a room very easily without the pendulum and it soon builds an impact on me. It occurred to me that if anyone could connect to a new means of dealing with it then it could well be someone with that sort of affinity.

That thought encouraged me as with growing excitement I began to check the 'information', the ideas and the thoughts that were coming into my mind, using the pendulum to ask the energy for 'yes' or 'no' answers to my questions. Was that word just some random thought or part of a structured process? Was this word an indicator of how to neutralise geopathic stress? Did it mean I should do this or that to deal with the problems? Can I take the stress out of people? Can I clear rooms or buildings? Can I use this or that to carry with me in order to protect myself? How well would it work for me? How well would it work for others?

Although I am not generally skilled as a dowser, other than being able to identify the physical influence of negative energies, the responses I was getting via the pendulum began to seem really encouraging. Over a number of days of further work, more and more thoughts, fresh ideas and possibilities emerged more clearly as the Intelligent Energies guided me towards techniques on which I could experiment.

The first tangible concept I found myself closing in on by this means was to try to create a convenient means of carrying protection against geopathic stress around with me wherever I went, so that I would no longer have to worry about being subjected to its effects when I was away from home. I particularly had in mind the problem of sleeping in hotels as I was making quite a lot of business trips in those days and from time to time inevitably encountered hotel rooms that gave me problems; the only way I could ensure I was comfortable wherever I went was to take the trusty bin liners with me. As effective as bin liners usually are, there is no doubt that they can be a bit of a pain to use and always raised the possibility that hotel staff would find out what I had put into the bed and think I was crazy! I was therefore keen to find something better than the liners, something portable that would give me some protection and which might also have the extra benefit of helping me when I was in someone else's office, meeting room or home where I would also often feel the impact of geopathic stress.

The words that came into my mind as I set about my task in earnest led to further ideas until, eventually, it seemed that the process had pushed me to develop a 'mixture' – a combination of ingredients which had a liquid base and which, therefore, I could drink. You would be forgiven for thinking that such a 'potion' is only marginally less crazy than putting bin liners under your mattress, but at least it was convenient and would stay secret – especially if I needed protection during a business meeting!

Through a combination of dowsing and using the muscle test that I described earlier, I became hopeful that what I had come up with really would be capable of warding off the distorted energy of geopathic stress. Although I trusted the dowsing and the muscle test that had confirmed the liquid would work for me, my rational brain also told me that real proof could only be found by testing it on site. I knew I would have to check it out at some location where I would otherwise have suffered the effects of the 'bad energy' and so I started the practice of carrying a tiny bottle of the mixture wherever I went. In all honesty I cannot recall the first time I did use the bottle in a real test but I know that I did use it many times on my business trips and eventually satisfied myself that it did indeed give me the energy protection I had been looking for. Through the input of Intelligent Energies I had arrived at something that was capable of being carried around with me and available to be taken whenever I found myself affected by the problem of geopathic stress. It was exactly what I had been prompted to find and I believed I now had the benefit of a much tidier and more discreet solution than the bin liners!

I persevered with dowsing and searching for other options; thanks to more ideas through the Intelligent Energies I next came to understand that the concoction would work perfectly well if I simply kept the bottle on my person – there was no need to take it orally. It seemed that, somehow, the mixture's energy field was capable of interacting with my body energy, or possibly acting directly on the force of geopathic stress. Although I had no clear idea of the actual mechanism I had developed, it seemed that the effect of the bottle was either to block the stress from invading my body energy or else it neutralised its impact once it did get through. I later used my methods to establish that it was the latter but either way I felt sure that the protection could take place while the mixture remained within the bottle; somehow that seems the most remarkable part!

Convinced as I was that my discovery had worked a number of times for me I could not shake off a feeling that I should seek some independent confirmation of its potency. No doubt the Intelligent Energies were encouraging this thought too – perhaps to give me reassurance and confidence that I was not deluding myself and that I did indeed have something that would do the trick for anyone. I do remember wondering if it were possible that, as a healer, I was somehow plugging into healing energy directly to help myself, and maybe bypassing the bottle and its contents altogether. Because of my interest in the subject of geopathic stress I had spoken on a number of occasions to Rolf Gordon, the author of the book *Are You Sleeping in a Safe Place?*, which is a book I highly recommend to anyone who would like an easy guide to this whole topic. Rolf had founded the Dulwich Health Society in London to publicise and tackle geopathic stress and was an authority on the subject. I knew that if anyone could give me an accurate and independent appraisal it would be Rolf.

Sadly Rolf had learned about the topic of geopathic stress following the death of his son from cancer. Rolf was the first person to tell me of research suggesting that a high proportion of cancer sufferers have spent time being affected by geopathic stress. I cannot vouch for that personally but I will say again that geopathic stress represents adverse energy from which it is recommended that we should all protect ourselves regardless of the exact implications. Once Rolf had come across the reality of geopathic stress and was convinced of the harm it can do, he devoted his life to publicising what he had learned; he became committed to the cause of helping people to avoid becoming affected.

Whenever I spoke to Rolf, either in person or over the phone, it was his habit to be constantly dowsing to help him generate responses; he would always be using the pendulum to check my general health and whatever else came to mind as the conversation went on. When I rang to ask what he thought about my mixture it was no surprise to hear that, as usual, he was working with the pendulum to get some answers. He quickly told me that his readings were confirming what I had already come to recognise and that, in his view, the mixture did indeed work to give protection.

This may not be much of a sample in terms of research, but at the time Rolf's confirmation was certainly good enough for me; it gave me great confidence that I was on to something really worthwhile. I sent Rolf some of the bottles so that he could take a closer look; he said he would get a friend of his who was also skilled in the field to check the mixture as well and a few days later back came the response that his friend too agreed with our conclusions. Rolf's contact had also given the added advice that the mixture would be better for the addition of alcohol as a preservative, in the same way that the Bach flower remedies are preserved.

Although I was mightily encouraged by the responses the two men had given me, the proof of the mixture could not only rely on the result of dowsing, it would have to come from more practical trials. Yes, the mixture had worked for me whenever I took it on my business and other trips, but how could I show by experiment that it worked for other people? My problem was that the effectiveness of the 'energy shield' could only be tested by someone who was able to know whether geopathic stress was present and who could also work out whether they were being affected – or being protected. This made it difficult to get an independent test organised until I could find someone else besides myself whom I knew would be able to experiment for me; I knew of no such person and so this area of my work then went quiet for a while – perhaps until the energies stepped in again!

One morning among the day's mail I found I had received my invitation to the wedding of Claire, the young ME patient I had been able to help a few years earlier; of course we were thrilled to renew our contact with her and in such happy circumstances. When we eventually met up at the reception we naturally began chatting about geopathic stress generally and her health in particular. I was delighted to hear that she had kept her strength through the years since I had treated her and was continuing to live a happy and successful life. Her wedding seemed an even more special occasion than usual because somehow it confirmed that those desperate times of struggling with ME were well and truly behind her. During our chat she happened to mention the bottle I had given her a long time previously in the hope that it would help keep her free of geopathic stress. I had totally forgotten that I had let her have one of the bottles when I had first developed them but was glad that I had, especially when she told me that it had been of great help to her on many occasions.

More than that, she had become as interested in the subject as I was and never lost the opportunity to tell others of her own experiences and to warn them of the dangers of this form of bad energy. In doing so she had sometimes mentioned the mixture I had given her, showing them the bottle by way of illustration. Claire told me of one person whom she could tell suffered from geopathic stress and said that, while giving him the benefit of her advice, she had also let him see the bottle. He took it and held it for a short time and then very quickly told her that he had felt it had made his fingers 'tingle'. This effect was news to me but I immediately saw it as another indication that things were happening for real and that the impact of the bottle and its contents was not a matter of self-deception or wishful thinking. Talking to Claire had provided me with another level of the proof that I needed in order to have the impetus and the confidence to go further. Although I did not know exactly how I was going to make any advance, I was very keen to continue to explore the ways of Intelligent Energies.

I continued with my practical healing and addressing the general issue of geopathic stress, telling everyone who would listen to me about its existence but even as I did so I was also working on other ways to help protect people in their houses and places of work. This had led me to another idea of neutralising its presence by 'healing' affected buildings, as one would send absent healing to treat a patient, or neutralise bad energy in an affected object. It would mean concentrating my healing on the building and its underground faults rather than a person or a possession, but perhaps it would work. When I mentioned this idea to Rolf Gordon, however, his advice was that this technique had already been tried before and the verdict was that although it may work for a short time the problem of geopathic stress soon reasserted itself. Nevertheless, I still tried it for myself as part of my own learning curve and did so both on site at affected houses and by absent treatment from a distance. Unfortunately I must admit that, eventually, I had to agree that it did not seem to have made any long-term gains for any of the properties.

Fortunately it was not long before the Intelligent Energies

weighed in again; yet more clairsentient influences set me off on a different tack, which also involved working on properties from a distance, but not just using healing. As usual, I had to sift the words and concepts that were coming into my mind as I was receiving the help I needed, but I eventually came up with another possibility which, however I tested it, was signalling to me that this time it would work well. Having fine-tuned it to its best effect, I started to use the new system wherever and whenever I could.

I found that the method worked for me every time and I now frequently use it as part of my work to clear homes and workplaces. It is my present preferred method, being far cheaper than machines and more convenient, not to say more professional, than the bin liners! It is the method I mentioned earlier when I talked about my client who had suffered brain haemorrhages, the headmaster working in the office which left him with constant headaches, the child with behavioural problems, and many other instances.

I have refined the system still further and plan to include it as a service from my website. On the site I again make it plain that you should satisfy yourself that any person or method you intend to use either to check for geopathic stress or to deal with it is genuine and competent to do so. You should explore the website of the British Dowsing Society to get help and look at other sites and books to understand more. Try dowsing for yourself or use the muscle test I described earlier – not just to guide you over whether any site is actually affected by geopathic stress, but also to show whether it will be safe after it has been treated. Do not be afraid to name any person you intend to ask for help as you check their abilities through the muscle test. Unfortunately we do not yet have convenient measuring devices to check geopathic stress levels independently; until science takes it more seriously we have to use our world of energies to inform us.

Having enjoyed success in creating my bottled mixture and then my method of neutralising the energy from properties, it was not long before I instinctively put a hold on the healing techniques that had been my life from the moment I first realised that I had an ability to help people. Instead I became certain that developing an even more direct and deliberate interaction with Intelligent Energies was the way forward for me. This new direction took shape when I suddenly found myself thinking about a small mole underneath my arm, one of those small sticky-out pink ones like the one that had unexpectedly cleared from Cathy whom I featured in my case studies. The mole had never bothered me much before but, probably prompted by another clairsentient message, it began to get to me until I got it into my head that I had to do something about it.

What happened next amounted to yet more evidence that it is indeed possible to make gains through healing energies despite the doubts of sceptics. The following is an account of how I developed my own means to access interactive energies in a way that gives more people than ever a chance to understand about healing at first hand. I make no specific claims about what is about to emerge other than that it is all true, fits squarely with everything I have been saying about Intelligent Energies and convinces me that no other explanation for what happened stands up.

Concentrating on the mole, I went through my, by now, familiar process of concentrating on what I wanted to be able to do and hoped for some help. Eventually the breakthrough resulted when it dawned on me that I was being attracted towards developing a healing-energy dimension of some sort;

I began to concentrate on how to clarify this and make such a thing work. I cannot give a full account of the process that followed partly because it was disjointed and it is difficult to describe – or even to remember – the individual thoughts and instincts that I went through. My thought processes, prompted by Intelligent Energies, led me gradually towards a new means of channelling healing using healing-energy cards, or patches, which would need to be specially formulated. Many evenings went into working my way towards the details of what gradually turned into an amazing healing opportunity.

The first patch to be revealed and tested was the response to that sudden notion to do something about my underarm mole. It took a while for the concept of a patch and the means to charge it with energy to emerge, but eventually it did and I worked my way through to something I could trial for myself. When I first tried the card I found that, although it didn't clear the mole away in one miraculous sweep, I was definitely conscious of feeling a sensation of tingling a few minutes after I first put it in place. I had no knowledge really of what to expect, or how long it might take to see any kind of result but I left it there for about half an hour before taking it off. There was nothing apparent to show for that first attempt at treatment but I was quietly thrilled by what was going on – even daring to believe that my new patch really would prove successful. Over the following few weeks I continued trying it from time to time for relatively short periods until one day I noticed that the mole had changed to a darker pink colour. Encouraged, I kept the patch on longer and over a few more days watched the pink colour of the mole gradually deepening. Within another two or three days of what became more or less constant treatment, the mole grew generally darker still until I noticed a dark purple line threaded round the base of the mole where it was attached to the side of my chest, under my arm. I then watched this line gradually move further up the mole, taking the darkening colour with it and heading towards the tip.

Once the whole of the mole had turned purple in this way it started to blacken uniformly and shrink; not long afterwards when I touched it the shrivelled mole simply came away between my finger and thumb. There was not the slightest pain as it came off; all I felt, for a short while afterwards, was a slight burning sensation almost like a raw chafed feeling, two centimetres or so across the area where the mole had been. It was slightly uncomfortable but not at all painful or even what you would call sore. Needless to say, I was delighted with the success of the whole venture which I had to admit seemed quite bizarre!

I wasn't really sure what to make of it all but somehow I knew this part of my journey was not over and that removing my harmless mole was not what this was about. Outside of healing and dowsing this was now the third example of specific personal collaboration with Intelligent Energies, following the new way of neutralising geopathic stress in properties at a distance and then the protective mixture I had bottled. For me, this meant there may be more still for me to find through Intelligent Energies and so, over several months, I looked further for the next step but found no new inspiration. It was yet another example of how timing has to be right before events come together – another instance of how we must respect the fact that we cannot always expect to turn on a tap of instant interaction just because it suits us. Just as we must go through the doors of opportunity when they open, the more we press against the doors that are closed the more tightly they will remain shut.

All I knew for now was that I seemed to have used the card to connect to the universal healing force in a similar way to the mechanism of healing by other means such as crystals, sound and the 'healing hands' with which I was more familiar. I also realised that messing around with moles was probably not a good idea and that I really needed a new focus!

This lack of progress continued until one day it 'occurred to' me that I had for many years been troubled on and off by indigestion and stomach acidity. Again, this was not a cosmic illness as these things go but there is no doubt it can be annoying and sometimes quite painful when it strikes – enough to move me to accept that my next project should be to see what could be done. It seemed obvious that the next stage in the sequence ought to be to investigate the potential of healing by patches by thinking about my acid indigestion and then see where it led me. I find it no easier to describe the sequence which followed than I could when I was writing about the way in which I found the means to deal with my mole. All I can say is that over some days I opened myself up to anything I could interpret from the energies until I felt I had mastered everything that was required – until I sensed that the signals I was picking up on had indeed led to some kind of new healing patch.

At the same time I was beginning to regard the card as something to boost a chakra as a means to pass on healing energies. Because acidity appears in the tummy area I decided to aim it at the tummy chakra which is believed to be yellow and so I chose that colour for the card; I 'thought' that keeping to it might give the patch an added boost. There is, of course, much more to the patch than its colour, but colour and shape are thought to be an added help in matters involving energy as part of a healing process so I thought I would give the patch every advantage I could.

However I also 'knew' that the major chakras are connected to the minor chakras as well as to the energy flows and the energy mass (or aura). There was, therefore, no way of telling where this was going to lead me!

As soon as I was able to try the new patch on the next occasion that I suffered a bout of acid indigestion, I was very impressed with what happened. I was delighted when the discomfort, which usually lasted for quite some time, eased and disappeared less than five minutes after putting the card on the chakra. I then removed the patch and found the discomfort came back. Replacing it was followed by relief once more. It was yet another breathtaking moment in my life as the Intelligent Energies yet again were supporting everything I have been saying!

Although I was thrilled with the way it had worked for me, once again I needed to establish whether it would prove as effective for someone else. I knew I would find it easier to find a willing guinea pig for this remedy than I did when I first tried to trial the geopathic stress bottle but there were still not many people I felt confident about rushing to talk to about my new concept. In any case none of the people whom I might expect to take me seriously had ever mentioned anything about indigestion to me so far as I knew. All I could do was to give a patch to each member of my family and ask them to use it if they, or anyone they knew, offered any sort of opportunity for a field trial. I then had to sit back and wait for feedback.

So far as I recall the first chance to check it out finally arrived when I received a telephone call from my son Dave when he was at university with his girlfriend Nicola. Dave asked if I could send some healing to Nicola who had developed an uncomfortable tummy; no details of what might have been eaten or drunk were offered or asked for but it was clearly enough of a problem for Nicola to be looking for a healer to give relief. Although this was not indigestion as such I decided that Nic's complaint might also be related to the yellow chakra and might therefore connect with the energy of the patch.

'Do you mean she has not tried the yellow patch?' I asked Dave. 'What yellow patch?' he replied. So much for my research panel! I reminded him that they both had been given a yellow card for more or less this circumstance – did they still have at least one between them they could try? Miraculously it turned out that they did and, even more miraculously, when I phoned back later Nicola was able to confirm that she had indeed enjoyed speedy relief. Note that I had to phone back; there are miracles and miracles but hoping for your kids to phone when you want something is asking too much of the cosmic forces!

Nevertheless, once they had confirmed that the patch had seemingly helped Nicola it amounted to a big step forward for me. I had now made two different healing patches triggered by three different problems – a troublesome mole, stomach acidity and an upset tummy. I was sure that both cards had been effective and one for someone other than me. Nicola was not someone who was likely to have been able to use it only as a focus to heal herself, as I might perhaps have done without realising it when I treated myself. What is more, Dave and Nic had seen it work too quickly for it to be the placebo effect; I would rule out placebo anyway because, at that point, Nicola could have had little or no confidence that the patch would work at all and we know that prior belief is crucial if placebo is to succeed. It all combined to show beyond doubt that I had developed something that could confidently be trialled more widely.

At this point however I knew that in doing so I had to give a strong warning. Although I had connected the yellow card to my own indigestion as a minor condition, excess acidity can lead to other serious complaints and complications, particularly in the longer term. I therefore reminded anyone who wanted a card for any purpose that it must not be used as a 'remedy' for anything without medical advice. As it happened, before I got round to offering it very widely to others to get their reactions I was prompted towards two more 'discoveries'.

First, I had been suffering from an unexplained pain in the crook of my thumb and index finger of my left hand. For some unaccountable reason, other than Intelligent Energies getting involved again, I was 'moved' to try holding the same patch between my painful thumb and finger. There was no logical reason for me to do so but I held it at the base of the joint for about five minutes and found to my amazement that the pain disappeared. It returned not very long after I had removed the patch, but when I put it back the discomfort was relieved once again. I found that the more I used the patch the easier my thumb became; this was a very puzzling turn of events but even more was to follow.

Months later I realised that, sometimes, I had been feeling more at ease than usual on occasions when I had to speak at big meetings or conferences. The only variable that I thought might account for this was that I had fallen into the practice of carrying a yellow patch in my shirt pocket. Although there was no reason to believe the card could be calming my nerves I began to carry one constantly to monitor its effects. Because it works to boost an energy chakra it is not always necessary to have the patch actually touching the skin, though I do like it to be as close as possible, so I decided it could stay in my shirt pocket. This more or less permanent experiment took a little time but convinced me that wearing the card really did seem to help ease my anxiety and brought my nerves much more under control in stressful situations. I also came to feel that it generally relaxed me far more than I had been used to regardless of whether I was up against any particular cause for anxiety.

As an aside, I subsequently learned that chiropractic techniques to adjust the spine do make links between finger pain, acidity and digestive disorders apparently due to nerve pathways becoming blocked and in need of release. I am also told that problems with the spine in the neck area could have an effect on breathing – which in turn inhibits relaxation and therefore public speaking. My acidity, Nicola's upset tummy and my finger pain may not be so disconnected as I thought; not only an interesting revelation to me, but possibly an illustration of why holistic treatment is to be encouraged and a hint as to why orthodox science doesn't always see the point!

What all of this meant for me in practice was that. I now had no doubts that my work with healing-energy patches had something to offer the world both in terms of accepting healing energies – there is no other way they can work except through the energies – but in so doing they also strengthen the case that I am making overall.

This is of course that we live in an extraordinary universe developed and nurtured on interaction with Intelligent Energies. There is no other realistic conclusion that can be drawn, not least from experiences such those which follow; all are genuine accounts that speak for themselves:

—— Stephen ——

On the morning of his wedding day Stephen turned up to collect my son David, who was to be Stephen's best man. It was clear that Stephen, who is always a lively character, was not at his best. He told us he had an upset stomach and was feeling nervous; the two problems were probably connected, which would be unsurprising on his big day.

I gave him a patch to try as he sat on our sofa and almost immediately he told us that the symptoms were easing and that he was feeling much better; within a few more minutes the discomfort had virtually disappeared.

He decided to keep the patch with him and went on to have a wonderful day, giving as relaxed a groom's speech as I have ever heard.

This was not all that happened that day as I found later!

—— Michael ——

I was seated next to Michael, Nicola's father, later at Stephen's wedding reception and once the meal had finished we parted company for a little while before I met up with him again at the wedding disco an hour or so later. By way of a courtesy greeting, I asked him how he was.

'Too full of food to enjoy this pint!' was his answer as he regarded his beer with an uncharacteristic lack of enthusiasm. Spotting this as a possible yellow chakra connection I immediately invited him to try the yellow patch, knowing him well enough to be sure that he would not expect anything of it even if he were prepared to try it at all!

So far as I recall Michael had known I was a healer but he certainly knew nothing about the patch in advance; I told him to see if it might help and, a bit to my surprise, he readily agreed to give it a chance. He placed it inside his shirt at the point where he felt uncomfortable and then, after about five minutes of social chat, I asked again how he was feeling; I was absolutely delighted when he told that the discomfort had now completely gone.

This was a very speedy and, for him, an unlikely success which encouraged us both to talk some more about the patch and its other possibilities. When I mentioned the possible links to muscular or joint disorders he quickly agreed to try it where he had the pain he experienced from what he said was an arthritic ankle which had begun interfering with his beloved golf.

He later reported back to me that he had used the patch for his golfing by putting it down his sock and that the pain had eased to the extent that he was able to enjoy his sport again without any problem.

That was not quite the end of it. Michael, not being a person to accept whatever he is told without giving it any thought, then set up an interesting experiment for himself, without in fact mentioning it to me until much later. Having found that he had no problem when he had put the patch in his sock, he tried taking it out halfway round the golf course to see what would happen; sure enough by the end of the round the pain was back.

As a variation to that, he then did the first nine holes of a round without the patch, by which time the pain was affecting him, so he then put the patch back in place to finish the round. The pain eased away again, allowing him to complete the round without difficulty. I was very grateful for confirmation that, at least in some circumstances, something was very definitely happening.

—— Daryl ——

I had given healing on a number of occasions over the years for Daryl who is a friend and was a neighbour at the time. One evening when a group of us were out socialising, and almost as soon as she arrived, she came over to tell me that her neck and shoulders were giving her pain. Daryl wanted me to do some contact healing on her there and then but, seeing another opportunity, I asked if she would try 'this patch I have come up with'; I added that if it did not help I would happily do some contact healing later. She agreed to try the patch, which I put at the base of her neck at the back of her shoulders and left her to it.

Very soon I was astonished when she looked over to me and said 'my neck has gone warm'. This was the first time that anyone had experienced such a reaction and I can tell you it impressed the hell out of me! Playing it cool, I said 'that's good, just see how it goes'. It was not the sort of social occasion that made it very easy for me to talk to her in detail about what had happened – alright, it was the pub quiz again (!) – but I do know that Daryl's pain eased at least to the extent that she did not feel any need to have the contact healing.

Although Daryl was the first person to alert me to the fact that sometimes the card could generate a sense of warmth when it was being used, she was by no means to be the last. I was particularly pleased that the experience had already occurred to Daryl when it cropped up again while I was chatting to a very senior regional figure at a business event one evening – not an occasion when I would have wanted to have been caught unawares about this effect that the card could bring about. Having told him something of my work I was pleased he had taken sufficient interest to ask me if there was a patch I could let him try; as I always carry some with me I gave him one to take a look at there and then. He held it for a few moments against a cyst of some kind on one of his fingers; he looked distinctly puzzled and then in his usual, non-excitable style simply said, 'It's gone hot … should it?'

That kind of sums it all up really. It doesn't do that noticeably for everyone but it does for a good proportion. I do sometimes notice slight tingling or, more often, tremors of flowing energy when I use it for myself, but whether or not the user experiences any sensation doesn't seem to make any difference to the feedback I get. What, if anything, a user feels is probably all a matter of how sensitive he or she is to their body and the healing process.

—— Harry ——

The patch that Harry used was actually passed on to him by a mutual friend who had taken it originally in the hope that it would help his son. The son had suffered a nasty fall from a height and was in considerable and constant pain. I was later told that the son had tried the patch and had felt heat at all the points where his injuries were but he did not notice any immediate improvement in his pain and said he did not wish to continue using it.

However, passing the patch on to Harry did both him and me a big favour. Harry was suffering from arthritis in both knees; he was not inclined to try the patch, simply because his belief system told him that there could not possibly be anything to it. His wife, on the other hand, had different ideas and, quite rightly, told him he had nothing to lose and that he had better get on with it! Non-sceptical wives and mothers have been a huge help to me in all aspects of my work with energies, far more so than many of their men would have been if they had been allowed their own way.

Having only one patch and two affected joints Harry held the patch between his knees and to his surprise he too noticed both of the joints getting warm. Very soon the pain eased and it was not long before he found he could bend his knees to put on his own socks and was able to walk normally upstairs. He told me that using the patch meant he had been able to do these simple things for himself for the first time in 14 years!

This is reminiscent of a similar case in which an older man tried one of the cards and told me that after holding it for about 25 minutes he had been able to make a fist with his hand for the first time in five years. This is not something that I expected and I do not make any specific claims about it other than that is how it turned out.

—— Greta ——

I had done some hands-on healing for Greta who had been very impressed with what it had done for her, particularly as she had never experienced healing before. I must have given her a patch to try as well because she later took one to her mother's house on one of her frequent visits.

In Greta's own words: *'I gave the patch to my mum who put it at the back of her neck where the pain that day was strongest. I had not crossed the room to sit down again when she told me her neck had gone hot. Pretty quickly she said that the pain was not half as bad as it had been immediately before she put the patch on.'*

Again the situation is there was no prior expectation, from the person who used my card, I was not even present and neither person there was aware that, in some cases, the patch did indeed cause anyone to report a sensation of warmth. Using the patch preceded a sense of heat followed by a measure of relief very swiftly.

It is hard to get away from the obvious conclusion that this sense of heat must stem from a 'stimulation' of the body's energy system because similar sensations are reported during 'hands on' healing.

— Gary —

I was told that Gary, the partner of one of my work colleagues, always suffered acid indigestion after his Sunday morning fried breakfast. This took the chakra healing back to its roots of course and I was highly delighted when my colleague later reported back that Gary had passed on the message that he was now able to enjoy his Sunday morning treat without paying the heavy price of acidity – his cholesterol levels though may be a different matter!

Pleased with his experience Gary mentioned the patch to his brother who was suffering from joint pain for which the medics had not so far been able to make a diagnosis. After he put the card on the painful area Gary's brother too reported feeling the warmth that the interaction with energies can bring and soon noticed the pains easing. He was therefore in the position of being able to enjoy some relief from his condition before it had even been properly diagnosed!

— Julie —

This is about another person I have never met, but who was given the patch by my friend and colleague Julie, someone to whom I had given the healing for a repetitive strain injury that I described in my first set of case studies. The problem experienced by Julie's friend was said to be sciatica and was bad enough to have kept her out of the pub for two weeks; this meant it was really important!

Julie's friend, someone else with no experience of healing, was not at all convinced that it could possibly do any good but was willing to test it out; she put the patch on her lower back and sat down to watch television. A little later she had to go upstairs and was on her way back down again before she realised that she had just walked up her stairs effortlessly with no pain, something she had not done so easily for a fortnight. The following Sunday's topic in the pub was about healing energies and chakra patches. As so often happens, the suggestion was made that the improvement was 'mind over matter', the vague and all too frequent excuse that is made by those who are not ready to accept there is a real mechanism to healing.

Julie's friend had a pretty good response, however, telling the group, 'I had put the patch on my back and forgotten all about it, I didn't expect it to work and was amazed when I afterwards realised I had been able to walk up and down the stairs without any trouble. My mind was not involved!' Good for her!

—— Nicola ——

As I have said, my son's partner Nicola has experienced healing a number of times including help for dealing with objects that were carrying bad energies. She is definitely not one to be persuaded of anything against her will, or contrary to her experiences, but exposure to the healing world has encouraged her to get involved herself so that she attended a dowsing course and also became a student of Indian head massage. I know nothing of this technique except that on one occasion she used me to practise on and I felt more relaxed the following week than I can ever remember!

When Nic was in Australia she managed to extend the repertoire of wearing patches while on a scuba diving trip. She is particularly prone to motion sickness which is apparently something that diving can bring on – not least on the boat being ferried to the diving spot! On one occasion she felt seasick and put the patch inside her wetsuit and within minutes she felt fine, the sickness disappeared and she was able to carry on enjoying her diving.

—— Brenda ——

My wife has been involved in many of my learning experiences in healing and similar matters; many of them would not have happened without her enthusiastic help. She is a keen singer and for many years performed with a local Gilbert and Sullivan society. In one production she had a part which involved dancing around in a circle; this soon brought on a problem of cramp in her foot which was probably the result of having to wear flat dancing pumps when she was only accustomed to footwear with some sort of heel.

Still on the look-out for opportunities to learn more I suggested she put one in each pump to see what would happen. What did happen was that the cramp did not appear during the performance that night and did not return for the remaining run of the show while she was using the patches. Cramp anywhere between knee and foot is still a problem she suffers from time to time; but if she stands on a card she usually finds the cramp eases away very quickly. Brenda often sees opportunities to offer the yellow cards to those she meets including:

- The lady on a trip from their church who used a card when she complained of a tummy disorder which quickly cleared.
- A friend who mentioned something similar as she was leaving the pub; as the designated driver she had drunk one too many acidic soft drinks. She knew nothing of the card but later agreed she had unexpectedly solved her problem by the time she had pulled out of the car park.
- A young friend who suffered badly with period pains

which regularly caused her to have a day or so off work due to the intensity of the pain. She found that after putting the healing patch on her tummy (the yellow chakra area) the pain greatly reduced. Her discomfort was not totally eliminated but eased sufficiently to mean she no longer took time off work.

—— Podge the dog ——

Podge is a schnauzer owned by a friend and helps demonstrate how using healing techniques on animals is one of the best ways to see if real help is being given; in such cases there is no room for anyone to argue that mind over matter or some sort of psychology has influenced the 'patient'. The dog had developed long term difficulties in walking that the vet had not positively diagnosed. Podge had suffered for a couple of years or so which limited her ability to take exercise; as a result she had put on weight which in turn reduced her level of exercise even further and so worsened the pain. Although the vet had provided medication it appeared to have no effect

For some time I had been keen to try a yellow patch on Podge and eventually asked her owner, Jean, if she would be willing to test one out. I was delighted, though a bit apprehensive, when she readily agreed. It seemed to us that the best way to use the patches in these circumstances would be to put some under the blanket of the dog's basket and wait to see what happened. A few weeks after I had dropped a couple of patches off for Jean to use I asked her if there had been any developments. Jean told me that after the cards had been put in place Podge began to find it easier to walk; she had then been able to increase her activity and had lost weight. She became very much healthier and very much happier. Jean later told me that Podge is now 'like a puppy'.

The cases I have shown do not represent the only times the card has shown good reason to press my argument that successful interactive energy healing has taken place. I have not yet conducted trials that would be regarded as scientifically or clinically convincing. At this stage I am not ready to do that but they remain events that help make my case about Intelligent Energies being active across the universe.

I can expand on that a little with regard to two more patches that have also emerged but have only had very limited use by other people so far. Again, I refer to them only to underline the possibilities opened up by Intelligent Energies and chakra healing. Like most of us my wife and I are sometimes prone to feeling 'down' at times; it is hard to know when slightly low moments give way to anxiety and when such feelings would be more accurately diagnosable as stress or even depression. Whatever the medical diagnoses, the feelings are real and can be very debilitating; I know from personal experience that when your spirits are low, and we healers believe that is probably a more literal expression than many people realise, there is nothing you can easily do to turn things round.

There is no appeal to logic, counting your blessings or even pinpointing exactly what the cause is. It just has to work its way out of your system and even with mild cases this can take days or even weeks.

I cannot recall whether it was me I wanted to bring out of one of these bouts or whether I was trying to help my wife but one way or another I set out to see if I could develop a card that might help. As I began work on this new patch I remember feeling anxious; I wanted to get results swiftly and was desperately hoping that I would quickly get the signals I needed. Perhaps hastened by my concerns the usual clairsentient process came into play almost immediately, as I recall, and thankfully soon led me to a new patch. We have both used this patch on odd occasions since and found ourselves feeling much better in a very short time.

As with the yellow patch I gave it a colour to reflect an energy centre; this time I chose green for the heart chakra – a point in the centre of the chest where the heart energy centre is held to be. The heart energy centre seemed an appropriate place on which to focus relief and as this chakra is considered to be the green one, green seemed to be the appropriate choice.

In my own case, I found my spirits rising in a matter of 15 to 20 minutes, but generally I have found most progress after the card has been carried for a day or two before it seems to be no longer needed. When she tried it seriously my wife too found very quickly the same degree of initial gains that I had enjoyed. To see her go from feeling very down to singing around the house in a couple of hours was all the evidence I needed.

It was not easy to get other people to test this patch for me; once again I needed to know someone well enough to know they were out of sorts in a similar way and to be able to ask them to experiment with a card. Eventually our friend Jean, for whom I had channelled healing several times for other matters, mentioned she was having bouts of anxiety and asked if there was anything I could do to help.

I immediately offered the green patch for her to try; she had already used the yellow one in connection with back pain so it was not too difficult to get her to give the green one a chance. Within a week or so she was reporting back that she was feeling much better but since she was under pressure at work she asked me if she could carry on using it. Of course I was delighted with the feedback and told her to keep the patch for as long as she wished.

Some weeks later she was in touch again to ask for another of the patches because she had just given her own to a colleague at work who was severely anxious, particularly about a forthcoming work-related inspection. She had bumped into Jean in the corridor, severely overwrought, and obviously at the end of her tether. At some point in her story she told Jean that she had been diagnosed by the doctor as suffering from stress-induced tonsillitis and that she was barely able to speak.

Jean told me she only had time to give her colleague a green patch and tell her to place it down her jumper, over her heart; there was no time apparently to say anything more and the colleague therefore knew nothing about what the card was for, or what it might do. Shortly afterwards the two met up again. 'What is that patch all about?' demanded Jean's colleague. 'Has it helped?' asked Jean. 'It certainly has, I feel much calmer', came the reply. Jean told me her colleague continued to improve from that day on and later went through the inspection without any trouble.

The next person to test the green patch was the sister of a former work colleague of mine who, from birth, had been suffering from a faulty heart mechanism which often left her very breathless. She visited me for healing, which I agreed to do if only to see if I could make her feel more comfortable, however briefly. The condition was a major physical abnormality and I did not want to think about making any concentrated effort to try to deal with that. During the session there was indeed some improvement in her breathing and in her colour immediately after the healing

We discussed healing while she was relaxing after I had been working on her and this inevitably brought up the topic of chakra healing patches. She readily offered to see if the new patch could help further in any way and put it in place on her chest. As soon as she put the patch on her heart centre, to my amazement, she immediately felt it go hot. Although, as I have said, this happens quite a lot with the yellow patch it is the only time, out of the few of us who had worn it, that anyone had told me they had felt warmth from the green one. It seems to me another sure sign that something is happening and that this patch too will add its weight to the things I believe in.

There is a postscript to that particular incident. Probably about 18 months later I got a call from Jean to ask if I would see her friend Erica for healing; it turned out that Erica was the one who had tried the green patch for work-related stress but whom I had never met and whose name I did not know. Of course I agreed to see her for any treatment I might be able to give. When Erica visited me she explained that she had recently been badly affected by a very stressful situation which had brought on strong pains. She had remembered to try the patch which, by this time, was long after I had first given it to her; Erica felt better after putting the card on her heart chakra but still felt she really needed something more which is why she wanted to visit me. The healing session, however, soon took some very surprising turns!

First Erica told me that when she had first tried the green card that Jean gave her, she had immediately felt her chest go hot. Although my client with the heart problem had been the first one to mention to me that it could generate heat I now knew that the first time it had actually happened was during that earlier treatment for Erica. Meeting her for the first time when she came for the healing now meant that my work with the healing-energy patches was given the additional boost of a second person reporting unexpected physical sensations while using one. This was of course an intriguing revelation, but more was to follow.

Before we actually started any healing Erica opened up by describing the sensation she was suffering as being like having a cylinder lodged there – 'like the cardboard centre of a toilet roll'. That may not be the most poetic description, but it was graphically clear and was to prove helpful to us in monitoring the progress of the healing. About ten minutes after I started hands on healing, Erica told me that the 'tube' felt 'flattened in the middle'. Not long after that she told me that the flat area had extended so that the problem had become more like a toothpaste tube that needed to be squeezed empty at one end; she added that she was now mentally trying to force the 'toothpaste blockage' out from that area. With no knowledge at all of visualisation techniques I suggested that she changed her imagery into that of an hour-glass with sand inside that was easily and gently running out; she did this and it was not then long before she was able to tell me that her feeling of having a cylinder in her chest had greatly eased.

There was then yet another twist in this session when Erica chose to mention that she was wearing two rings on a chain around her neck; it soon transpired that both rings had belonged to people undergoing great health-related anxiety. Mindful as ever of the capacity for adverse energy to be passed on through possessions, I offered to use my usual technique to clear both rings. I did this for her and it was not long before Erica announced that she no longer felt any discomfort at all. However, when I used the pendulum to dowse the rings to see if the bad energy had been cleared I found I was getting an elliptical orbit as part of the 'yes' response rather than the usual perfect circle. To me, this meant we were on the right track but we were still missing something about the rings that needed to be dealt with. Another of those clairsentient moments led me to discover that Erica's sister also had a ring from the same person as Erica which the pendulum told me also needed to be cleared. As soon as I had done this and checked with the pendulum it swung into a perfect 'yes' – the bad energies were gone! I have to say the whole session proved a fascinating healing experience for both healer and client.

By the time I actually met Erica I had already been led towards one more healing-energy card; this one was after my wife had begun to develop hay fever about four years previously. Although this had been a relatively mild irritation at first, it was becoming much more troublesome and was threatening to ruin a holiday we were having at the time in Cornwall. I went through my customary process of trying to work with Intelligent Energies to channel the right wavelength of healing energy into a new patch for her; quite quickly I came up with one which, according to the signals I was receiving, would be able to help relieve the symptoms of her uncomfortable problem.

My wife put it over her heart centre since fixing it to her eyes and nose, where the problem was manifesting itself (around the indigo chakra) was clearly out of the question! She never feels sensations while these patches are in place, no feelings of warmth or anything, so we left it there and later set off from the holiday cottage to drive about twenty miles to St Ives. About two hours after she had started to wear the patch, and about half an hour into the drive out, my wife suddenly announced that all the sensations of hay fever had pretty much disappeared. Cautious as ever we both realised that the relief might be to do with the fact that we had moved out of the area of the cottage and possibly away from the source of her discomfort and so we suspended judgement for a while. I was pretty hopeful that moving away from the cottage was not the reason for her relief since the hay fever had been proving a growing problem for some time no matter where we were; thankfully, when we returned there was no recurrence of the symptoms and she stayed free of it from then on.

I cannot be certain what the future holds for the healing energy cards; my direct experiences have been positive and I am in no doubt that they will come to be seen as an effective treatment. However, I need trials and research to move this area of my work along and hope to make this happen in due course through my website. In the meantime I have been concentrating on researching and writing my book, a hugely enjoyable task if a time-consuming one, not least in terms of sharing the wider ramifications of a universe built on energies – the mission I set myself once I realised the power of the forces around us. In the final chapter I want to pull together the threads of everything I have learned so far about the whole new world which I have discovered – the discovery that gave my book its title and which can change your life.

11

JOINING FORCES
hands across the universe

'There is no logical way to the discovery of these elemental laws. There is only the way of intuition, which is helped by a feeling for the order lying behind the appearance'

Albert Einstein

For me to have worked for so long as a healer, using the gift of 'healing hands' to help others, gave me the inspiration and the confidence to pursue the questions about what else the healing mechanism could do - and where else it fits into our universe and our lives. As I have been explaining of course, what I came to recognise is that it is not so much 'the' healing mechanism that offers us more; rather it is that healing is possible because of the interactive and integrated structure of universal energies – something that we have to take into account if we seriously wish to understand what is going on all around us.

Einstein's sense of the order that crosses the universe and of the reality of intuition, nicely expresses the world that I have discovered. Of course he was not addressing the sort of detail that I have covered nor does he go on to consider directly the day-to-day effects that are possible when we work with the ways of a universe such as he describes. Nonetheless his words fit gloriously with the forces that are essential to our universe; for me what really matter are the opportunities that these forces can deliver when we do see the universe as it really is and then learn how to work with it.

That is why I have given this 'order of the universe' and the ways in which we are all affected by it, a fresh identity as the 'Fourth Perspective'. Sadly, despite Einstein's intuitive grasp, the breathtaking interconnected working structure I have been defining is not generally recognised in modern thinking. Most of the western world, in particular, remains unaware of the means by which we can change or improve our individual lives through forces that were better understood and more effectively used centuries ago. To write those words is to invite instant criticism and even ridicule; yet the fact remains that I sent healing to 'George in Glasgow' by a mechanism that consciously understands what I am trying to do – and then helps me to do it.

To know this is so means everything; it is not about whether or not something exists such as angels or ghosts, nor whether someone who claims psychic gifts is good, bad or a cheat. Those things are important in the same way as how highly relevant it might be to know how competent is your local plumber but that is not why I have written this book. I have written about everything I know because we should all know it if we are to make the most of our personal lives and be a part of a balanced existence. To know about healing and other energies is not just a matter of gaining a better academic understanding about the way the universe works; there is much more at stake than that and I want to bring the threads of all this together as a final chapter.

As I was beginning the final draft of this chapter, claims came through that scientists have managed to create a new species of their own by combining a bacterium with computer-generated human input. They believe they can control this hybrid but I have to say I am far from convinced they are right. The bacterium will have energy that is capable of reacting with Intelligent Energies for the good of the entity which is interacting – that is, the bacterium; I do not see how scientists can control that interaction any more than they can control how viruses mutate. I am not questioning the security of their experiments and am not in a position to know whether or not there are real dangers in what they are doing. My point is that if science does not recognise and allow for the impact of Intelligent Energies on living organisms then the judgements they make will be incomplete; sooner or later and with further advances they may well prove unsafe. If there is genuine life within their new hybrid the scientific framework is going to be found desperately wanting; that is something that now matters greatly in principle and perhaps already in practice.

Cosmic Intelligent Energies interact with us all the time whether or not we happen to realise it. There was nobody around to ask them to generate the universe but they made the start and then led a process to bring life on earth by introducing the essential genetic mutations of natural selection. Eventually human consciousness reached a level that allowed us to communicate directly with forces powerful enough to have generated our fantastically complex universe. The energies that are ever-present and are responsible for the precision of everything in creation became able to respond to us specifically in all sorts of ways that invite us to find the means to reciprocate. We can interact through specific techniques that we can accomplish personally and can also enjoy the 'psychic' gifts practised by those such as healers and others; we can seek communication through beliefs in a divine God or simply listen to the thoughts that are inspired subconsciously – those clairsentient moments that strike us all from time to time.

Professor Brian Cox is making a well-deserved reputation for himself as a fine public communicator in matters of the cosmos and particle physics. Giving a lecture to celebrities at the end of 2011 he described how manipulating the particles in a diamond (by rubbing it vigorously) all the other electrons in the universe had to shift in order to accommodate the result of his rubbing action! He even introduced this part of his lecture with the words: 'everything is connected to everything else'.

For the professor this does not explain what he referred to as 'mystical' healing; and of course he is right. Natural healing is explained by the interaction of energies that I have been writing about, but what the professor has done is to confirm that science accepts that interactive universal connections are real enough. This does make the interactive transfer of information and of healing perfectly realistic events.

Universal energies can guide us and work in our favour if we open ourselves up no matter what route we choose: meditation, Tai Chi, yoga, prayer, visualisation or any number of other avenues that all lead back to the practical and spiritual values inherent in Intelligent Energies. They bring us benefits as part of an amazing web that does work for us, directly and indirectly, personally and generally throughout our lives. The more we use that web consciously, the more we will be in tune with it and the greater will be its influence for us; our links will be stronger and we will be better able to channel its support into our lives and the lives of others.

Even when we do not seek direct contact with them, however, the energies are always an integral part of our lives as they inspire and guide us. Those scientific advances which were made by individuals who had no obvious reason to see them coming are a good illustration of what is possible, as is the route I unexpectedly took to develop my healing-energy cards. Because they happen at the subconscious level, inadvertent connections such as those are easy for us to latch on to, though harder to recognise for what they are. I have long believed that inspiration which strikes people in creative fields such as song-writing, music or artistic composition comes from an interaction with energies. I was therefore impressed to hear country song-writer Nancy Griffith saying that she did not believe she invented songs personally but that they were 'blowing in the wind', waiting to be captured; she held that the gift of the writer was to 'reach out and grab them'.

I have a lot of sympathy with those thoughts which reinforce my notion of Intelligent Energies in principle and in practice; in writing this book there were times when it all came together smoothly and almost effortlessly and other times when it didn't. When the muse isn't flowing, my efforts to force the pace are useless; the words that I choose nearly always have to be rewritten when I see them again later, or they simply do not reach the page at all!

To acknowledge the inspirational influence of the interactive energies is not to diminish the creative work of anyone in the arts any more than I was being rude to scientists who did not have the apparent credentials to come to the conclusions that they did. Whatever the source of ideas or the information that emerges apparently from nowhere, a great deal of skill and effort has to be put into shaping it into a final product. I am happy to acknowledge that I have been repeatedly blessed with input from Intelligent Energies to move me from convinced sceptic to even more convinced, moderate psychic; I have also put twenty years of my life into trying to make the most I could of the links I have built.

We have all heard of hundreds of possible examples of how Intelligent Energies interact in our lives even if it has taken until now for the mechanisms to be sensibly explained. From angels to Zen Buddhism, they may take different forms and have different functions, but ultimately they all depend on the interaction of energies. If we embrace this perspective fully, we become free to explore a new world however we wish and then to connect to whatever strikes a chord with us as individuals. The internet is the modern way to search and to learn, of course, but I recommend that you see this as an initial filter and then rely on books by responsible authors and reputable publishers to give you greater depth before you commit to anything. Just because this universe of energies is real enough doesn't mean that people will not dig pitfalls for you or seek to take advantage.

Sensible care and a deal of caution to advance steadily is all you really need in order to get closer to Intelligent Energies and what they can do. There is much you can try for yourself – the muscle test and pendulum dowsing that I described earlier would be good starting points to check your own potential. In addition visualisation, or cosmic ordering as it is now becoming known, might also appeal; this is a technique in which by visualising what you wish to secure for yourself you can make things happen. It is not something I am personally very familiar with but I would suggest that you do not expect instant success from the moment you first try; as with all skills, unless you get a lucky first hit, it takes time and some dedication to get results. Whatever you try be prepared to put the effort in, be sincere and practise, practise, practise.

It took me time and experience to develop as a healer but the start of it was the effort I made to make my connection with the energies via the book about Sai Baba that had inspired me. Although I did not recognise it at the time I was indeed making my connection to the energies. Even though I was relying on Sai Baba's words and had not at that time learned much about the energies, I was still making the link that everyone must make if they are to benefit from them. My first faltering experience as a healer was triggered about three weeks later; my first attempts at dowsing for geopathic stress on the other hand proved highly effective immediately. The lesson, therefore, is that working with the energies is a reality but it can be unpredictable and variable; the connection is often tenuous and elusive at first so do not expect easy results, though if you are talented or perhaps if there are other issues working in your favour you might quickly surprise yourself.

I am encouraging as many people as possible to open their minds and find their own understanding of the state that I call the Fourth Perspective partly because it will change your life for the better and partly also to raise awareness of the validity of the many happenings that cause problems for the scientific framework. It really is time we broke the old mould – a point I would like to make by asking you to imagine what life might be like for more advanced civilisations that may exist elsewhere in the galaxy or the wider universe. Think about it for a moment – what do you see? Stereotypically, what most people would say they expected in advanced 'alien' cultures out there across the cosmos would be bigger and better science: advances that allow those beings to make journeys through space or undertake time travel; to possess superior weaponry, gigantic computers, robots and advanced technology at every turn. We are not attuned to consider a reality in which civilisations have discovered the way in which the universe is working through the subatomic energies; or that they may have applied knowledge of interactive cosmic forces to preserve and protect their world, boosting nature and making the most of natural resources in a more civilised sustainable way. We do not imagine that along with technical advances they might have clung on to the deeper understanding that comes from living with nature.

OK, I accept that we take our lead on alien worlds from science fiction, and of course smooth-running cultures, at one with each other and their planet, are not usually the setting for best-selling books and Oscar-winning films. But even so it is easy to see how our familiar reliance on science has prepared us to believe that a hi-tech route of ever more sophisticated machinery is the only plausible direction for true progress to be made. Only if we strip out our own familiarities and free ourselves to think more creatively are we likely to consider that other intelligent forms might fully understand the major energy mechanisms throughout the universe and have long been able to acknowledge them far better than we generally do on earth.

Simply because I can interact with healing energies and can send them instantly to anywhere on the planet I know that advanced intelligent life must sooner or later have recognised them and drawn them into their culture, the way everything in every world actually does connect back to energies. Intelligent life would be well aware of the benefits of working with the cosmic forces that interact with the energies of all living things as we all float in those energy fields that comprise and shape the universe. They would communicate naturally and consciously with the universal forces, whether or not they referred to a divine God and regardless of whether ceremonies, routines or the introduction of 'worship' was their means of communication.

Would they perhaps have recognised and conducted their lives around the principle of karma? On our earth, this is a feature of Hinduism and Buddhism which, in simple terms, teaches that 'what goes round comes round'. In other words the good that we do comes back to us in some way, and so does any harm for which we might be responsible; it is claimed as a part of this philosophy that our actions shape our destiny over many lifetimes. Such possibilities might be seen clearly enough by advanced intelligent beings, not necessarily as a conscious judgement from a 'personal' God but possibly as an unavoidable mechanical feature of energies: positive words, thoughts and deeds automatically attracting the benefit of similar good energies and vice versa – harmful actions attracting negative consequences. All of this might well be regarded as non-controversial, something that happens as automatically as water flowing down their hillsides.

Closer to home and more specifically is it, theoretically, possible that a more advanced civilisation than ours might invent a means to heal the sick through the manipulation of subatomic particles; might we expect our scientists on earth to be able to do the same in two or three hundred years' time? I think there would be many who would regard that as highly likely but in our present-day environment when healers point out that we have actually already done so it is mostly dismissed as impossible. The reason for that, of course, is that we expect advances to arise out of the work of scientists; if they cannot yet channel subatomic particles as a healing mechanism and the theory remains outside their present framework then we think nobody else can already be there!

The main message in this book is entirely new – that Intelligent Energies exist as a force at the subatomic level and guided both the accumulation of the universe and the evolution of life; this message fills the gaps in our scientific model, explains the world of psychic happenings and provides practical evidence for the presence of God. These energies represent the common thread that I mentioned at the outset, the common thread that allows all aspects of western culture – governments, academia, society generally and health providers in particular – to recognise that scientific truths, psychic powers and spiritual values are all equally valid. All three make up the material pieces of our one universe, all imperfectly understood but all equally relevant to our lives and the way in which everything works.

Because it is a familiar area to me, and one that is largely misunderstood, I have stressed how the broad lack of knowledge about healing within the whole medical establishment diminishes potential and obstructs possible advances in the care we can give people. I gave one example of this when I talked about Jim, my client who almost died and had to undergo very significant surgery after delays to his diagnosis and treatment. Those delays could have been avoided if, as a healer, I had been in a position from which to give information to his GP that I could expect to have been taken seriously. Another, more mundane illustration, occurred recently when someone asked me for help with a painful thumb. She had no idea what she had done to it, but I gave some contact healing that improved things for a few days before she got in touch again, this time to ask for absent healing because it was more convenient and she still had some pain.

As well as being more convenient, absent healing can also be very useful because it will go straight to the source or sources of what is wrong with a client. There is no possibility of being diverted by my conscious interventions as can happen when I search physically with my hands for the best contact-healing point. I know that wherever the 'absent' energy automatically goes to work on the body of a client it will be exactly where the biggest problem has originated. Because of this it was very interesting to me when my client rang later to say that, before sending her off to sleep, the healing produced vibrations in the joint of her thumb, the base of her first finger, her wrist and her shoulder. She also confirmed the healing had considerably eased the pain again.

From the locations to which the healing energy had been attracted we concluded that her problem had probably been caused by a fall she had not really noticed during one of her ju-jitsu lessons, something we had not worked out before. Although orthodox medicine might have identified that without help from a healer, it does not alter the principle that the system with which healers work would be able to contribute much to patients' health issues if it were ever to become a recognised and respected part of the health infrastructure.

That is just one small example of why we need to see everything more clearly; it is just as easy to see examples on the larger scale. In early 2010 a UK government advisory group, the Science and Technology Committee, recommended that the National Health Service should cease funding homeopathy. The reason given was that they believed it to be a treatment with results no better than the placebo effect. Interestingly, this judgement ignores the fact that orthodox medicines can be licensed even though they may be no more than 30–35 per cent effective which is less than some placebo results.

The percentage success rate of homeopathy is therefore not out of line with some drugs which have been accepted, which means that the clinical data may not be the Committee's real issue. Perhaps a better clue lies in the fact that committee members admitted they do consider the explanations for how homeopathy acts to be scientifically implausible; science cannot explain why homeopathy would work so that's that! Scientists are certain that homeopathy contains no active ingredient, but they are wrong; it contains powerful energy. It just does not contain anything that fits into the area that science knows about. Homeopathic practitioners and patients are satisfied with the results in practice but none of that counts.

Interestingly to me the same official committee report also has something more to say about the placebo to which they compared the homeopathy; the report explains that the placebo works when patients get better because of their belief in their treatment and that it usually relies on 'some degree of deception'. This of course vindicates my arguments that healing does not equate to placebos because most healers' patients do not expect to get better and nearly always say so; furthermore, none of them expects the warmth or other sensations that almost always accompany healing but which are never mentioned as being present during placebo trials. I doubt that homeopathy is delivered in the way that placebos are administered either but the Committee did not spot that!

I do not really mean to keep bashing science in all of this; nor am I particularly addressing the Science and Technology Committee. Rather I am attacking a culture that has arisen over the centuries which relies too heavily on what I have shown to be incomplete scientific authority. We all know that science has opened up the world, literally in terms of travel and communication, and metaphorically in how it has come to understand practical truths about nature and the universe. It has made enormous strides in every field, including in matters of health and medicine, which are topics that particularly resonate with me as a different kind of health practitioner. As well as the fruits of science that we do see around us, we can add a long list of achievements that have brought us here, along with a good many propositions that have had their day but are still testaments to human ingenuity. Those successes have understandably given science its powerful platform and I suspect few of us would wish to give up all that we know and the benefits we enjoy, in order to have lived in an earlier period of history with none of our present understanding and technological advances.

However, we should not lose sight of the fact that those early 'scientists' who erected standing stones as part of their culture also had brilliant minds. They did not merely display astonishing mathematical, astronomical and engineering abilities, they also showed an awareness, sensitivity and spirituality in being so strongly motivated to design and construct these amazing features. In doing so they got far closer to nature, the changing seasons and the real cosmos than has our modern culture for all our rockets, lunar landings, Martian probes and chemical discoveries.

Those who founded beliefs based on interacting with the universal energy, and then built religions as a means to organise their beliefs, knew something that science has forgotten. Those of us who practise 'non-science' continue to prove millions of times over that there is a dimension missing from what is usually represented as the rational, totally science-based view of our world. To adopt a Fourth Perspective is to take a more unified view of the world and the universe, one in which we would all find a place for the truths that are inherent in the three familiar, but disjointed, existing perspectives that run from history through to the present day. We can accept known scientific facts and the way in which the modern world is run but must also accept values and truths from historic perspectives that have since been left behind by a technological society. The key lies in those threads of energy that run through the whole of existence with their power to interact. They are the threads of cosmic Intelligent Energies as well as body energy, the energies that are carried and given off by objects and those that are part of the earth itself – energies that are beneficial or helpful and others that are, or can become, harmful.

To acknowledge the presence of these energies is a simple enough principle but one that changes everything in our mainstream understanding. The evidence throughout my book leads us to realise that the interaction of these energies not only accounts for a structured universe, it justifies the claims of genuine psychics throughout the ages, especially in the field of healing which shows such tangible results. Recognising energy as the definitive factor to connect 'mind, body and spirit' also opens us up to explore the value of many techniques including meditation, yoga, Tai Chi and similar practices. The effect of energies in combining 'thoughts' with the physical body explains some health issues, both adverse and beneficial; some of the effects of positive or negative thinking are known to medical science but the mechanisms are not. Wherever you look energies have their place and leave their mark.

The power that works with us as Intelligent Energies is probably the same force that is defined differently and worshipped through religions; alternatively, it could be a subsidiary force established by the more familiar divinity as the means to drive the development of the universe. In neither case is God actually 'replaced' in what I have to say. The presence of the universal energy demonstrates the foundations for belief in God and confirms why we should communicate at such a cosmic level. We can do so through structured links, including those shaped by religion if we wish, or through other more personal means – whatever suits us as individuals.

There is also an argument for saying that since the Intelligent Energies interact with our body energy they mingle and become a part of us. The energy is then within us, in a way that makes it 'personal' for us; we are quite possibly surrounded and at a physical level joined by a force that is literally as close to us as it is possible to be. As close as any 'person' God could be and as close as, if not closer than, any physical person could be – close enough to be actually a part of us and our energies; close enough also to give, receive and spread the universal love at the heart of religious belief and driving all positive human interaction.

The 'Renaissance' I claimed from the beginning, the view that I have named the Fourth Perspective, takes a mix of tradition and new revelations in order to develop a fresh practical and philosophical outlook. It unites metaphysical 'unscientific' elements that are around us with the twenty-first-century understanding of the world and better equips us to contribute to greater future advances. It puts a fresh slant on current issues such as the impact of electronic fields, cancer clusters and the little-known health factor of geopathic stress; until we recognise the reality of all this we continue to make life unnecessarily difficult at every level.

Thankfully there are reasons to believe that we are now at a time when a much more unified view of reality may be more acceptable to a wider range of people and in greater numbers than has ever been possible before. As I have been mentioning, scientists are being forced to tackle their own new dimension.

The dark matter I mentioned is perhaps the most dramatic and most telling example but as scientists learn more through quantum physics they are now expanding and challenging the science of the past; the clockwork universe is now more old-fashioned than healing hands!

Subatomic theories continue to change everything about the way we look at the universe. Intelligent Energy fields, almost by definition, come into this category of subatomic particles – an area that scientists want to look into so seriously that they have built the Large Hadron Collider in Switzerand at a cost of £6 billion to help them. There really is no logical reason to believe that Intelligent Energies do not exist as a property somewhere in the new fields that science already knows or continues to propose. It surely need not be long before this vital key to understanding the universe, already familiar to psychics, will start to be equally acknowledged in scientific quarters as it is among many free-thinking individuals from all backgrounds.

I was particularly interested to see that the late C. S. Lewis, author of *The Chronicles of Narnia*, was one of those eminent thinkers to believe that the universe is not as bleak and empty as the way scientists have dissected and understood it; he held it to be far more alive and to have far more meaning than is commonly recognised.

In religion and beliefs about God, it is also true to say that opinions and fresh approaches have come alive. There are many past doctrines that are being hotly debated and which provide openings for new attitudes to flourish among believers and non-believers alike – a coming together that may help bring down the old barriers that divided beliefs.

In my own general field people are joining in, recognising the nature of mind, body and spirit as, despite the cynics, millions explore healing and other therapies. Their experiences continue to add further insights and confidence in the benefits and practicalities of interactive energies.

Care for the environment is rising quickly up the agenda; this is critical for the planet but appreciating such principles might go on to connect us better to the controversial Gaia theory about the nature of earth proposed by James Lovelock. His hypothesis respects the earth as a living organism that is regulated interactively through micro-organisms in the biosphere to maintain its stability; it is easy to see how the powers of cosmic Intelligent Energies tie in with his theory of a living earth and resonate also with other philosophies.

For almost fifty years the Findhorn Foundation based in Kinross has actively practised a philosophy that I can appreciate from my own experiences and beliefs. The following is taken form their website – and I am very grateful for the Findhorn Foundation's permission to do so:

The founding principles of the Findhorn Foundation and community have remained at the centre of all our activities over the years, they are

- *deep inner listening, and acting from that source of wisdom*
- *co-creation with the intelligence of nature*
- *service to the world.*

How we express these principles through our activities, continues to change and grow, reflecting both the evolution of the consciousness of the community and the needs of the world around us, locally and globally.

Deep inner listening was applied to the task of growing the first garden at Findhorn, which the founders – Eileen Caddy, Peter Caddy and Dorothy Maclean – engaged in as a way to supplement their diet by growing their own food. The inner source of wisdom they contacted daily included the intelligence of nature, and when they listened to and applied the wisdom they received, the garden flourished. As they progressed in their practice of attunement to the intelligence of nature, they came to understand that they were actually engaged in a process of co-creation with nature. This new understanding, and its results in the Findhorn garden, were the catalysts for inspiring others to work in this way, and launched Findhorn onto the world stage.

In the case of the Foundation and those who have been a part of its growth over the decades, there is much more to this than philosophy and rhetoric; their practical achievements and way of life would have been impossible without the tangible support and guidance from 'the source of life'. My terminology, and certainly my own terms of reference, may be slightly different but the energies I have encountered and have now written about are part of the same universal pattern. They do indeed work for us, and with us, in a whole range of ways that make a difference. To know this offers everyone the confidence and the opportunity to find their own new way of life with renewed belief in a Whole New World!

APPENDIX
What happens now?

www.intelligentenergies.com

Find us online and stay up to date

- Jeff's Blog
- News and Updates
- Feedback
- Your questions answered

Join our efforts to explore a whole new world!

intelligentenergies

APPENDIX
Healing-energy cards

I have devoted more or less a whole chapter of this book to the subject of healing-energy cards. The instances I have talked about are the first public reports of my experiences with the cards and the feedback I have had from others who used them – not all of whom were amongst my healing clients.

In the book I reach my initial conclusions drawn from my beliefs as a healer and from the events that I describe. Next I hope to be able to work with bona-fide researchers from any appropriate background willing to help – or to sponsor – further investigation and wider trials. I would like to hear from anyone able to help.

— APPENDIX —
Geopathic stress

I am keen to encourage wider, multi-disciplinary research into the existence, nature and potential effects of geopathic stress. Overall, geopathic stress is a topic that most people are unaware exists; that is something which needs to be changed – and the sooner the better!

Some (highly) technical data about the physics already exists and needs to be gathered and reviewed by scientists or academics. There are also many more personal accounts linked to individuals and organisations that need to be seen and understood by every one of us. Much is on the internet though - like all internet topics - care has to be taken over the bona-fides of those who post the information. My website www.intelligentenergies.com is a helpful starting point.

Unfortunately the present picture reflects a main theme of my book: there is more than one perspective to take into account when we look at our world and our universe! There are technological means to help tackle the issue of geopathic stress as well as complementary techniques including Feng-Shui and my own method using Intelligent Energies.

Do not simply take my word for it; I urge you to use the muscle test (simple kinesiology) or dowsing – both are explained in the book and on my website – to establish whether you or those you know may be affected by geopathic stress. You can also use the same means to satisfy yourself as to how you might find effective help from genuine sources.

I also urge everyone to pass on the knowledge that they gain. I intend to press publicly for more research into this topic and more publicity in the hope that it can be brought fully into the open for everyone's sake.

— APPENDIX —
Share the Fourth Perspective!

'All religions, arts and sciences are branches of the same tree'

Albert Einstein

In 'It's a Whole New World!' I have told my story to help others see ways to improve their lives whether their needs are many or few. I hope to introduce many more people to the potential of 'healing hands' and give insights into other benefits for mind body and spirit based on interaction between energies. Too much doubt and negativity have been attached to many of the topics I cover in the book and I hope that I have done something to counter that – to help change perspectives and encourage a greater freedom for people to explore how the world really works. Whatever you discover – tell others!

Thank you and very best wishes

Jeff Jeffries